Theories of Crime Through Popular Culture

Sarah E. Daly
Editor

Theories of Crime Through Popular Culture

palgrave
macmillan

Editor
Sarah E. Daly
Saint Vincent College
Latrobe, PA, USA

ISBN 978-3-030-54433-1   ISBN 978-3-030-54434-8   (eBook)
https://doi.org/10.1007/978-3-030-54434-8

Cover illustration: Syed Shabab / EyeEm

This Palgrave Macmillan imprint is published by the registered company Springer Nature Switzerland AG.
The registered company address is: Gewerbestrasse 11, 6330 Cham, Switzerland

For the dedicated instructors, educators, and staff members who make learning happen every day, and for the students whose enthusiasm make it a joy to teach

Preface

In 2019, I was driving in the car with Justin, and we heard "Fantastic Voyage" by Coolio on the radio. I started pointing out elements of the song that represent various elements of criminological theory, and it led to an interesting discussion. From there, I realized how my own love of the discipline is pervasive even in my personal life, and I wanted to share the idea. I thought it would be both fun and beneficial for students to understand how criminologists can apply these theories to films, television, music, and more, even when those artifacts are not overtly related to criminal justice or criminology. It is easy to point out criminal justice issues or criminological theories at work in *Law & Order* or *Criminal Minds*, but less so when watching *The Bachelor* or playing *Super Mario Brothers*.

Around the same time, I had also tweeted about the emotional burden of criminal justice research. It can be exhausting, depressing, and overwhelming at times. I asked others in the field for the ways that they cope, and I learned that many shared the same sentiments. As this project came to life, I also realized that it was an opportunity to do something *different* within our field. We rarely have the opportunity to be so creative or free-flowing or even, dare I say, fun, so this project became a source of entertainment. Contrary to popular belief, professors and academics do other things aside from research and teaching, but perhaps predictably, we never really remove our criminology hat.

This collection of essays is the work of dedicated professors and criminologists who want to share the ways they see the world and apply theory and research to even the most unexpected topics. I encourage students and educators to do the same in their lives and to find criminological theories at work in the most mundane or non-criminal justice environments. The authors have added their own personal touches, infused their personalities throughout the readings, and honestly enjoyed writing these chapters. They are more stylistically diverse and unique than standard journal articles or academic books, and that was encouraged and celebrated throughout this process. We did not want writing or reading about criminological theories to be a tedious mandate, but rather a fun exercise that can allow students to peek into the thoughts and personalities of those who have contributed. Further, I wanted to use the opportunity to demonstrate the processes and thoughts of those at varying stages in their careers and criminological studies, showcasing undergraduate and graduate students, doctoral candidates, and seasoned professors.

Criminological theories and their elements are around us every day, and as those who seek to participate and work in the criminal justice system, we have a responsibility to recognize these as the foundation for an understanding of human behavior in all forms. I hope that readers have as much fun reading these chapters as the authors did writing them, and I look forward to seeing similar exercises from young scholars and other academics. Academics, instructors, and students are encouraged to email me their own applications of theory for possible inclusion in future volumes.

Latrobe, PA   Sarah E. Daly

Acknowledgment

This book would not have been possible without the dedication and excellence of many people. It has been an honor to work with everyone on this fun and exciting project.

First and foremost, I have to thank the team at Palgrave Macmillan who were open to the idea and have provided meaningful insight and direction throughout the process. Our editor, Josie Taylor, was fantastic in providing feedback about the content, cost, and aims for the book. Liam Inscoe-Jones, our editorial assistant, has been supportive in offering information about deadlines, formatting, and finalization of the manuscript. I am thankful to have worked with such wonderful people and an organization that values this project.

Academic Twitter truly came together for this project. Through a vast network of criminologists, I met incredible people online who have contributed to this book. Just when we all think that the internet is generally terrible, something amazing comes to life from social media, and I am grateful that it was a resource that produced something positive and tangible.

The authors whose work appears in this book have been a joy. They have miraculously submitted all drafts and reviews on time and with shrewd and meaningful input. I am amazed that even at the end of semester slogs, midterm madness, and a pandemic, they have been punctual and thoughtful. Even more, their excitement about this project has pushed me to work better, faster, and harder to make this idea a reality. From students, to practitioners, to academics, everyone has worked to make their interest in and love of criminological theory accessible for students and the general reader. I have consistently been in awe of the authors who were there for all the right reasons and let down their academic walls. They jumped at the chance to apply elements of our job to our favorite forms of entertainment and the students who relished the opportunity to apply what they were learning in the classroom. Thank you to all of you taking time out of your personal and professional lives to share in this project.

Additionally, those students who helped me to organize emails, reviews, and drafts made my life infinitely easier. Thank you to Teresa Zambotti and Derek Fether for their help and for keeping me sane throughout this process.

Thank you to my colleagues and department at Saint Vincent College who supported me in this and other endeavors and recognized the importance of accessibility and pedagogical tools. Saint Vincent College is an educational environment that focuses on teaching and educating, and it has allowed me the academic freedom and creativity to pursue endeavors such as this. I am sure that many other deans and chairs would scoff at a junior criminology faculty member writing a piece on Michael Scott of *The Office*, but Dean Gary Quinlivan and my chair, Bruce Antkowiak, have been encouraging and supportive of this project. Similarly, Drs. Kayla Jachimowski and Eric Kocian in my department not only contributed to this project but also initially supported the idea and shared excitement about the project. As usual, Sandy Frye is the glue who keeps us all together and keeps the department running, and Eva Kunkel helps us in every way possible.

Finally, thank you to my friends and family who support me in all my professional goals and share and tolerate my enthusiasm about criminology. My mom, Marie Daly, is the best publicist I know and the most supportive person on earth, and my initial conversations with Justin Perry—who always listens to me ramble on about criminological theory—led to the idea for this book. My personal and professional life would be far less meaningful and full without people to share these experiences and achievements, and I am grateful to those I love for their support and their encouragement.

Contents

Notes on Contributors

Rachel Baumann, M.S. holds an M.S. in criminology from Saint Vincent College in Latrobe, Pennsylvania, and a B.S. in computer science with a concentration in cyber-security. Although her interest mainly focuses on cybercrime, an important skill in this field is understanding people and learning why they do the things they do. She is new to publishing her work, but she is always ready to learn new things and gain experiences when opportunities present themselves. She is an eDiscovery Specialist with Arconic.

Breanna Boppre, Ph.D. is an assistant professor in the School of Criminal Justice at Wichita State University. Her research examines how gender and race shape system-involvement as well as the impacts of correctional policies and practices. Her work appears in the *International Journal of Offender Therapy and Comparative Criminology*, *Corrections Policy, Practice, and Research*, *Victims & Offenders*, and *The Journal of Ethnicity in Criminal Justice*.

Andrea R. Borrego, Ph.D. is Assistant Professor of Criminal Justice and Criminology at Metropolitan State University. Her main areas of research include police use of force, LGBTQ victimization, and community perceptions of prisons.

Sarah E. Daly, Ph.D. is an assistant professor in the Criminology, Law, and Society department at Saint Vincent College in Latrobe, Pennsylvania. Before her career in academia, she was a high school Spanish teacher and school counselor in New Jersey. Her research includes work on school violence, mass and active shootings, and gender-based violence. She holds degrees in criminal justice, school counseling and applied psychology, and Spanish literature from Rutgers University, University of Pennsylvania, and University of Notre Dame, respectively.

Jared M. Hanneman, Ph.D. is an assistant professor in the Department of Sociology and Criminal Justice Studies at Thiel College in Greenville, Pennsylvania—a small, Lutheran-affiliated college in the liberal arts tradition located about an hour and a half from Pittsburgh and Cleveland. He holds a Ph.D. in sociology from the Graduate School and University Center of the City University of New York, an M.A. in sociology from University of Pittsburgh, and a B.A. in sociology, microbiology, and philosophy from Miami University in Oxford, Ohio.

Lauren Humby, Ph.D. is a lecturer in the School of Law and Criminal Justice at the University of Southern Queensland in Australia. Her research interests focus on therapeutic animal-centric practices that encourage rehabilitation, reintegration, and desistance.

Kayla G. Jachimowski, Ph.D. is an assistant professor in the Criminology, Law, and Society department at Saint Vincent College in Latrobe, Pennsylvania. Her primary areas of research include the intersection of mental health and criminal justice and statistical methodology in criminology research.

Jill A. Kehoe, Ph.D. is an assistant professor of criminal justice at City University of New York (CUNY) LaGuardia Community College. Her current work focuses on offender and situational characteristics of LGBTQ hate crimes. She has one-year-old twins and hopes that she will be able to watch the final season of *Game of Thrones*, let alone write about it.

Kristopher Kell is a master's student in criminology at Saint Vincent College. He majored in sociology as an undergraduate and has plans to continue his education in a doctoral program upon completion of his degree. He also works as a graduate assistant at the Fred Rogers Center, and his research interests include drug addictions and sexual deviance.

Eric J. Kocian, Ph.D. is an associate professor in the Criminology, Law, and Society department at Saint Vincent College in Latrobe, Pennsylvania. He has a true passion for the field of criminology and continually makes great efforts to expand his knowledge and teaching abilities in all areas of the discipline. He takes great pride in formulating honest, caring, and personal relationships with his students. He does his best to assist them with the comprehension of material in class while helping them decide where their vocational path will lead them when they leave Saint Vincent College and how they can best serve God and mankind. His relationship with God remains the most important thing in his life, and he is grateful to have such wonderful, loving, and supportive family members and friends in close proximity who remind him of His graces and blessings on a continual basis. He enjoys weightlifting, running, swimming, basketball, good movies, Notre Dame Football, and the New England Patriots.

Ryan J. Lemmon, M.S. is a criminology graduate student at Saint Vincent College. He graduated from Waynesburg University with a dual major in criminal justice administration and social sciences. He is interested in research on criminological theories as well as effective and safe law enforcement practices. He plans on working with a law enforcement agency in some capacity in the future.

Morgan P. Murphy, M.S. is a doctoral student at University of Central Florida where she studies the effects of young adults' direct and indirect exposure to gun violence. She graduated from Saint Vincent College with her master's degree in criminology in 2019 and her bachelor's degree in criminology in 2018.

Chad Painter, M.S. is a graduate of the criminology master's program at Saint Vincent College where he also earned his undergraduate degree. He is pursuing a career in law enforcement.

Paige L. Parsley, M.S. is a doctoral student at Indiana University of Pennsylvania. She graduated from Saint Vincent College and earned her master's degree in criminology in 2018. Her area of research focuses on policing and biosocial criminology.

Shon M. Reed is a doctoral student in the Department of Criminology and Criminal Justice at University of Nevada, Las Vegas. His primary research interests focus on masculinity and crime, gendered system responses to victimization, criminological theory, and white nationalism. His work has been published in *Child Abuse & Neglect* and the *Journal of Drug Issues*.

Colton D. Robinson, M.S. holds a master's degree in criminology from Saint Vincent College where he also completed his bachelor's degree. During his academic career, Colton has written many research papers, presented at an academic conference, and designed an ongoing study focusing on the public perceptions of police-worn body cameras. As one who has a love for helping others and ensuring their safety, Colton aspires to become an officer of law enforcement and has worked in juvenile probation agencies.

David Safin is Assistant Professor of Communication at Saint Vincent College in Latrobe, Pennsylvania. He holds a Master of Fine Arts in Film and Digital Technology from Chatham University in Pittsburgh where he completed the thesis, "You Had to Be There: Documentary Techniques in Narrative Comedies." His areas of interest include video production, television criticism, documentary, and film studies.

Cory Schnell, Ph.D. is an assistant professor at University of South Carolina. He holds a Ph.D. from Rutgers University. His research interests include policing, place-based criminology, and quantitative methods.

Victoria A. Sytsma, Ph.D. is an assistant professor in the Department of Sociology at Queen's University. Her research interests include policing, applied research, and open-air drug markets.

Rachel E. Vanetta is a master's student in criminology at Saint Vincent College. She graduated in 2019 with her bachelor's degree, and she plans on attending law school upon completion.

Andrew Wilczak, Ph.D. is Associate Professor of Criminology and Sociology at Wilkes University. His research interests include exploring the relationship between youth violence and victimization and both mental health and status attainment in early adulthood, with a specific focus on gender and race differences in these processes. He has a doctorate in sociology from Bowling Green State University and a master's degree in criminology and criminal justice from Eastern Michigan University.

Dana Winters, Ph.D. is the Director of Simple Interactions and Academic Programs for the Fred Rogers Center for Early Learning and Children's Media at Saint Vincent College in Latrobe, Pennsylvania. Through projects involving children's helpers across many diverse settings, including child care, school systems, community programs, residential care, and children's hospitals, she communicates and reflects what is simple and deep about work in service of children and their families. Dana holds a Ph.D. in administrative and policy studies from University of Pittsburgh, an M.A. in education from Indiana University of Pennsylvania, and a B.A. in sociology from Saint Vincent College.

List of Figures

List of Tables

An Introduction to Criminological Theory and Popular Culture

1

Paige L. Parsley and Morgan P. Murphy

An Overview of Criminology

Criminology aims to understand and explain criminal behavior and crime through observation and extensive research. The overarching idea is that in understanding criminal behavior, criminologists can better construct programs and policies and suggest changes that will prove beneficial in reducing or eliminating crime. As crime evolves and changes, so do the approaches to studying it. As such, criminology is always a growing field, with new information and insights developing every day.

The field does not study offenders alone but also considers the role that victims, law enforcement, environment, and community play in producing or inhibiting crime. In doing so, criminology recognizes that crime is not the result of a single person or characteristic, nor does it only affect the offender. Rather, many factors culminate and lead to criminal behavior. Furthermore, criminology takes into account that crime not only affects offenders, but also victims, community members, and members of the criminal justice system. In exploring all of the facets of crime

P. L. Parsley (✉)
Indiana University of Pennsylvania, Indiana, PA, USA
e-mail: P.L.Parsley@iup.edu

M. P. Murphy
University of Central Florida, Orlando, FL, USA
e-mail: morgan.murphy@knights.ucf.edu

© The Author(s) 2021
S. E. Daly (ed.), *Theories of Crime Through Popular Culture*,
https://doi.org/10.1007/978-3-030-54434-8_1

1

and possible explanations for criminal behavior, criminologists are better able to create a full picture of crime and its occurrences.

Theories as Essential Curriculum

Theory serves as the foundation of criminology. Simply put, a theory acts as a sensible way for people to understand and help explain criminal behavior and activity (Bernard, Vold, Snipes, & Gerould, 2016). Theories begin with the observation of a particular circumstance and are composed of logical, related concepts that allow criminologists to understand and explain possible reasons as to why the circumstance occurred (Kubrin, Stucky, & Krohn, 2009). By their nature, theories are systematic and provide researchers with the same methods and meaning by which to replicate and understand phenomena (Kubrin et al., 2009).

It is important to note that theories are not simply criminologists' personal opinions as to how and why crime occurs. Rather, theories are entrenched in research, applicable to multiple situations, and easily proven or disproven by other researchers (Akers, Sellers, & Jennings, 2017). Overall, learning about criminological theories provides students with the tools to better understand the underlying reasons for crime.

Applying and Observing Theories at Work

Individuals' perceptions of crime and criminal justice can be shaped through popular culture. For example, movies, television shows, music, commercials, and art are all sources of entertainment that can possibly shape an individual's perception. These sources of entertainment are able to affect what the public believes about crime and related institutions, particularly if the public has little exposure to or knowledge about actual crimes. Some popular examples of entertainment are shows such as *Law & Order*, *CSI*, and *NYPD Blue*. Other examples of popular criminology include the television show *Oz*, a 7-Up television commercial, the movie *Lean on Me*, and hip-hop music.

Yousman (2009) examines the ways in which the HBO television drama, *Oz*, legitimizes both the expansion of the prison-industrial complex and the prevalence of inhumane prison environments. He highlights the hyperviolence and the framing of race and class within the television series, and he explains that viewers enjoyed the violence that was depicted in the series. Many of the viewers expressed how realistic they believed the portrayed prison life was, while also noting that they had never been to jail or prison in their lifetime. The series depicted 72 deaths throughout the six seasons, and the vast majority of those deaths were portrayed as homicides. In contrast to the television show's depiction of prison life and violence, the most prevalent leading causes of death in prison are suicide, disease, or old age (Yousman, 2009). As a result, individuals' perceptions of prison life were shaped based on the television show of the HBO television show *Oz*.

A 7-Up television commercial created by Young & Rubicam caused an uproar when they based a commercial on the old saying, "Don't drop the soap." The commercial begins with the protagonist in a prison, who drops a can of 7-Up. He then turns to the camera and says, "I'm not picking that up." Next, the actor sits in a cell with an incarcerated individual who has his arm around him. The actor goes on to say, "When you drink 7-Up, everyone is your friend." A few seconds later, the actor says "OK, that is enough being friends." The commercial then fades to black, but viewers are still able to hear the actor say "Hey, where are you going?"

The commercial was later removed from television after two months as a result of the nature of the ad. The activist group, Stop Prisoner Rape, led the campaign to have the ad taken off of television. The organization believed that the ad was making light of and joking about prison rape, and they argued that it would skew individuals' perceptions of prison rape (Whitehead, 2010). When television shows and ads make prison rape jokes, they normalize the idea of prison rape. As an idea—in this case, prison rape—becomes normalized, there is a possibility that it is not taken as seriously as it should be, and it becomes a part of common rhetoric about and widely accepted beliefs.

Another example of criminological theories in popular culture is the movie, *Lean on Me*. Based on a New Jersey high school principal, Joe Clark, a Black educator, who was hired in order to improve the conditions of a predominantly African-American high school and, primarily, to raise students' test scores in order to prevent the state from taking over the school. In his first act as principal, Clark expels 300 students that were "identified" as drug dealers or troublemakers. Clark not only expelled students, but he also fired teachers that did not agree with his radical measures.

Irwin Hyman (1989) discusses how the movie is misleading and how easily society can be deceived when offered an easy solution. After the movie was released, there was public support for Clark and his tough-guy antics. Individuals even cheered for his actions against the students and teachers. If these radical tactics were used on a parent's child, they would not be cheering for Clarks' tactics but would be arguing against them.

Hyman (1989) argues that if these tactics were used by a white principal, then the principal and tactics would be racist. However, since they were performed by an African American principal, they are not. In reality, the takeover of the school by the state was never a threat. Furthermore, the test scores of Clark's students on the New Jersey High School Proficiency Test were the lowest in the state for 1986 through 1988 (Hyman, 1989).

Regarding popular criminology, the concern is that *Lean on Me* could shape individuals' perceptions of the public-school system. For example, an individual could reasonably conclude that expelling "troublemakers" is an efficient way to quickly improve a school environment. Moreover, audiences could view Clark's radical actions as acceptable or even desirable when considering options for improving a school system if they were to base their opinions on the movie alone. As such, the movie paints a particularly unrealistic, somewhat dangerous standard for viewers.

Hip-hop music is another source of popular culture that has the potential to affect individuals' perceptions of society. Due to lyrics that are commonly used, hip-hop music is widely associated with violence (Taylor & Taylor, 2007). For example, the popular song "Murder on My Mind" by YNW Melly was in the top 20 on the Billboard Hot 100 and was also No. 1 on Apple Music (Anderson, 2019; Eustice, 2019). The popular song refers to YNW Melly shooting and killing two of his friends. Melly even turned himself in to the police and was charged with two counts of first-degree murder (Hopkins, 2019). The use of explicit, violent lyrics can encourage or lead many youths to copy and act out the lyrics that they hear in songs, though there are other legal concerns about freedom of speech, hip-hop and other music as art rather than a glorification of violence. Individuals, most likely youth, could be affected by hip-hop music and what they believe about music and crime. The study of criminological theories present in hip-hop could be a unique pedagogical tool as well as a historical evaluation and artistic representation of a specific time period. Further, it can highlight the ways in which popular culture can affect views and perspectives about groups of people, leading to a larger discussion of popular criminology.

Popular Criminology and This Book

Popular criminology is a conceptual approach used to interrogate popular understandings of crime and criminal justice and examine the interconnections between crime culture and media (Kohm, 2017). Movies, television shows, music, art, and literature are a few sources of popular criminology that criminologists use. Popular criminology as a field of study could expand the ways in which scholars approach the study of crime and criminal behavior. This book provides several examples of how criminologists can apply criminological theory to popular culture.

The layout of this book is designed to give students insight into how criminologists think about issues. In applying criminological theory to popular culture, the authors show how deeply criminological theory pervades everyday life, not only for the authors themselves but also for the subjects about which they write. The book will change the lens through which students look at the world around them and encourage them to consider the theoretical underpinnings of the books, movies, and music that they love.

As students read, they should notice that each chapter differs from the next in both topic and approach. While this design may seem unusual for students, particularly those who have only encountered only more formal texts, it will show them that there is not one single "right way" to think about criminology. In fact, it is these nuances in how criminologists think and consider topics that create new ways to consider criminological issues. The importance of innovative thinking is invaluable, as it keeps the criminology field moving forward and progressing.

Students will also note that each author has his or her own writing style and process through which they convey their findings. Unlike peer-reviewed journal articles that have a specific layout and rigid requirements, this book allowed the authors more freedom to express their points of view regarding popular criminology and theoretical thinking. The strengths of this design are twofold: (1) Writing a chapter was fun for the authors, rather than an exercise in checking off a list of requirements for a peer-reviewed journal article. (2) Students are able to observe that success in the criminological field is not necessarily determined by a particular writing style or format, but rather the ability to think critically and articulate findings.

Moving Forward

From here, it is our greatest hope that students take the idea of applying criminological theories to popular culture and do the same. Whether the songs that students listen to remind them of strain theory or they recognize that the plot of the movie they are watching has a plot riddled with elements of deterrence that heightened level of thinking is our goal.

References

Akers, R. L., Sellers, C. S., & Jennings, W. G. (2017). *Criminological theories: Introduction, evaluation, and application (7th ed.)*. New York, NY: Oxford University Press.

Anderson, T. (2019, February 28). YNW Melly's "Murder on My Mind" Blasts into Top 20 on Billboard Hot 100. *Billboard*. Retrieved from https://www.billboard.com/articles/columns/chart-beat/8500550/ynw-melly-murder-my-mind-top-20-billboard-hot-100

Bernard, T. J., Vold, G. B., Snipes, J. B., & Gerould, A. L. (2016). *Vold's theoretical criminology (7th ed.)*. New York: Oxford University Press.

Eustice, K. (2019, February 16). YNW Melly's "Murder on My Mind" Nabs No. 1 Spot on Apple Music Amid Murder Charges. *HipHopDX*. Retrieved from https://hiphopdx.com/news/id.50328/title.ynw-mellys-murder-on-my-mind-nabs-no-1-spot-on-apple-music-amid-murder-charges

Hopkins, A. (2019, April 3). YNW Melly's "Murder on My Mind" Takes on New Meaning After Double Murder Charges. *Miami New Times*. Retrieved from https://www.miaminewtimes.com/music/ynw-mellys-murder-on-my-mind-takes-on-new-meaning-after-double-murder-charges-11086114

Hyman, I. A. (1989). The Make-Believe World of "Lean on Me". *The Education Digest, 55*(3), 20–23. https://doi.org/10.1107/s0108768107031758/bs5044sup1.cif

Kohm, S. (2017). Popular Criminology. *Oxford Research Encyclopedia of Criminology and Criminal Justice*. https://doi.org/10.1093/acrefore/9780190264079.013.158

Kubrin, C. E., Stucky, T. D., & Krohn, M. D. (2009). *Researching theories of crime and deviance*. New York, NY: Oxford University Press.

Taylor, C., & Taylor, V. (2007). Hip Hop Is Now: An Evolving Youth Culture. *Reclaiming Children and Youth: The Journal of Strength-Based Interventions, 15*(4), 210–213.

Whitehead, J. (2010, June 21). 7-Up Pulls TV Ad After Civil Rights Groups Cry Foul Over Prison Rape Joke. *Campaign US*. Retrieved from https://www.campaignlive.com/article/7-up-pulls-tv-ad-civil-rights-groups-cry-foul-prison-rape-joke/146481

Yousman, B. (2009). Inside Oz: Hyperviolence, Race and Class Nightmares, and the Engrossing Spectacle of Terror. *Communication and Critical/Cultural Studies, 6*(3), 265–284. https://doi.org/10.1080/14791420903049728

Deterrence Theory and *Batman*

The Dark Knight of Deterrence

Eric J. Kocian

"Why bats, Master Wayne?" asked Alfred, as Bruce Wayne molded a throwing weapon into the shape of the nocturnal creature. "Bats frighten me. It's time my enemies share my dread" (Nolan, 2005, 0:59). Batman comic books, movies, and television series hover around the theme of a billionaire orphan assuming the role of the Batman in order to fight crime and keep the people of Gotham City safe from those who prey upon its citizens. Like many other superhero characters, Bruce Wayne suffered a tremendous loss earlier in his life when he witnessed the murder of his parents, Martha and Thomas Wayne. This event sparked a flame inside young Bruce to fight crime and victimization, relying on his extreme intellect, rigorous training, and vast family fortune.

Yet, despite the high-tech devices and weapons found on his Bat-belt, the state of the art computers and intelligence software in the Bat cave, and the military-style land (Batmobile), sea (Batsub), and aircraft (Batwing) vehicles, the tool utilized most by Batman in bringing about justice was the element of fear. Before his passing, Thomas Wayne taught young Bruce the valuable lesson that "all creatures feel fear" (Nolan, 2005, 0:11). It was a life lesson that Bruce Wayne came to fully understand and master to protect Gotham, as evidenced by his life's work and the manner he fulfilled it.

E. J. Kocian (✉)
Saint Vincent College, Latrobe, PA, USA
e-mail: eric.kocian@stvincent.edu

Long before Bruce Wayne became Batman, taking to the streets with a hatred of evil and a desire to bring about justice; turning fear against those who prey on the fearful, Cesare Beccaria published his book *On Crimes and Punishments*. Beccaria's 1764 manuscript on criminal law reform received instant interest and appreciation for his unique perspectives on crime, those who partake in criminal behaviors, and those who seek to punish them accordingly. Beccaria argued that the law needed to be impartial, with equal sanctions applied to anyone who engaged in antisocial behaviors, but in a manner mild and humane and proportional to the crime (Beccaria, 1764/1986).

In the world of criminology, Beccaria's work epitomizes classical theory. The starting premise for classical criminology theories is that human behavior is a result of free will: a rational calculation of risk/reward or pain/pleasure. Behavior, according to classical criminologists, assumes a cost-benefit analysis (Akers & Sellers, 2009; Bernard, Snipes, & Gerould, 2016). In other words, people make decisions based on the extent they believe their choice of behavior options will maximize their pleasure and/or minimize their pain.

Crime occurs when the perceived benefits or pleasures of a certain act outweigh the perceived costs, or when people pursue their own self-interests because effective punishment is lacking (Cullen & Agnew, 2003). They argue,

> All individuals choose to obey or violate the law by a rational calculation of the risk of pain versus potential pleasure derived from an act. In contemplating a criminal act, they take into account the probable legal penalties and the likelihood they will be caught. (Akers, 2000, p. 16)

Beccaria argued that punishments should be such that the cost of crime exceeds the rewards of crime, *deterring* people from engaging in criminal behaviors out of fear of being punished (Akers & Sellers, 2009; Bernard et al., 2016).

When dissecting the constructs of Beccaria's deterrence theory, the element of fear remains apparent. All creatures feel fear. This was a lesson both Cesare Beccaria and Bruce Wayne (Batman) taught humanity in their own, unique ways. The purpose of this chapter is to explore the many ways in which Beccaria's deterrence theory cloaks itself in the cowl of the Caped Crusader character in order to provide a better understanding of Beccaria's Batman, also known as The Dark Knight of Deterrence.

Two Facets, Same Subject

Specific deterrence and general deterrence operate similarly to that of Bruce Wayne and Batman: two identities, but the same subject. Bruce Wayne, the eccentric billionaire playboy, focused his attention and efforts on running Wayne enterprises and making sound financial decisions that benefitted his individual lifestyle. Batman, on the other hand, the vigilante crime-fighter, focused his attention and efforts on scouring the city streets in search of villains. He did so to ensure Gotham citizens were protected, in order to benefit society as a whole.

Deterrence theory can best be understood and viewed in terms of specific deterrence and general deterrence, two identities dealing with the same subject matter. Specific deterrence focuses on the individual and the punishment he or she suffered as a result of a crime or forbidden behavior in which they were caught and punished. When that individual is given the opportunity to engage in said behavior again, for which he or she was previously punished, theoretically speaking, the person will choose not to do it again out of fear of the impending punishment (Akers & Sellers, 2009).

An example of how specific deterrence works theoretically can be found in the sentiments of media personality and model, Paris Hilton. In 2007, Paris Hilton was arrested for driving with a suspended license following her driving under the influence (DUI) arrest. She was sentenced to serve 45 days in jail, serving 23 days before being placed on house arrest. In an interview with Larry King following her release, Paris said she would "never again drink and drive and that her time in jail was 'a time-out in life'" (HULIQ, 2007, n.p.). The punishment instilled in Paris Hilton a fear about choosing to drink and drive and, as a result of the reprimand she received, she will choose not to partake in that behavior again.

General deterrence, on the other hand, operates a little differently with attention paid to how the punishment of someone else affects all others in society. The general deterrent effect occurs when someone in society is caught and punished for a crime. The wrongdoer serves as an example and theoretically speaking, others in society will choose not to engage in the same type of behavior out of fear they will be punished similarly. The punishment for bad behavior serves as an example to others in society, and it is believed they will be afraid to engage in the same behavior for which someone else was punished (Akers & Sellers, 2009).

In keeping with the Paris Hilton example, her punishment (jail time) for driving under the influence of alcohol and driving with a suspended license should deter others from committing the crimes she committed. The other members of society knew what she did because of her celebrity status. They knew what the punishment was that followed as a result of the news coverage. Therefore, fear of punishment would cause them to make a different choice when placed in a similar situation to Hilton's.

Commissioner Jim Gordon best realized the impact of a general deterrent effect as a result of Batman's efforts in Gotham. Commissioner Gordon maximized that value by striking fear into criminals, most notably with his use of the Bat-signal. The Bat-signal was a large projection light housed on the rooftop of the Gotham City Police Department and, when lit, cast a brilliant Bat-symbol across the Gotham nightline. This signal served as a way to communicate with Batman and alert him that his efforts were required, but it also served as a means to strike fear into potential lawbreakers by letting them know Batman could be in the general vicinity (DC Database, n.d.).

As mentioned previously, classical theorists assume human beings are guided by their own free will, and decisions for law-abiding behaviors and law violations are the result of personal choice (Beccaria, 1764/1986). If behavior, including crime, is a result of choice and individuals exercise their free will to engage in such behaviors, Beccaria stressed the idea of deterrence through punishment in order to decrease criminal behaviors. As stated earlier, this calculation is rooted in the individual's prior experience with punishment, either specifically or generally (Akers, 2000). Crime, according to this line of thinking, essentially would be controlled by the law if the perceived "cost" or punishment for a violation of a behavior outweighed the perceived reward.

If criminals believed Batman lurked about in the shadows, waiting to punish those who violated the law, deterrence theory would suggest people would be too afraid to offend because the cost of unlawful behavior outweighed the potential reward. The potential for physical confrontation with Batman and his brand of justice, coupled with the likelihood of punishment from Gotham's legal brand of justice, made it advantageous for people to obey the law. In short, it would not be worth the risk of engaging in whatever nefarious act considered because the risk outweighed the reward: an essential concept to the theory. This has often been referred to as the felicific calculus principle, where people seek to obtain an agreeable balance of pleasure and pain (Schmalleger & Bartollas, 2008).

Holy Ingredients, Batman (The Swiftness, Certainty, and Severity of Punishment)

From 1966 through 1968, Adam West held the title role of Batman in the famed television series (IMDb TV, n.d.). Anytime he or his trusty sidekick, Robin, would find themselves in a battle throwing punches at evildoers, words insinuating the power their punches carried would flash across the scene. This lets viewers know how those blows resonated in the minds and bodies of the culprits. It was unmistakable to viewers of all ages that the lawbreakers were being punished by Batman (and Robin).

Beccaria argued the main objective of punishment should be deterrence. "To be deterred, offenders must stop to weigh the costs and benefits, be aware of the penalties, find those penalties intolerable, and have other more attractive options" (Vincent & Hofer, 1994, p. 11). In order to achieve deterrence, punishments should be based on the principles of celerity (swiftness), certainty, and severity proportional to the crime (Akers, 2000; Beccaria, 1764/1986; Cullen & Agnew, 2003).

Celerity, or swiftness, refers to the amount of time that passes between the commission of an illegal act and the implementation of punishment on that individual. The more "swift" or immediate a punishment follows an unwanted behavior, the more meaningful and useful the punishment will be to the individual and perhaps society as a whole (Akers, 2000). Beccaria (1764/1986) stated in his book, *On Crimes and Punishments*, "the more prompt the punishment is and the sooner it follows the crime, the more just and useful it will be" (p. 36).

In applying swiftness to Batman and his brand of justice to assess how effective he was in satisfying Beccaria's first requirement for deterrence, one can make the argument that the Dark Knight delivered his punishment in a most expeditious manner. Whether Batman restrained criminals at the scene of the crime without much of a struggle or he delivered a beat-down before incapacitating them, the vigilante crime-fighter brought about "street-style" justice immediately. Compared to the criminal justice system, where due process and the rights of the accused delay punishment for those convicted or pleading guilty to a crime, Batman measured out and administered punishment more rapidly than any formal, governmental system could for aforementioned reasons.

Proportional severity of punishment deals with the strength or intensity of an imposed punishment when a specific behavior has occurred (Gray, Miranne III, Ward, &Menke, 1982). Severity concerns fitting the amount of punishment in proportion to the damage the crime had on society. The punishment remanded to the offender should be such that it is severe enough to outweigh the benefits of the crime, but not overly severe, as unjust punishments will not deter (Akers, 2000; Beccaria, 1764/1986).

When looking at the level of severity Batman levied toward criminals, he appears to have found the perfect balance of rigor and harshness. His level of force (severity) depended on the seriousness of the crime and the threats posed by the individuals perpetrating them. From all cinematic and literary accounts, Batman levied his most stern punishments on those who posed the biggest threats to the overall well-being of society. Batman continually dug deeper into his repertoire of reprimands to provide appropriate penance for those who sinned against humanity. Whether it be the Joker, the Penguin, Bane, or the Riddler, it is hard to argue that the common thief or drug dealer was dealt with as harshly as those terrorists who endangered the citizens of Gotham the most. To the observer, Batman's recipe of reckoning captured the perfect balance of retribution and equity toward all he served.

Certainty deals with the chances that an individual will be punished for an illegal or unwanted behavior (Gray et al., 1982). Increasing the certainty of punishment if someone engages in an illegal behavior decreases the probability that the individual will continue to engage in illegal behavior because of the perceived likelihood of being punished (Akers, 2000; Beccaria, 1764/1986). In deterrence research, certainty remains the most important of the three elements (Beccaria, 1764/1986; Bernard et al., 2016). Certainty of punishment remains the most difficult to attain and/or assess, even with child-rearing practices or violations of criminal statutes. Not all crimes or violations are reported and oftentimes, people successfully complete criminal acts multiple times before getting caught.

While it remains impossible to punish every single time a bad behavior occurs, the idea Batman (and other deterrence theorists) subscribe to looks for ways to increase the certainty of punishment. "The certainty of punishment, even if it be moderate, will always make a stronger impression than the fear of another which is more terrible but combined with the hope of impunity; even the least evils, when they are certain, always terrify men's minds" (Bernard et al., 2016, p. 9).

In the final scene of *Batman Begins*, Jim Gordon reports the progress of Batman's efforts to him by stating, "You really started something here; bad cops running scared; hope in the streets..." to which Batman responds, "We can bring Gotham back" (Nolan, 2005, 2:09). This entire conversation serves homage to Beccaria's respect for the certainty of punishment and the idea that Batman's efforts are helping to meet that requirement.

Further proof of Batman triumphing in achieving the perception of certainty that criminals will be punished takes place in *The Dark Knight* when the Joker first meets with the mob bosses of Gotham. The Joker begins by saying, "Let's wind the clocks back a year. These cops and lawyers would never cross you. What happened? Did your balls drop off? I know why you are afraid to go out at night: The Batman" (Nolan, 2008, 0:23–0:24). Although never directly referenced by Gordon or the Joker, the certainty of punishment manifested in Batman's pursuit of justice facilitated both his sense of deterrence and justice.

Batman's and Beccaria's Boundaries

Throughout the history of the Batman comic books and cinematic portrayals, questions about Batman and his taking of human life have been debated. Some contest that Batman killed the Joker in a 1988 comic book episode, entitled *The Killing Joke*, while others argue the Batman did not take the Joker's life at that time (Burlingame, 2017; Crump, 2013).

In Christopher Nolan's *Batman Begins*, the final step for Bruce Wayne's training to become a member of the League of Shadows required him to execute a farmer accused of stealing his neighbor's land and killing him. Bruce Wayne confesses that he is no executioner and that the man should be tried for the accusations against him. Bruce is told that his compassion is a weakness his enemies will not share, to which he responds, "That's why it's so important: it separates us from them. This man should be tried" (Nolan, 2005, 0:36). Batman's appreciation for human life rests on the same foundation as Beccaria's work, regardless of whether or not Batman killed the Joker or other villains most dangerous to society. Batman recognizes the benefits of utilizing the criminal justice system and not punishing overly harshly, conceding that incarceration provides a more equitable outcome than death.

Beccaria believed that capital punishment was not a right, but instead was a war of the nation against a citizen and not useful or necessary, with the exception of two rare circumstances. Beccaria's first argument in favor of capital punishment occurred when the security of the nation was threatened by the existence of someone whose mere life presence produced the threat of a revolution. The second justification for the use of capital punishment provided by Beccaria involved the scenario where death served as the one and only deterrent to discourage others from committing crimes (Beccaria, 1764/1986).

Alfred, in a comic book speech, said, "There are reasons not to kill. We've discussed these before. To say that murder is immoral is too vague. Killing, even once, even with reasons, strips you of your humanity" (White, 2019, p. 151). Alfred's soliloquy resonated throughout the Batcave and echoed Beccaria's creed concerning the taking of a human life. Batman does allow for exceptions and, while not explicitly stated, they pertain to conditions similar to those expressed by Beccaria.

Four specific instances exist where Batman either allowed a wrongdoer to perish or purposely caused their death. All four occurrences involved exceptionally sinister and remarkably dangerous extremists who accounted for the innumerable deaths of Gotham citizens. Batman's justification for said actions revolved around the notion that their capture and imprisonment would not guarantee adequate protection for society, due to their abilities to escape/orchestrate crimes from jail and/or their destructive actions were so heinous an example needed to be made out of them (White, 2019). The rational parallels Beccaria's seamlessly. After blockading a door, ensuring a Soviet Union assassin would die, rather than apprehend him, Batman thought to himself, "Sometimes circumstances are such that rules pervert justice. I'm not in the business to protect rules. I serve justice" (White, 2019, p. 160).

Becoming Legends

The philosophies, practices, and punitive ideologies between Batman and Beccaria harmonize impeccably. Both men similarly hypothesized human nature, prescribed parallel courses of action to curtail unwanted behaviors, and realized the importance of guarding against abuses and atrocities associated with punishment. Their respective work remains in the upper echelons of respect and acclaim of their corresponding fields and persists as the subject of countless opinions, educated debates, and rigorous studies. Essential to properly understanding either composition entails recognizing and appreciating how fear of punishment influences human behavior. Bruce Wayne articulated it best before his training began when he proclaimed, "I seek the means to fight injustice; to turn fear against those who prey on the fearful" (Nolan, 2005, 0:08).

As a result of their masterpieces in their given concentrations, both Batman and Beccaria live on as literary classics. Deterrence theory remains the posterchild for the classical school of criminology while Batman posters hang about comic bookstores, movie theaters, and the walls of Caped Crusader fans' bedrooms. Their impact remains mythical, leaving readers and aficionados to wonder how men like Cesare Beccaria and Bruce Wayne, neither with any unearthly superpowers to speak of, could elevate themselves to such lofty heights. Perhaps the answer to such inquiry can be found in the words spoken to Bruce Wayne early on during his training; "If you make yourself more than just a man, if you devote yourself to an ideal, and if they can't stop you, then you become something else entirely… a legend, Mr. Wayne" (Nolan, 2005, 0:05). Suffice it to say, amongst other things, Batman and Beccaria remain legends of deterrence and crusaders for criminology.

Discussion Questions

1. Deterrence theory focuses more on punishment than it does on rehabilitation. Can Deterrence Theory remain relevant during times when the Criminal Justice

System focuses more on rehabilitation and education than it does on punishment and incapacitation?

2. Deterrence theory assumes people make decisions on the extent they wish to maximize pleasure and/or minimize pain. Do you think human beings are rational creatures or do you believe behavior is more determined by forces outside of our control?

3. Critics argue that deterrence theory is not effective at altering behavior compared to other theories. Think about raising an infant or house-training a pet. When you witness a behavior you wish to change in that child or pet, what methods do you find to be most successful? Do those methods coincide with deterrence theory or are they in direct opposition to deterrence theory?

4. What are some policy recommendations you can suggest using deterrence theory as the theoretical foundation for your argument?

5. Deterrence theory states that certainty is the most important element of punishment and severity is the least important element of punishment. Why do you think we have a tendency in the criminal justice system to focus more on severity of punishment than certainty of punishment?

References

Akers, R. L. (2000). *Criminological Theories: Introduction, Evaluation, and Application* (8th ed.). Los Angeles, CA: Roxbury Publishing Company.

Akers, R. L., & Sellers, C. S. (2009). *Criminological Theories: Introduction, Evaluation, and Application* (5th ed.). New York, NY: Oxford University Press.

Beccaria, C. (1986). *On Crimes and Punishments* (D. Young, Trans.). Indianapolis, IN: Hackett Publishing. (Original work published 1764).

Bernard, T. J., Snipes, J. B., & Gerould, A. L. (2016). *Vold's Theoretical Criminology* (7th ed.). New York, NY: Oxford University Press.

Burlingame, R. (2017). Did Batman Kill the Joker in Alan Moores' The Killing Joke? Retrieved from https://comicbook.com/blog/2013/08/16/did-batman-kill-the-joker-in-alan-moores-the-killing-joke/

Crump, A. (2013). Did Batman Kill the Joker at the End of Killing Joke? *Movie News Screen Rant.* Retrieved from https://screenrant.com/the-killing-joke-batman-killed-joker-grant-morrison/

Cullen, F. T., & Agnew, R. (2003). *Criminological Theory: Past to Present* (2nd ed.). Los Angeles, CA: Roxbury Publishing Company.

DC Database. (n.d.). Bat-Signal. Retrieved from https://dc.fandom.com/wiki/Bat-Signal

Gray, L. N., Miranne III, A. C., Ward, D. A., & Menke, B. (1982). A Game Theoretical Analysis of the Components of Punishment. *Social Psychology Quarterly, 45*(4), 206–212.

HULIQ. (2007). Paris Hilton Tells She Will Never Drink and Drive. Retrieved from http://www.huliq.com/25843/paris-hilton-tells-she-will-never-drink-and-drive

IMDb TV. (n.d.). Batman. Retrieved from https://www.imdb.com/title/tt0059968/

Nolan, C. (Director). (2005). *Batman Begins* [Motion Picture]. Burbank, CA: Warner Brothers Entertainment Inc. Blue Ray.

Nolan, C. (Director). (2008). *The Dark Knight* [Motion Picture]. Burbank, CA: Warner Brothers Entertainment Inc. Blue Ray.

Schmalleger, F., & Bartollas, C. (2008). *Juvenile Delinquency*. Boston, MA: Pearson Education, Inc..

Vincent, B. S., & Hofer, P. J. (1994). *The Consequences of Mandatory Minimum Prison Terms: A Summary of Recent Findings*. Washington, DC: Federal Judicial Center.

White, M. D. (2019). *Batman and Ethics*. Hoboken, NJ: Wiley Blackwell.

Social Learning Theory and *Mean Girls*

3

"You Can't Sit with Us": An Application of Social Learning Theory

Kayla G. Jachimowski, Ryan J. Lemmon
and Rachel E. Vanetta

A Brief Introduction to Social Learning Theory

Social learning theories focus on the process, application, and learning of criminal or delinquent behaviors during the socialization of juveniles. More specifically, how those who are close to the juvenile, for example, teachers, family members, religious leaders, or peers can affect the ways in which an individual interacts with the world and people around them. Consider the concept of "hate." It is a well-held notion that hate is a learned behavior; the constant exposure to negative feelings, contacts, or ideology can plant the seeds that lead to violent, hateful encounters. Similarly, social learning theorists believe that crime and delinquency are learned, though the specifics of how the behaviors are learned vary between the theories. Most theorists credit Edwin Sutherland's differential association theory as the start of more modern-day social learning theories. Ronald Akers (1994) articulates that his theory is a "reformulation and extension" of Sutherland's take on learned criminal behavior (as cited in Cullen & Agnew, 2011, p. 130).

While there are many social learning theories to consider, both empirically and historically, this chapter focuses on three theories: differential association theory (Sutherland 1947), differential reinforcement theory (Burgess & Akers, 1966), and

K. G. Jachimowski (✉) · R. J. Lemmon · R. E. Vanetta
Saint Vincent College, Latrobe, PA, USA
e-mail: kayla.jachimowski@stvincent.edu

© The Author(s) 2021
S. E. Daly (ed.), *Theories of Crime Through Popular Culture*,
https://doi.org/10.1007/978-3-030-54434-8_3

social learning theory (SLT) (Akers, 1994). The chapter is broken into two parts. First, it is an overview of two of the theories mentioned above and their relevance as it builds to understanding the application of SLT. Second, the movie *Mean Girls* was chosen specifically because of its pop culture icon status. In addition to the awards, nominations, and celebrity mentions, the movie has topped charts for its witty portrayal of high school, the adaption of a screenplay from a book, and the memorable quotes the authors continue to use throughout this chapter. Sutherland, and other social learning theorists, suggests that peer-groups play a critical role in learned behavior; as such, the authors of this chapter picked a piece of media that focuses explicitly on the hardships of peer relationships in high school at that.

Differential Association

Edwin Sutherland's (1939) differential association is the first complete look at what would later become a cornerstone for social learning theorists. However, it is worth mentioning that he spent eight years perfecting his theory (as cited in Cullen & Agnew, 2011). In Sutherland's theory, the emphasis was not on *how* behavior was learned, but rather *what* was learned. He believed that was the only difference between conforming to societal norms and engaging in criminal behavior (Williams & McShane, 2010). Unfortunately, given the complexities of his nine propositions (discussed below) and the empirical nightmare of attempting to test some of the central concepts, differential association was frequently critiqued as a theory that cannot achieve empirical validity. In fact, despite attempts, Lanier, Henry, and Anastasia (2015) suggest that, even though some concepts have received support, the evidence suggests the theory is too complex and unclear to be successfully tested.

It is well beyond the scope of this book chapter to discuss, in detail, Sutherland's nine propositions of differential association. However, it is essential to know them to understand how Akers (1994) expands on the part of these concepts. Additionally, the second theory discussed, differential reinforcement, also stems from these proposed processes of how individuals begin engaging in criminal behavior. The authors have provided these, in brief, in Fig. 3.1. However, they would like to emphasize that learning theorists maintain that criminal behavior is learned and spent the next 60 or so years attempting to define and expand on the concepts presented in Sutherland's differential association theory. Furthermore, Burgess and Akers (1966) maintained several of the general propositions proposed by Sutherland while clarifying their position (see Fig. 3.2).

1. Criminal behavior is learned
2. Criminal behavior is learned through interactions with other persons in a process of communication.
3. The principal part of the learning of criminal behavior occurs within intimate personal groups.
4. When criminal behavior is learned, the learning includes (a) techniques of committing the crime, which are sometimes very complicated sometimes very simple; (b) the specific direction of motive, drives, rationalizations, and attitudes.
5. The specific direction of motives and drive is learned from definitions of the legal codes as favorable or unfavorable.
6. A person becomes delinquent because of an excess of definitions favorable to violation of law.
7. Differential associations may vary in frequency, duration, priority, and intensity.
8. The process of learning criminal behavior by association with criminal and anti-criminal patterns involves all of the mechanisms that are involved in any other learning.
9. While criminal behavior is an expression of general needs and values, it is not explained by those general needs and values since non-criminal behavior is an expression of the same needs and values.

Fig. 3.1 Nine propositions of differential association theory. (Note: Figure adapted from the propositions in Sutherland, E. H., Cressey, D. R., & Luckenbill, D. F. (1992). *Principles of Criminology*. Dix Hills, NY: General Hall)

Differential Reinforcement (Burgess & Akers, 1966)

Initially, three theorists attempted to address the limitations of Sutherland's differential association theory, C. Ray Jeffery (1965) and Burgess and Akers (1966), by blending Sutherland's theory with an emphasis on Skinner's concept of operant conditioning (Lanier et al., 2015). Simply speaking, this is the idea that behaviors can be adapted following a series of punishments and reinforcements. Tibbetts (2015) suggested that due to the nature of academia being too "intradisciplinary," it is likely Sutherland would have considered adding operant conditioning to his theory had it been a more well-known concept (p. 142). After deciding that Jeffrey's (1965) definitions and concepts of learning theory still lacked clarity, Burgess and Akers made attempts to reformulate learning theories to concepts that were more testable than the ones proposed (Williams & McShane, 2010). Most specifically, Burgess and Akers (1966) approached differential reinforcement from a position of punishment, specifically that punishment could be positive if it leads to a decrease in unwanted behavior.

1. Criminal behavior is learned according to the principles of operant conditioning
2. Deviant behavior is learned both in nonsocial situations that are reinforcing or discriminating and through that social interactions in which the behavior of other persons is reinforcing or discriminating for such criminal behavior
3. The central proposition of learning criminal behavior is found in groups which make up most of the individual's reinforcement.
4. Specific skills, techniques, avoidance tactics, and attitudes are functions of the effective and available reinforcers and the existing reinforcement contingencies.
5. Classes of behaviors which are learned and frequently occurring, are reinforcements which are effective, available, and reinforced by the norms were the reinforcers are applied.
6. Criminal behavior is a function of learning behaviors (criminal in nature) that is more highly reinforced when compared to noncriminal behavior.
7. Learned criminal behavior is directly related to the probability, frequency, and amount of reinforcement of the behavior. These interactions rely on the attitudes, norms, and inclinations of the group.

Fig. 3.2 Seven propositions of differential reinforcement theory. (Note: Figure adapted from the propositions in Burgess, R., & Akers, R. (1966). A Differential Association-Reinforcement Theory of Criminal Behavior. *Social Problems, 14*, 131)

Secondly, though all their propositions can be seen in Fig. 3.2, an emphasis on differential reinforcement is the role of imitation and modeling in reinforcing behaviors across the spectrum of what is socially acceptable. Influenced by the work of Bandura, which suggests that while operant conditioning is vital as a form of conditioning, they maintained that individuals can learn simply by watching the actions of other people. Arguably, Bandura plays an extremely important role in Burgess and Akers (1966) theory of differential reinforcement because it focuses on how the modeling of behaviors of adults and, relevant to this chapter, peers can change how a juvenile mimics behaviors, which are favorable (this is outside of the legality of said behavior).

As with all criminological theories, there are criticisms of this theory. Most notably, the theory is criticized that its propositions continue to be tautological (Tibbetts, 2015). Simply put, it cannot be specified, which variables presented in Burgess and Akers' (1966) differential reinforcement theory come first in their list of propositions. Even more specifically, Tibbetts (2015) offers the example that if individuals are offending because they have seen others offend, and they have seen positive results from criminal behavior, it makes sense that they would believe criminal behavior is good and increase the likelihood of offending. Secondly, it is still challenging to determine the association of peers and whether that occurs before or after the delinquent behavior. However, despite these criticisms, differential association theory is possibly the most empirically valid theory outside of those who fall under integrated criminological theories (Tibbetts, 2015).

Both of these theories play an enormous role in understanding the necessary foundations of Akers' SLT because they have informed the understanding of the direction of how criminal behavior may be learned. One point the authors wish to make is the distinction between micro- and macro-level theories: most simply put, individual-level theories (micro-level theories) versus group-level theories (macro-level theories). This difference is important because criminological theories have difficulty explaining differences among groups of people, that is, socioeconomic status, sex, race, geographical locations, to name a few. Sutherland's *differential association* and Burgess and Akers' *differential reinforcement* are micro-level theories (meaning their focus is on individuals). Neither theory attempts to extrapolate their concepts as macro-level (focusing on groups). Akers' SLT was extended in 1998 to do just that—apply criminal learning propositions across groups of people.

Social Learning Theory: Learned Behavior

Social learning theory is a criminological theory used to explain deviant behavior. The theory contends that criminal behavior is driven by variables that both motivate and control undesirable behaviors. These variables can both encourage and undermine conformity, depending on different factors (Cullen & Agnew, 2003). Ronald Akers, the founder of SLT, revitalized differential association theory, incorporating the language of operant conditioning. Akers wrote that criminal behavior is learned in both social and nonsocial situations. The social situations he referenced are reinforcing or discriminative through social interactions. How people act in these social interactions are also reinforcing or discriminative for criminal behavior (Vold, Bernard, & Snipes, 1998). Essentially, social and nonsocial situations and interactions with people in these situations and exposure to their behavior prove to be reinforcing or discriminative stimuli for criminal behavior.

Operant conditioning holds that an organism (in this case, a person) learns how to get what they want from their environment. In operant conditioning, rewards and punishments are used to reinforce either conforming or undesirable behaviors. In other words, operant conditioning is a means of learning by association. Behaviors are reinforced through reward and punishment and through expectations that are learned through watching what happens to others. Later, Akers added modeling to SLT, believing that a large portion of learning takes place by observing the consequences that behaviors have for others who exhibit them (Vold et al., 1998).

Means Girls Summary

Mean Girls (2004) is a movie about the inner workings of a high school and its culture. The film script was written by Tina Fey, who also stars as Ms. Norbury. The film was inspired by a nonfiction book called *Queen Bees & Wannabes* by Rosalind Wiseman. The book discusses school culture and cliques within schools. It describes how girls dress up in revealing costumes for Halloween and how friends have impacted girls. Wiseman discusses her time in classrooms when she asks girls to shut their eyes and raise their hand if a friend had gossiped about them, talked behind their back, or forced them not to be friends with certain people. There was a quote from one girl that she did not believe that those things happened at her school since she did not believe there were exclusive cliques in the school. Many of these quotes from the book are an inspiration for scenes within the movie (Zuckerman, 2014).

The movie begins by introducing the main character, a new student named Cady Heron, who was homeschooled for 16 years in Africa. Cady, coming into an American high school, provides a unique look at how the culture of a high school can influence a person's behavior. Cady has to learn how to navigate the school's social hierarchy and culture with the help of other students. Cady first makes friends with the social outcasts of the school, Janice and Damien. Janice and Damien have past negative interactions with the popular girls in the school. The popular girls bully Janice and Damien, which causes them to be social outcasts. The popular group of girls within the school is nicknamed "The Plastics." The Plastics consist of three girls named Gretchen Wieners, Karen Smith, and the leader of the group, Regina George. Janice and Damien hatch a plan for revenge on The Plastics. Because Regina approaches Cady about sitting with them at lunch, Janice and Damien have Cady infiltrate The Plastics to take revenge on Regina George.

The Plastics begin to accept Cady within the group and begin to influence Cady's behaviors. Cady begins to sit with The Plastics for the rest of the week to move the revenge plan forward. When The Plastics and Cady go to the mall for a shopping trip, Cady begins to discuss how she might want to join the mathletes. Regina, Karen, and Gretchen all tell her that it would be social suicide to participate in mathletes. This thinking is the beginning of Cady making academic sacrifices for the approval of The Plastics. Cady almost fails her calculus course due to the influence of The Plastics. The influence of The Plastics changes Cady's perception of the importance of her excellent grades. They also influence Cady's perceptions of body image as well. Cady only believed there to be "only fat or skinny," but The Plastics introduce her to the perspective that there could be more things wrong with a person's body other than just being fat or skinny. After this, Cady begins to see negative body image issues as acceptable and engages in them herself due to the influence of The Plastics.

After their shopping trip, The Plastics show Cady a book that they call the Burn Book. The Burn Book is a scrapbook filled with pictures of students and faculty at the school with negative comments written about each person in the school. Later within the movie, Ms. Norbury, Cady's math teacher, confronts Cady about her deliberately failing her exams. When Ms. Norbury confronts Cady, Cady puts Ms. Norbury in the Burn Book, saying that she is a "sad old drug pusher."

Cady begins to develop a crush on Aaron Samuels, who is in her math class. Aaron is not very good at math, so Cady begins to fail math assignments and tests for reasons to study with Aaron even though she knows the answers. Aaron is also Regina's ex-boyfriend, making the situation precarious. Cady goes to a Halloween party as an ex-wife (an ugly, unappealing costume), while the rest of the girls are dressed in very revealing costumes. Cady is made fun of for her choice in costumes since it does not follow the status quo of the school. Regina then finds out about Cady's crush on Aaron and decides that she and Aaron should get back together. Throughout the movie, Cady begins to unravel Regina's popularity by using weight gaining bars from Cady's time in Africa, having Aaron break up with Regina, turning Karen and Gretchen against her, and becoming the leader of The Plastics herself. One of the most iconic scenes within the movie is the winter talent show when The Plastics perform to "Jingle Bell Rock" in revealing Santa costumes. The dance starts the riff between Gretchen, Karen, and Regina. As Regina gains weight and loses the support of Gretchen and Karen, Cady starts to lead the group herself.

As the revenge plot ends, Regina decides to leak The Burn Book to the school and, to conceal the fact that that she created it, she puts herself in the book. With Gretchen, Karen, and Cady being the only people not in the Burn Book, they are the prime suspects. Cady, in the end, takes responsibility for the Burn Book and subsequently, the rumors, disappointment, hurt feelings, bullying, and consequences, though not completely without motivation, as one of the rumors is that Ms. Norbury sold drugs to the students. Upon Ms. Norbury's investigation as a drug dealer, Cady steps up and admits fault. As punishment for her contribution to The Burn Book, Cady is forced to join the mathletes for their upcoming competition. Cady and the mathletes win the competition and make it back in time to attend the school's Spring Fling dance; this is important as she has the opportunity to address the juniors and seniors when she wins Spring Fling Queen. During her speech, she talks about how everyone is royalty at the dance and metaphorically that popularity is fleeting. The final scene pans through the different characters and how they found cohesion outside of The Plastics. At last, there is peace at the school.

Mean Girls had an immense cultural impact on society. There are memorable quotes from the movie that are still known in 2020. Quotes such as "I'm not a regular mom, I'm a cool mom" and "on Wednesdays, we wear pink" are famous lines in the movie. Scenes within the movie are relatable to what high schoolers have endured in the past, present, and possibly future. The movie shows the variety of cliques that could be seen within a high school that most people can relate to at least one of the cliques. The movie inspired a theme for Ariana Grande's music video for *Thank You, Next*. In the music video, celebrities were cast to play different characters from the movie. As of January 26, 2020, the video has been viewed 472,673,873 times since it premiered on November 30, 2018 (Grande, 2018). Sixteen years after the movie was released, it still provides references in society's culture.

Social Learning Theory in *Mean Girls*

The movie *Mean Girls* is an excellent teaching tool for SLT because the main character, Cady, is essentially a blank slate going into high school for the first time. Before this point in her life, she had been homeschooled. She also had quite an unconventional childhood, spending 12 years in Africa because her parents were zoologists. Because of this, high school was new to her, and she was vulnerable to the influence of others. Later in the movie, she began associating with a group of notoriously superficial, petty, and sometimes vicious girls known as The Plastics. Gradually, she began to lose herself and resemble the peers she had associations with, exhibiting learned behaviors. The evolution of her definitions and behaviors is a significant motif in the plot of the movie.

The movie portrays the four elements of SLT very well. Akers and Burgess established four key learning processes that occur when an individual learns behaviors: differential association, definitions (general and specific), differential reinforcement, and imitation (Cullen & Agnew, 2003). These four concepts play a prevalent role throughout the entirety of the movie and are observable at different points.

Differential Association

The first of the four main elements of SLT is differential association. The central premise of SLT is that behaviors, both deviant and nondeviant, are learned and reinforced. Differential association is the process of an individual being exposed to normalized definitions of certain acts and behaviors. These definitions could either be favorable or unfavorable to deviant behaviors (Cullen & Agnew, 2003). According to Akers, differential association is the most important source of social learning (Vold et al., 1998).

There are two dimensions to differential association: a behavioral interactional dimension and a normative dimension. The behavioral interactional dimension refers to the direct association and interaction with others who engage in specific behaviors. Simply put, it is around peers who act a certain way. The normative dimension is the different pattern of typical behaviors and values, which the individual is exposed to through this association (Cullen & Agnew, 2003). These are the norms and values the person is exposed to through these interactions. In the context of *Mean Girls*, the differential association is Cady frequently socializing with The Plastics, who frequently engage in behaviors which most would consider undesirable. They then normalize these behaviors and share their values with Cady. In SLT, these social groups expose the individual to definitions and models to imitate (Akers & Sellers, 2009).

According to differential association, the group that the individual decides to interact with provides the social context for the mechanisms of SLT. This peer group does not just expose the individual to the definitions, they model the behaviors and definitions so the individual can imitate them, and, when they do, the group reinforces the behavior. Differential association consists of two types of social groups: primary and secondary groups. The primary group is the most important group (Akers & Sellers, 2009). It consists of family, friends, and other close relationships that can model and reinforce behaviors. The secondary group consists of neighbors, church figures, teachers, authority figures, and other relationships that may not be close family or friends. However, it can still serve a role in differential association (Cullen & Agnew, 2003). In the film, Cady spends a significant amount of time with The Plastics and often values their opinions and desires their approval. Therefore, they most likely serve as a primary group for Cady, often modeling and reinforcing undesirable behaviors. However, when she is not with The Plastics and is with Janis and Damian, her values and interactions are vastly different because they represent a different influence on her, and when she spends significant amounts of time with them, her behaviors differ from when she is with The Plastics.

There are variables in differential association that can affect the immediate impact and permanency of the associations. There are four variables associated with differential association (see Fig. 3.3).

Primarily, the permanency of these associations will be impacted by how early the association occurs in the lives of the individual, how long the association lasts, and the frequency and intensity of the relationships and interactions. The stronger

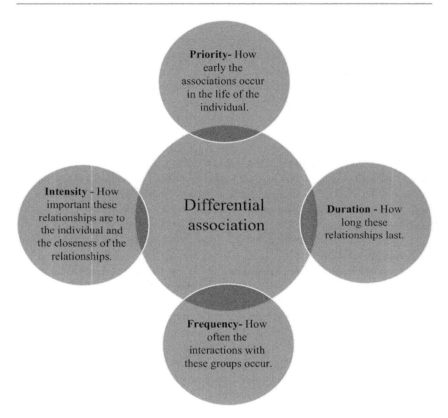

Fig. 3.3 Variables of differential association. (Note: Figure adapted from the propositions Akers, R. L. (1985). *Deviant Behavior: A Social Learning Approach*. Belmont, CA: Wadsworth)

these variables are, the more common their effects on the lasting behaviors of the individual may be (Cullen & Agnew, 2003).

Differential association can be observed in the movie *Mean Girls*. In the movie, the main character, Cady, begins to associate with a group of vicious, superficial girls who engage in what most would consider undesirable behaviors. At first, Cady is appalled by many of their actions. However, it eventually becomes clear that she does seek approval of the leader of the group, Regina George, despite how much she claims to dislike her. These girls become a primary group for Cady, and they model several negative behaviors for her and alter her definitions about what is and is not acceptable behavior. Eventually, Cady starts to believe that being in The Plastics and doing the horrible things is better than not being in The Plastics at all, and her actions reflect this belief.

As the movie continues, a bright motif begins to form that Cady is slowing turning into Regina George, doing the same horrible things she did. An example of this would be the three-way phone call. In this instance, Regina calls Cady to gossip about another girl in the group and gets Cady to agree. Immediately after, it is revealed that the other girl is on the line with them, listening to the conversation. Later in the movie, Cady does this same thing to Regina and exhibits several other learned, manipulative behaviors.

Another example would be Cady's definitions regarding The Burn Book. This is a book that The Plastics had created where they write vindictive, slanderous remarks about most of the students and teachers in their high school. At first, Cady is appalled by this and has an unfavorable definition of what the girls are doing. However, as the movie progresses, and she spends more time with The Plastics, her definitions change, harmful behaviors are reinforced, and she begins to imitate the actions that initially appalled her. These actions all start with her association with the girls and the significant amount of time she spends with them.

Definitions

The second element of SLT is definitions. Definitions are the individual's attitudes and meaning that they attach to a specific behavior. Simply put, these are the rationalizations, situational definitions, and other evaluative and moral beliefs that an individual uses to define behavior as right or wrong. There are two types of definitions that a person can have: general and specific (Cullen & Agnew, 2003). General definitions are religious, moral, and other conventional values that are held by the individual, favorable to conforming behaviors and unfavorable to deviant behaviors (Akers & Sellers, 2009). Specific definitions, or those favorable to deviant behaviors, often lead people to undesirable behaviors that they rationalize and justify. For example, people may consider stealing morally wrong. Also, they may feel that it is important for people to obey theft laws. However, they may not see anything morally wrong with using drugs, leading them to rationalize that it is acceptable to violate drug possession laws (Cullen & Agnew, 2003). They will consider some specific definitions of deviant actions that are morally reprehensible and rationalize others as morally acceptable because specific definitions reflect the meaning they attach to behaviors and actions (Vold et al., 1998).

If the individual holds attitudes and values that disapprove of deviant acts, they are likely to refrain from engaging in these acts. Conversely, if their attitudes approve or rationalize deviant behaviors, they are likely to do them (Vold et al., 1998). This can lead people to create definitions that justify or rationalize specific behaviors. These are called neutralizing definitions. An individual may view a specific act or behavior as something that is generally morally reprehensible, but they may rationalize why it is acceptable for them to do it. However, though they may consider it acceptable for them to do it, they may still consider it unacceptable for others to imitate their actions (Akers & Sellers, 2009). Cullen and Agnew (2003) wrote that neutralizing definitions include verbalizations, rationalizations, techniques of neutralization, accounts, disclaimers, and moral disengagement. Neutralizing definitions may appear as feelings and statements that justify behaviors or remove responsibility from the individual. They may include feelings and statements such as "I can't help myself," "I am not responsible," or "They deserved it" (Cullen & Agnew, 2003).

Neutralizing definitions are developed through imitation and differential reinforcement. They affect the individual, both cognitively and behaviorally. Cognitively, they create a mentality that increases the likelihood that someone will commit an act when an opportunity presents itself. Behaviorally, they affect the commission of deviant or criminal behaviors by acting as internal discriminative stimuli (which operate as cues to signal the individual as to what responses are appropriate or expected in a situation) (Akers & Sellers, 2009).

In *Mean Girls*, the restructuring of Cady's definitions is apparent. For example, when The Plastics and Cady are in Regina George's room after the shopping trip, The Plastics begin to judge their bodies very harshly and negatively, commenting on minuscule details that Cady never even thought to notice before. Her voice-over claims that she thought that there was "only fat or skinny, apparently, there can be a lot of things wrong with your body." Then, after this experience, Cady begins to define this idea of body image as acceptable and starts to do it herself.

In another scene, Cady begins to purposely fail math class to talk to Aaron, a high school boy she is romantically interested in. When she first starts the school year, it is clear that she is knowledgeable and a very driven student who would never jeopardize her grades for a romantic interest. However, Cady begins to think that failing math is okay since she is trying to get Aaron's attention, and these actions are in congruence with something The Plastics would do. Her definitions for good grades in school begin to shift drastically.

Another example of this is when she first saw the Burn Book. When she first sees it, she does not approve of it. She views it as something terrible. However, she accidentally makes a remark about Damien that is written in the book and is positively reinforced by The Plastics. She begins to view the book more favorably and, later, writes a comment about her teacher selling drugs (which is false). She goes from viewing this book as bullying to a more acceptable definition, even using it as the movie progresses. Her definitions on this topic change. Again, her definitions on this matter change due to her association with The Plastics, leading her to engage in undesirable actions she would not have at the start of the movie.

Differential Reinforcement

Differential reinforcement is the third element of SLT. Differential reinforcement is when the individual considers potential ramifications that follow certain behaviors. Simply put, these are the consequences of actions. People generally engage in behaviors that they believe will result in reward and generally refrain from activities that they think result in punishment (Vold et al., 1998).

This element holds that an individual's future actions and behaviors depend on the past, present, and anticipated ramifications for their actions. The odds of a behavior reoccurring in the future depend on reward outcomes, the reaction to their behaviors, whether they obtain approval, and if they get some sort of physical reward (money, food, pleasant feelings) (Cullen & Agnew, 2003). In order to extinguish a behavior, SLT holds that positive and negative reinforcement is necessary. Positive reinforcement is essentially punishment. This involves attaching a painful or unpleasant consequence to an action. Negative reinforcement or removing the reward of a pleasant outcome associated with the action is also necessary. There are variables associated with reinforcement, such as amount, frequency, or probability. Simply put, this is the amount of reinforcement, how often it is given, and the probability of it occurring (Cullen & Agnew, 2003).

Inversely, the behavior may achieve positive results and social reinforcement within the group of peers. The greater the value or amount of supportive reinforcement for a person's behavior, the more it will be reinforced, and this makes a higher probability that it will recur in the future. After the initiation of the behavior has begun, the social and nonsocial reinforcers impact whether acts will be repeated in the future. The definitions that the individual creates are also affected by the consequences, not just the behaviors (Cullen & Agnew, 2003). Social reinforcement, social context, moral attitudes, and other variables affect whether an individual experiences the acts as pleasant or unpleasant (Akers & Sellers, 2009).

Differential reinforcement is also prevalent in the movie. Again, the Burn Book scene is an example of this. Cady accidentally remarks on Damien's sexuality. The Plastics laugh and applaud, positively reinforcing Cady's comment. She then makes comments in the future in the book because she receives social validation from the people from whom she sought approval. In weighing the actions, she has to consider the benefits and drawbacks of her actions. Typically, she is given the choice of participating in The Plastic's antics and gaining social validation and friendship or rejecting their behaviors and losing the approval and the friendship, both of which she desires. Ultimately, the more Cady associates with Regina and The Plastics, the more attention, recognition, popularity, and social validation she receives. These reinforcers incentivize her to continue imitating Regina (the final stage of SLT) because, in her mind, she is obtaining the desired consequence, reinforcing her actions.

Imitation

The final element of SLT, imitation, is when the individual engages in behaviors, they observe others doing. Whether an individual will imitate the behavior depends on the variables discussed earlier. It also includes the characteristics of the model, the specific behavior, and the consequences they receive for doing it. Simply put, the individual mimics the behaviors they see in the group they associate with.

There are several examples of this to be seen throughout the movie. The evolution of Cady's feelings and behaviors regarding the Burn Book proves yet another example. The three-way call scene is another. Regina uses the three-way call on Cady earlier, and she uses it on Regina later. These behaviors are imitated after The Plastics provide Cady with a model.

However, one of the stronger examples of imitation in the movie is what happens within Regina George's family. Regina's mother, in the few scenes she is in, proves to be a very shallow, superficial, and emotionally immature mother, allowing Regina to behave very promiscuously, offering Cady alcohol as a minor, and having had cosmetic surgery. Regina follows suit in some way as she is promiscuous, shallow, self-obsessed, and emotionally immature as well. However, in the single scene in which she appears, Regina's little sister is dancing provocatively. At the same time, at a very young age, showing the behaviors learned through primary groups, the definitions the women in that family had created, the differential reinforcement, and, ultimately, imitation.

Sequence and Feedback Effects

Akers stressed that social learning is a complex process with reciprocal and feedback effects (Cullen & Agnew, 2003). He proposed a specific sequence of events by which learning behavior takes place (Vold et al., 1998). The sequence originates

Fig. 3.4 Social learning theory: A process. (Note: Figure adapted from the propositions Burgess, R. L., & Akers, R. L. (1966). A Differential Association: Reinforcement Theory of Criminal Behavior. *Social Problems, 14,* 128–147.

with the differential association of the individual with other individuals who have a favorable definition of criminal behaviors. These people then model the behavior for the individual to imitate. After this process has begun, differential reinforcement will dictate which behaviors will continue and which will cease.

The four elements are all pivotal components of an underlying process, which dictates what they will do when the opportunity for a deviant behavior occurs (Cullen & Agnew, 2003). Whether the individual will engage in deviant behaviors depends on learned definitions, imitation of deviant models, and the anticipated consequences reinforcement produces the initial deviant act. The facilitative effects of these variables continue in the repetition of acts, although imitation becomes less critical than it was in the first commission of the act (Akers & Sellers, 2009) (Fig. 3.4).

Conclusion

The societal impact that *Mean Girls* has had on society for 16 years makes the movie a pop culture icon. Since the movie allows for the viewers to learn how individuals change their behaviors to fit a social circle, applying SLT to the movie is simple. While there are examples that could be interpreted outside of those given by the authors, the examples given were the best way to describe the learning process within this movie. Showing the shaping of an individual new to a public high school environment shows an interesting perspective on high schools even if it is just within a movie. Using pop culture icons and criminological theories allows for more perspectives on how pop culture shapes society and what perspectives the writers, producers, and directors seem to include into their movies, books, and television shows.

Discussion Questions

1. Consider Cady's sudden change of heart when Mrs. Norbury is going to be arrested. Do you think SLT can be used to explain this change in behavior? Make sure to support your answer.

2. Given the other criminological theories discussed in this text, what other theories do you think work well to explain *Mean Girls* or situations within the movie?
3. The chapter discusses imitation as one way Cady begins acting like "The Plastics." Using your own examples, describe how researchers can use imitation to better understand peer-groups and juvenile delinquency.

References

Akers, R. L. (1985). *Deviant Behavior: A Social Learning Approach*. Belmont, CA: Wadsworth.
Akers, R. L. (1994). *Criminological Theories: Introduction, Evaluation, and Application* (3rd ed.). Los Angeles, CA: Roxbury Press.
Akers, R. L., & Sellers, C. (2009). *Criminological Theories: Introduction, Evaluation, and Application*. New York: Oxford University Press, 90–95.
Ariana Grande. (2018, November 30). *Ariana Grande – Thank U, Next* [Video]. YouTube. Retrieved from https://www.youtube.com/watch?v=gl1aHhXnN1k
Burgess, R. L., & Akers, R. L. (1966). A Differential Association: Reinforcement Theory of Criminal Behavior. *Social Problems, 14*, 128–147.
Cullen, F. T., & Agnew, R. (2003). *Criminological Theory Past to Present: Essential Readings*. Los Angeles, CA: Roxbury Publishing Company.
Cullen, F. T., & Agnew, R. (2011). *Criminological Theory Past to Present: Essential Readings*. Los Angeles, CA: Oxford University Press.
Lanier, M. M., Henry, S., & Anastasia, D. J. M. (2015). *Essential Criminology* (4th ed.). Boulder, CO: Westview Press.
Sutherland, E. H. (1939). *Principles of Criminology* (3rd ed.). Philadelphia: J. B. Lippincott.
Sutherland, E. H. (1947). *Principles of Criminology*. Philadelphia, PA: J. B. Lippincott.
Sutherland, E. H., Cressey, D. R., & Luckenbill, D. F. (1992). *Principles of Criminology* (11th ed.). Dix Hills, NY: General Hall.
Tibbetts, S. G. (2015). *Criminological Theory: The Essentials* (2nd ed.). Thousand Oaks, CA: SAGE Publications, Inc.
Vold, G. B., Bernard, T. J., & Snipes, J. (1998). *Criminological Theory*. New York, NY: Oxford University Press.
Williams, F. P., & McShane, M. D. (2010). *Criminological Theory* (5th ed.). Upper Saddle River, NJ: Prentice Hall.
Zuckerman, E. (2014, April 28). The Author Who Inspired 'Mean Girls' Talks Its 10th Anniversary. Retrieved January 24, 2020, from https://www.theatlantic.com/culture/archive/2014/04/revisiting-mean-girls-with-rosalind-wiseman/361283/

General Strain Theory and *The White Shadow*

4

Off the Court: Understanding Agnew's General Strain Theory Through TV's *The White Shadow*

David Safin

Decades after its modest run on network television, *The White Shadow* (CBS, 1978–1981) is often identified as being the program Bruce Paltrow created before his more recognized and acclaimed series, *St. Elsewhere* (NBC, 1982–1988). It is also regarded for being a training ground for Thomas Carter, Kevin Hooks, and Timothy Van Patten, who acted in the series, but went on to more successful careers behind the camera. On its own, however, *The White Shadow* only managed to achieve cult status despite being regarded as groundbreaking (Botte, 2018). Its premise was simple. Following a career-ending injury, professional basketball player, Ken Reeves, was recruited by his old friend and former college classmate, Jim Willis, to serve as the head coach of the boys' basketball team at Carver, an inner city high school populated, mostly, by African-Americans. Early episodes played like a fish-out-of-water tale, as Reeves, who is white, adjusted to his situation and vice versa.

Over the course of 3 seasons and 54 episodes, Coach Reeves helped students with issues such as addiction, alcoholism, gambling, parental abuse, prostitution, and teen pregnancy. In doing so, he demonstrated that regardless of the circumstances, his tactic of relentless discipline, motivation, and above all, loyalty would remain steady, and the appreciation the players felt toward him intensified as his stay extended. His unwavering credo was that success in basketball would lead to

D. Safin (✉)
Saint Vincent College, Latrobe, PA, USA
e-mail: david.safin@stvincent.edu

33

a funded college education, which he often described as a "ticket out" of their environment. By immersing himself into his players' lives, he enrolled in a crash course in the difficulties they were forced to endure on a near-daily basis, and vicariously, the audience went along for a ride not often exhibited on network television.

General Strain Theory: An Introduction

In an interview with the *New York Post*, actor Thomas Carter, who portrayed player James Hayward, noted, "It really made you think about where these kids, many of them African-American, really live. What kind of things do they have to deal with every day? What are the consequences, what are the costs, of their environment? So much of it, I don't remember it being done before anywhere on television" (Botte, 2018).

Carter's thoughts regarding the "costs" of the players' "environment" are representative of scholar Robert Agnew's general strain theory (GST). In it, Agnew argues that "people engage in crime because they experience strains" in their daily lives. "Strains," as defined by Agnew, are "events or conditions that are disliked by an individual." He delineates "strains" in three general ways—an individual losing "something they value," being treated in an "aversive or negative manner," and/or being "unable to achieve their goals" (Agnew, 2006 p. 190). In *The White Shadow*, Coach Reeves learned quickly that success on the court hinged not just on his practice schedules and game plans, but also on his ability to help manage the strains faced by his players.

For example, in the series' fifth episode, "Pregnant Pause" (January 1, 1979), Reeves was chastised by Principal Willis for advice given to a player, Milton Reese, who had just been informed that his girlfriend, Darlene, was pregnant. Distressed and in search of counsel, Reese asked the coach what he would do in this situation. Reeves, who was born in Queens and educated in Boston, replied, "Where I come from, it is simple—you ring the bell, you marry the girl." Consequently, Reese quit school with an eye toward marriage. Later, Reeves was summoned to the principal's office where Willis, the stern yet patient patriarch of Carver, asserted via a pointed lecture, "Ken, you don't come from the ghetto. You don't know the pressures these kids have to face."

Willis' discourse was a calming intervention in response to a heated reprimand delivered by the assistant principal, Cybil Buchanin, who declared Reeves' guidance to be irresponsible for he "imposed his own values" on one of his players. Throughout the series, Buchanin played the role of Reeves' foil as she was often frustrated by his methods. While she was unyielding in her role as his administrative superior, their relationship ultimately evolved into one of mutual respect. In "Pregnant Pause," Reeves said in response to an apology from Buchanin, "I like a good fight, and you're the only one who will go toe-to-toe with me."

After calming down, Buchanin stressed that she wished Reeves had given Reese multiple alternatives because his counsel only made matters worse. Later, Reeves convinced Reese to return to school, work toward a college scholarship, and promise to marry his girlfriend after high school. Reese heeded this advice, but Darlene was left unsatisfied with his lack of immediate commitment. After some surreptitious investigating, Reeves learned that Darlene was not, nor was she ever, pregnant. Fearful that Reese would leave her if he received a college scholarship, she feigned the pregnancy in order to coax Reese into proposing marriage. Her fear of losing Reese is what Agnew would define as an "anticipated strain." Agnew contends that "anticipated strains may upset individuals and lead to criminal coping" (p. 192). While her actions were not illegal, they were certainly drastic. Her assertion that she was pregnant, therefore, negatively affected Reese because by quitting school, he would not be able to achieve his goal of a college scholarship.

Reeves' initial advice, therefore, added strain to Reese's life, and it took Assistant Principal Buchanin to point that out to him. Reeves believed he was teaching Reese responsibility, but when she asked, "how long do you think it'll take for an immature, 17-year-old, unemployed black kid from the ghetto to renege on that responsibility?" Reeves realized that perhaps his role as an advisor was not as black and white as he originally thought. The episode concluded with Reese back at practice grateful for the support offered by his coach, and Darlene in counseling at the behest of Assistant Principal Buchanin. Amid this situation, Reeves stressed to his superiors that he was brought in not to coach "players," but to coach "people." While he admitted he might have overstepped his boundaries in his efforts to solve the problem, he was unapologetic in his approach. His ability to maintain a sense of equilibrium in spite of the many challenges facing him, as he did in "Pregnant Pause," was the fulcrum of the series' run.

Detachment from Conventional Others

The potential for succumbing to the pressure caused by strains via deviant or criminal behavior looms over the head of each of the players, so Reeves used a strategy called "direct control" to prevent them from resorting to such conduct. "Direct control" is a type of social control in which someone sets rules, monitors behavior, and consistently sanctions violations (p. 193). Reeves asserted this method as his primary means of authority to his team at the conclusion of the pilot episode (November 27, 1978), when he declared in the locker room after their first victory, "I'm going to be leaning on you guys, and I'll be behind you every step of the way." Brash guard, Morris Thorpe, slyly grinned and responded, "Yeah, like a white shadow."

The level of control Coach Reeves could exert over his players was called into question in the episode "That Old Gang of Mine" (January 15, 1979). In it, Ricardo "Ricky" Gomez was cut from the team, not by the coach, but by the administration due to poor academic performance. They stressed that the move was "in the best interest of the student." Upon receiving the news that he had been removed from the team, Gomez was unfazed because he assumed his coach "fixed it." When Reeves responded that he had not, Gomez firmly asserted that his poor performance was not his fault. Reeves snapped, "look, you can't go through life blaming everybody else for your own problems. I'm sorry, Gomez. I don't make the rules." Before storming out of Reeves' office, Gomez replied, "Yeah. Sure you don't."

After being removed from the team, Gomez's bond with the institution of school weakened, and he began cutting class. During his "retreat from conventional others," Gomez, the only Mexican American on the team, rejoined a street gang called "The Aztecas" (p. 195). His transformation was symbolized by his choice to don a leather jacket bearing their insignia in favor of his Carver varsity coat. When Reeves saw him cleaning out his locker, he asked if the "Aztecas" jacket was new. Gomez replied, "Nope. I had it a long time. I just haven't worn it lately." When asked why he was once again hanging with this delinquent group, he responded that he had "nothing better to do."

Frustrated that he had no say in Gomez's dismissal, Reeves pleaded with Buchanin to overturn her decision. In his appeal, he insisted that being on the basketball team was what kept Gomez in school. He added, "He's got to feel like belongs somewhere, that he belongs to something. If it's not the team, it's going to be that gang." Agnew would concur with Reeves' contention, theorizing "individuals who cannot achieve status through conventional channels, like educational or occupational success, often join criminal gangs because the gang makes them feel important, respected, and/or feared" (p. 196).

In response to his plea for leniency, Buchanin told Reeves that if he wished to uncover what truly caused Gomez's dismissal; he should talk directly with his teachers. Among the subjects of his inquiry was Carver's English teacher, Miss Newkirk. When asked for her rationale for failing Gomez, she declared it was due to his not completing a book report. Gomez had wanted to write his report on the story of Emiliano Zapata, but Miss Newkirk would only accept reports on one of two books—*Little Women* or *The Autobiography of Malcolm X*, neither of which interested Gomez.

Reeves' survey of the faculty led him to conclude that Gomez was being ill-treated due to his race. He further argued that this "demeaning treatment" lessened his "emotional bond" with his teachers, which led to a reduction in his "investment in conventional activities" like studying and completing assignments (p. 195). Reeves revealed this opinion in an impassioned speech at a faculty meeting in which he stated, "Gomez isn't failing Carver. Carver is failing Gomez, and he's the one being punished for it." After meeting resistance from members of the faculty, Reeves continued, "Do any of you care that Gomez feels like a failure, and he doesn't know why. Right now, he is roaming around the streets with some gang trying to get back what's left of his self-esteem because you've taken away from him possibly the one thing that was keeping him out of trouble."

Reeves' monologue was effective. He managed to convince Miss Newkirk to allow Gomez to do a report on *The Biography of Pancho Villa*. He also organized the other players on the team to develop what they playfully entitled, "The New Chicano Studies Program." They asserted that Gomez would not fail any more biology or history exams. This increased level of "social support" yielded positive results, as Gomez's subsequent book report was deemed passable, and he was permitted to rejoin the team (p. 197). The episode concluded with Gomez studying for an exam with several of his teammates.

The Cost of Criminal Coping

Reeves' experience with Gomez was a stark lesson on how strains can be generated from within, but in the season 2 episode "Needle" (November 26, 1979), he witnessed how external forces can also produce such a situation. In it, team captain James Hayward's 15-year-old cousin, Jason, died of an overdose of heroin. Robert Agnew calls Hayward's subsequent feeling of shock as a "vicarious strain," which he defines as a "strain experienced by others around an individual, especially close others like family members and friends" (p. 191). Agnew further argues that strains of this sort increase the probability of crime because individuals might "seek revenge against those who had victimized their family" or they might attempt to "prevent the perpetrators from causing further harm" (p. 192).

During a police officer's overview of the situation that led to Jason's demise, a distraught Hayward exhibited low levels of confidence in the officer's desire to bring the perpetrator to justice. The officer assured him that the police would do "everything they can," which did little to assuage Hayward's concerns. Later in the episode, Hayward followed up with a police detective. With little to report, the investigator repeated, "we're doing all we can," which only exasperated Hayward further. This dissatisfaction propelled him on a clandestine investigation of his own. After discovering the name and whereabouts of the dealer, Hayward set out to exact revenge.

Concerned for their friend, a few members of the team reached out to Hayward with hopes of changing his mind. When their efforts were unsuccessful, Thorpe approached the coach and informed him about Hayward's plan. An incredulous Reeves responded, "You're actually telling me that James Hayward is going to kill somebody?" Thorpe reasserted his contention that Hayward was plotting that level of revenge. Reeves, then, lectured Thorpe that a matter like this was the responsibility of the police. Clearly aggravated, Thorpe stated, "you really ain't from this neck of the woods, are you?"

Thorpe, like others on the team, shared Hayward's belief that finding the man responsible for Jason's death was not a high priority for the police. Roused by Thorpe's words, Reeves took to the streets in an effort to find Hayward before he was able to execute his plan. When his search proved successful, he made one final plea to Hayward. "Your cousin is dead. Killing this guy is not going to pull him out of the ground." After a brief back and forth, Reeves continued, "if you do this, you will not have just killed your cousin. You will have killed off your entire family, Hayward!" In tears, Hayward replied, "He was only fifteen years old!" Reeves responded, "Your kid brother's only five. You can't make him a victim too."

Undeterred, Hayward shoved the coach and ran away. Later that night, he confronted the dealer, Trotter, armed with a handgun. Having knocked him to the ground, Hayward pointed the gun in Trotter's face. Sobbing, he called out "please, God, let it come. Please, God, please!" But Hayward could not bring himself to pull the trigger. He told Trotter, "your time is going to come, man," before hurriedly leaving. The next day, before practice, Hayward admitted to Reeves that he could not shoot the man. When Reeves attempted to explain what he thought had stopped him, Hayward cut him off, proclaiming, "oh, come on, Coach. You don't know why, 'cause I don't even know why, man."

Reeves accepted his answer, and gestured toward the gym, as it was time for practice. What Hayward could not yet articulate was his realization that even though he could not resolve his strain through proper legal channels, the cost of committing murder was too high. Reeves' words were true. Hayward was too important to his mother, little brother, and those relatives left coping with Jason's untimely death. As a result, he proved Agnew's theory correct; "many individuals avoid criminal coping because the costs of crime are high for them" (p. 196).

Basketball as a Conventional Coping Resource

The season 2 episode "The Death of Me Yet?" (March 11, 1980) opened with a montage of basketball highlights compiled atop an address being delivered by Coach Reeves. "I want you to think about where you guys were two years ago, and where you are now. Because when we started, there wasn't one among you who believed enough in yourselves to think that you could ever get this far." Where they were was the cusp of a division title. All that stood between them and a trip to the city championship was a single victory. Laser-focused on the task at hand, Reeves' team handily defeated Keeler landing them a spot in the city championship game against Westmere at the sports arena in downtown Los Angeles.

The episode played like a series finale, as its tone was reflexive in nature. Reeves' pre-game words only reinforced that sentiment, as did his pensive stroll through the locker room the following day. As his gaze panned the players' lockers, aural flashbacks from earlier episodes played underneath. He continued his walk into the empty gymnasium where his eyes locked onto a single sign adhered to the wall, "BEAT WESTMERE." His reflection was interrupted by Assistant Principal Buchanin, who asked that they meet in her office.

Soon after defeating Keeler, the team held a victory party at the home of their equipment manager, Phil Jefferson. Their level of enthusiasm was reflected in how quickly they consumed their local alcohol supply, and senior Curtis Jackson, the least inebriated among the team, was charged with going to the liquor store to purchase more. Upon completing his purchase, two armed burglars stormed the register, demanding all of its contents. When the cashier pulled out a gun in his own defense, the burglars shot him and Jackson, killing them both.

This was the news Buchanin delivered to Reeves after his contemplative promenade through his facilities. Blindsided and upset, Reeves returned to the locker room, where he was visited by Miss Plunkett, a teacher who Reeves had been seeing socially. Reeves confided to her, "I managed to delude myself into thinking that I, well, that basketball could protect them from things like this." He went so far as to suggest that the team might not play the championship game, but he would leave that decision to his team. Unbeknownst to him, the team had already met privately and unanimously decided that they would play the game as scheduled.

Concurrent to his receipt of this terrible news, Reeves was contacted by a representative from the athletic department at Moorpark College, an affluent, private institution in need of a new basketball coach. His feelings of distress and disillusionment fueled his curiosity, as he visited the campus willing to hear their offer. The pristine and decadent campus featured a brand new, state-of-the-art athletic facility, but the lure that pulled Reeves to it most was the outward absence of the strains that plagued his tenure at Carver. There was, to him, no good reason to remain in his current position.

His decision to leave Carver for Moorpark was all but a foregone conclusion, when he returned to campus for practice. To his surprise, the team was waiting in the locker room, ready to confront him about the possibility of his leaving them for greener pastures. Defensive and angry, Reeves initially stated it was none of their business, but quickly realized that they deserved an answer. He confessed that he had been offered a job, but had not yet committed. Later, while the team ran laps after an efficient practice, Reeves returned to his office in the locker room, only to find a young man standing at one of the lockers. It was Jackson's younger brother, Willie, and he was there to retrieve his brother's belongings. The two engaged in a brief conversation about basketball, and in it, Willie emphatically stated that he hoped to, one day, play for Reeves because his older brother said that he was "the best—even for a white man."

Wanting to learn more about him, Reeves offered Willie a ride home. During their trek, Reeves peppered Willie with the same questions he asked of his players—questions about his family, his life, and his aspirations. While Willie was unsure how to answer Reeves' broad philosophical questions, he was confident that he "would always play basketball" because it is "the only time that I don't have to think about things I don't want to think about. Like when my father told me about my brother, I concentrated on putting the ball through the hoop."

Conclusion

Willie's words reminded Reeves that for those who suit up in Carver orange, basketball is not so much about the ends of leaving their environment, but more a means to surviving it. Basketball is an institution to which they could form a strong, emotional bond. It improves their "conventional coping skills," increases their "social support," and limits their "association with delinquent peers"—all strategies Agnew says aid in reducing the "likelihood that individuals will respond to strains with crime" (p. 197).

Basketball was why Reeves' players spent much of their free time cruising for pick-up games, hardly ever took off their varsity jackets, and wanted to play the championship game as scheduled despite losing one of their close friends to violence. It took Willie to remind Reeves why he took this job in the first place, and why he would continue at it "for years to come." Reeves revealed to his team that he'd be staying at Carver just prior to their taking the court, and not surprisingly, they went on to win the city championship.

At the subsequent trophy presentation, Reeves publicly summarized what two years of on-the-job training taught him about life in the inner city, and the role basketball played in it. He proclaimed, "I'm proud of my team because I think they proved to all of us that no matter what the adversity, no matter what the problems, you can overcome almost anything, as long as you have the will to win."

Discussion Questions

1. For those who have watched *The White Shadow*, what other methods of social support did Coach Reeves offer to his players? How did they help his players cope with their strains?
2. For those who have watched *The White Shadow*, what other strains did the members of the Carver High basketball team face? How did they manage those strains?
3. What other television shows or feature films have used the trope of a teacher/coach using methods of direct control as a means to prevent young people from resorting to crime?

References

Agnew, R. (2006). *Pressured into Crime: An Overview of General Strain Theory*. Los Angeles, CA: Roxbury Publisher.
Botte, P. (2018, November 27). Cult-classic 'The White Shadow' Still Resonates 40 Years Later. *New York Post*. Retrieved from https://nypost.com/2018/11/27/cult-classic-the-white-shadow-still-resonates-40-years-later/

Episodes

Pilot (Season 1, Episode 1)
Paltrow, B. (Writer), & Cooper, J. (Director). (1978). Pilot [Television series episode]. In Paltrow, B. (Executive Producer), *The White Shadow*. Los Angeles, CA: Columbia Broadcasting System.

Pregnant Pause (Season 1, Episode 5)
Bochco, S. (Writer), & Cooper, J. (Director). (1979). Pregnant Pause [Television series episode]. In Paltrow, B. (Executive Producer), *The White Shadow*. Los Angeles, CA: Columbia Broadcasting System.

That Old Gang of Mine (Season 1, Episode 7)
Rubin, M., & Kott, G. (Writers), & Paltrow, B. (Director). (1979). That Old Gang of Mine [Television series episode]. In Paltrow, B. (Executive Producer), *The White Shadow*. Los Angeles, CA: Columbia Broadcasting System.

Needle (Season 2, Episode 9)
Falsey, J. (Writer), & Lobl, V. (Director). (1979). Needle [Television series episode]. In Paltrow, B. (Executive Producer), *The White Shadow*. Los Angeles, CA: Columbia Broadcasting System.

The Death of Me Yet? (Season 2, Episode 22)
Rubin, M. (Writer), & Lobl, V. (Director). (1980). The Death of Me Yet? [Television series episode]. In Paltrow, B. (Executive Producer), *The White Shadow*. Los Angeles, CA: Columbia Broadcasting System.

Anomie and *The Purge*

5

Release the Beast: Purging for the American Dream

Andrea R. Borrego

The America depicted by *The Purge* films creates a social structure focused on economic success, as well as participation in the once-a-year purge. Economic success and purge participation are not mutually exclusive. In order for the economy to thrive and to keep crime rates down, citizens must purge on the sanctioned night. The lower and middle classes depicted in the films, however, experience the purge disproportionately from the top 1%. Access to safety through security systems, reinforced housing, and weapons vary among the social classes. The lower class experiences obstacles to stay safe during the purge and struggle to make ends meet the other 364 days outside of the purge. Institutionalized norms enacted by the New Founding Fathers of America (NFFA) through the purge are not sustainable, and they begin to lose their power to regulate citizens' behavior. The resulting society is one of anomie and strain.

Merton's Anomie

The "American Dream" involves achieving success by gaining material wealth and money. The idea has become institutionalized through American culture, which constantly advertises that everyone and anyone can achieve riches and social status

A. R. Borrego (✉)
Metropolitan State University of Denver, Denver, CO, USA
e-mail: aborreg1@msudenver.edu

© The Author(s) 2021
S. E. Daly (ed.), *Theories of Crime Through Popular Culture*,
https://doi.org/10.1007/978-3-030-54434-8_5

through hard work and ambition (Merton, 1968). Monetary success, however, can be indefinite in that people always want more and what is to be earned is relative to each individual and their social position (Merton, 1968). Economic success is relative to each individual and not everyone is privy to the same resources. Societal structure, such as social position, networks, and access to opportunities, shapes the various avenues individuals have for achieving the American Dream. Overemphasis on cultural goals, coupled with lack of options and opportunities, leads to what Emile Durkheim, a French sociologist, termed as "anomie," or normlessness.

Robert K. Merton (1938, 1968) applied Durkheim's idea of anomie to the discrepancy between America's culturally defined goals (i.e., economic success) and the structure in place that differentially allows for attainment, as well as avenues for attainment. Not everyone can achieve the American Dream of prosperity due to societal and personal limitations, which can cause strain. The pervasive cultural emphasis on ambition or the never-quit mentality pressurizes individuals to find the most effective way to achieve wealth and status. Methods for achieving wealth and status may or may not be legitimate, creating instability in society or anomie (Merton, 1968). Certain groups of society must choose how to adapt to the institutionalized ideas of success knowing that they cannot always pull themselves up by their bootstraps and make their way up the "corporate ladder." Merton's theory of anomie/strain explores the different ways in which individuals adapt to the apparent discrepancies of culturally defined objectives of success and the limitations on opportunities and resources to achieve those goals. In particular, Merton outlines five ways in which individuals adapt to cultural goals and institutionalized means: conformity, innovation, ritualism, retreatism, and rebellion.

The Purge Universe

In order to understand Merton's anomie/strain theory, this chapter uses the backdrop of the different *Purge* films produced by Blumhouse Productions. In the film series, the NFFA gain political power and enact the 28th Amendment to create the purge. "The purge" is a 12-hour period in which all crime, including murder, is legal. Four main films that comprise what we will call, in this chapter, the Purge universe:[1]

---

[1] The films are presented as they occur in the Purge universe timeline and not according to their release dates.

- *The First Purge* takes place in 2017, portraying the first purge as a government-sanctioned social experiment at a Staten Island low-income housing project that eventually starts the nationwide practice, despite protests. In order to ensure participation, citizens are offered US$5000 to stay on the island during the purge period. They are paid even more to participate (i.e., commit a crime). The government monitors participation through the use of video-linked contact eye lenses.
- *The Purge* takes place in 2022, five years after the first social experiment. The film not only focuses on one family but also portrays how society has embraced the yearly purge, which is evident through the various industries that have emerged, such as high-tech security systems and purge insurance.
- *The Purge: Anarchy* is set in the greater Los Angeles area and depicts what happens in the surrounding city a year after the previous film. The film follows a group of individuals who are brought together through varying circumstances: a mother–daughter duo taken from the public housing units by mercenaries; a police officer seeking revenge on a man who killed his son in a drunk driving incident; and a couple running from a group of individuals who capture and sell people to a wealthy society to hunt and kill on purge night. Overall, the film portrays how groups of varying social situations engage in the purge. This film also introduces anti-purge activists who begin to fight back against the NFFA.
- *The Purge: Election Year* follows a presidential nominee, Charlie Roan, who is running on the platform of repealing the 28th Amendment, which would end the purge, spurred by her witnessing the death of her family on purge night. During the present purge period, government officials and mercenaries hunt her down in an assassination attempt as government officials are fair game this purge season. Accompanying storylines depict the challenges the working class face, such as increased insurance premiums and homemade security systems (i.e., sitting on the roof of one's property with a shotgun), as well as the underground rebellion that provides medical services, a hideout, and a plan to assassinate the NFFA presidential nominee.

As you learn about anomie and strain, imagine yourself in the *Purge* universe. Imagine that the government supports and encourages engagement in crime, including murder, for 12 hours once a year, every year. Society is now built around the yearly purge. Organizations, businesses, and the media focus on and profit from the purge the other 364 days, weaving the purge into the social fabric of American society.

Society, Anomie, and Strain

"As your elected president, with my fellow New Founding Fathers, we make this promise. We will revive this country. The American Dream is dead. We will do whatever it takes to let you dream again," a message made by President Bracken in *The First Purge* (Blum et al., 2018) blares on the television representing the NFFA. The NFFA political party was created as a third option to republicans and democrats in response to an American society that was looking for a change. Citizens were increasingly angry due to a collapsing economy, high crime, high unemployment, and a bankrupt government that could not take care of its citizens (Blum et al., 2018). In 2014, the NFFA supported a social experiment by a psychologist that hypothesized that people will behave better when they are allowed to act out their frustrations without experiencing the repercussions (Blum et al., 2018). By 2023, six years after the first purge experiment, America had experienced an unemployment rate below 5%, a nearly nonexistent crime rate, and a relatively low percentage of people living below the poverty line (Blum et al., 2014). It appears as if the NFFA had created a societal oasis by allowing citizens to purge, or engage in all types of crime, for one night each year.

According to Merton (1968), "a cardinal American virtue, 'ambition,' promotes a cardinal American vice, 'deviant behavior'" (p. 200). In particular, Merton's (1938, 1968) sociological theory focuses on how social structure and anomie promote deviant behavior and nonconformity to social norms. He rejects the notion that deviance is a result of humanity's primal impulse for evil and focused on how social structure influenced conformist and deviant behavior (Merton, 1968). Anomie manifests when the pressure to conform and achieve economic success promotes individual competition that overrides a sense of community and working toward a collective good (Messner & Rosenfeld, 2013). Citizens, in turn, feel the strain to compete and achieve through any means necessary. Furthermore, individual means or resources an individual has to achieve are potentially limited by social stratification. The way the society is structured, with fewer opportunities for the poor and more opportunities for the middle class and rich, creates obstacles in achieving the American Dream that exacerbate strains (Merton, 1968).

Merton, however, rejects the propositions of the Chicago School that macro-level, structural characteristics allow crime to flourish in inner-city, lower socioeconomic areas (Lilly, Cullen, & Ball, 2019). Merton (1968) argues that poverty is not enough to produce high rates of crime and deviance. Rather, Merton (1968) hypothesizes that factors innate to American society across all levels of the socioeconomic continuum explained crime and deviance. In particular, American culture emphasizes (1) ambition toward the same goals no matter what one's social status because goals are open to everyone; (2) if at first you do not succeed, try again; and (3) if one truly fails, it is because they lost ambition (Merton, 1968). The overemphasis on ambition perpetuates the idea of success but fails to provide means and opportunities for an achievement other than the message "keep trying." As individuals are so focused on their own ambitions, they fail to see how societal structure limits certain groups' opportunities and access to the necessary means for achieving the American Dream (Merton, 1968).

The varying socioeconomic levels in America create differential experiences while constantly promoting the same goal for all: the American Dream. The American Dream can be described as "material comforts and individual opportunities of a middle-class lifestyle: a car, a house, education for the children, and a secure retirement" (Messner & Rosenfeld, 2013, p. 7). Citizens are constantly bombarded with marketing that glamorizes material wealth. Media portrays the rags to riches story as uniquely American; anyone can become successful if they can just get to America. Structural differences, however, limit opportunities and resources to achieve the American Dream through legitimate, institutionalized normative behaviors (Merton, 1968). Institutionalized normative behaviors include receiving a proper education, finding and maintaining gainful employment, investing in material wealth to keep earning, and following the law. For large segments of the country, following that path is not possible. For example, individuals from lower socioeconomic communities do not have the same school systems as middle-class suburbia and, in turn, do not have the same access to higher education. The lack of educational opportunities may lead to a lack of better-paying jobs to gain material wealth.

The ambition to gain economic success is ever prevalent, but constant failure to achieve such goals can lead to feelings of strain. Individuals may then be persuaded by ambition and strain to find alternative actions to achieve the universal cultural goals of society. Alternative actions could involve legitimate (i.e., law-abiding actions) or illegitimate (i.e., law-violating and norm-violating actions). Thus, the limitations experienced by individuals turn into strains, which leave individuals figuring out how to adapt to societal pressure with the American Dream constantly looming over their heads.

While society limits opportunities and resources for certain socioeconomic groups, the social structure also imposes certain norms or behaviors that are common and acceptable. Anomie occurs when cultural norms and goals do not match certain groups' abilities to follow culturally prescribed behaviors (Merton, 1968). What follows is crime and deviance from social normative behaviors. The overemphasis of achieving success results in pressure being placed on individuals to obtain their goals through whatever means necessary. While not all individuals will turn to crime and deviance, deviant behavior has a pattern as explained through five different typologies proposed by Merton (1968).

The American Dream in a New Society

This is your Emergency Broadcast System announcing the commencement of The Annual Purge sanctioned by the US Government. (Blum et al., 2014)

The premise of *The Purge* films highlights the cultural goals of economic success, decreased crime, and participation in the purge. Crime becomes legal and is encouraged for one night every year to continue to keep crime and poverty rates down (Blum et al., 2014). According to Merton (1938), individuals must adapt to the culturally defined goals and institutionally acceptable means. American life in the Purge universe retains the same culturally defined goals, but the institutionally acceptable means have changed. Purging is now the institutionally acceptable means to promote prosperity and gain what you want. Not purging is viewed as non-normative behavior because it does not support the goal of economic success in the United States. Nonparticipation undermines the social norms and behaviors outlined by broader society, creating anomie. Furthermore, nonparticipation varies for different social classes. Just as Merton (1959) suggested, "differential access to the approved opportunities for those variously located in the social structure" (p. 6) will result in feelings of strain.

Universalism and Inequality

Government officials of ranking 10 have been granted immunity from the Purge and shall not be harmed. (Blum et al., 2014)

Regardless of the different eras of social change that American society has experienced, inequality remains pervasive. The distribution of wealth and income is continually concentrated among a small percentage of citizens (Messner & Rosenfeld, 2013). Despite income segregation, the idea of the American Dream has endured across all social classes. In actuality, inequality may be needed to continue to motivate citizens to support the idea of the American Dream to compete for monetary gain (Messner & Rosenfeld, 2013), as is exemplified in the Purge universe. Poverty and inequality do not occur in a vacuum but are rather interrelated with other social and cultural values (Merton, 1938). In particular, the universally accepted American Dream devalues other institutional goals and promotes the idea that monetary gain is the only marker of success, which leads to a social structure that perpetually causes strain among individuals (Messner & Rosenfeld, 2013). For example, in the Purge universe, the purge is not seen as a morally defunct practice. Rather, it is a way for society to flourish. During the other 364 days, society in the Purge universe markets security systems, costumes, and murder tourism (a practice where people from other countries flock to American to participate in the purge) to continually promote the purge as the only way to a better America.

The government in the Purge universe realizes that in order for the purge to be successful, society must adopt it as an acceptable way to achieve the universally agreed-upon goal of the American Dream. In *The First Purge*, the NFFA sold the idea of the purge by dangling money in front of the citizens in a low-income neighborhood if they participated. In response to the question of whether or not people would participate one character proclaimed, "People pissed. They ain't got no money. They ain't got no food. They gotta release their anger. If they participate, it's going to be for that paper" (Blum et al., 2018). By focusing on the inequality already structured within society, the NFFA and the government created a market economy for engaging in the purge in order to control the population.

In the following years, the purge became the way of American society. The government no longer had to entice citizens to purge with actual money as the idea of the universally coveted American Dream was sufficient alone. By improving society through a reduction in crime and poverty, citizens believed that purging was the answer to upward mobility, or so it seemed. In order for the purge to work, the government had to perpetuate inequality through the social structure to pressurize citizens into participating. This was exemplified by choosing to implement the first purge experiment in a low-income neighborhood. During the experiment in *The First Purge*, the social scientist that created the idea of the purge realized that the government was using mercenaries to make it seem like people are purging so that the experiment would seem successful and become law (Blum et al., 2018).

In *The Purge: Anarchy*, the government also manipulates the system to create the social structure necessary for economic gain. The main characters discover that mercenaries target low-income housing projects in Los Angeles in order to reduce the number of low-income citizens. The mercenaries use surveillance systems to track individuals and target entire housing buildings (Blum et al., 2014). They easily break down the virtually nonexistent security systems to depopulate lower socioeconomic communities. In doing so, the government reduces the poverty rate, continues to tout the success of the purge, and perpetuates the necessary sociocultural conditions to promote conformity and competition.

Additionally, the first film, *The Purge*, highlights the relationship between safety inequality and income inequality. Citizens of the lower socioeconomic communities have less access to safety measures during the purge. In *The Purge*, the main character, James Sandin, sells high-tech security systems to the wealthy to ensure safety among middle- and upper-class societies. Alternatively, homemade security systems of wooden planks and deadbolts, as seen in *The Purge: Anarchy*, can be easily breached, which can force lower-income groups into purge participation whether they like it or not. Social stratification bounds responses to the structurally induced strain caused by the creation of the purge by the government. In essence, the purge is a way for the government to create barriers to economic success for the lower class or to perpetuate inequality and build a society that conforms to the values of the NFFA. Purge participation then becomes a *choice* for the wealthy, who can purchase poor people to slaughter in the comfort of their own homes or pay individuals to kidnap people to hunt, as seen in *The Purge: Anarchy*. Lower-class individuals who choose to purge do so at their own risk of falling victim to other purgers, but they are also not guaranteed safety should they choose to refrain. Thus, the Purge universe exemplifies how opportunities and means, or lack thereof, influence individual choices and actions based on social stratification.

Merton's Five Modes of Adaptation

Individuals who experience obstacles to opportunities, and subsequent strain, must decide how to adapt, which includes a two-step process. First, individuals must choose if they buy into the cultural goals being pushed by society. That is, do they buy into the American Dream? Second, they must decide what actions they want to take to achieve those goals. Merton (1968) discusses these actions in terms of legitimate or illegitimate means. Legitimate means refer to norm-following behaviors, such as getting a job to earn money. Illegitimate means refer to norm-violating actions, such as selling drugs to make money. Thus, deviant behavior can be seen as a rejection of the universal goals of economic success and/or the rejection of achieving the American Dream through institutionalized (i.e., socially acceptable) means or behaviors.

Conformity. Merton (1957, 1968) argued that most people conform to societal norms. In particular, conformists buy into the goals of success and they engage in legitimate means to achieve those goals, even if they experience obstacles. Conformists buy into the cultural goals of economic success, as well as the means to achieve those goals (Merton, 1968). Within the Purge universe, legitimate means refer to engagement in the purge. Individuals who support the purge demonstrate their adherence by purging once a year. They buy into products, marketing, and institutions that continue to promote the purge. The Skeletor character from *The First Purge* best exemplifies the conformist mentality. As he gets ready to purge, he yells "Founding Fathers! Pay me! Save me!" (Blum et al., 2018). He both buys into the idea of getting money and purging to earn that money.

Innovators. Individuals who buy into the cultural goals of economic success, but engage in creative, law- and norm-violating behaviors to achieve those goals are innovators. Essentially, innovators engage in deviant behavior to overcome the obstacles blocking them from achieving their goals. In the Purge universe, innovators buy into the goals of economic success but do not engage in the violent crime associated with the purge. They do, however, engage in other acts that support cultural goals. For example, in *The Purge: Anarchy*, young men drive around the city finding individuals to target during the purge. The characters Shane and Liz find that their vehicle brakes have been cut before the commencement of the purge. After the purge begins, the young men that cut their brake line continue to follow them. Later in the film, the young men capture Shane and Liz and sell them to a wealthy club located at a secretive location in the city so they can be auctioned off and hunted (Blum et al., 2014). The young men accept the cultural goals of economic success but find other creative ways to earn their money. They technically engage in deviant behavior by cutting the brake line before the purge begins and use that to their advantage during the purge.

Panhandlers engaging in law-violating behavior prior to the beginning of purge night provide another illustration of innovators. On her way home, Eva encounters panhandlers that are trying to sell her black-market weapons. The panhandler gets in her face to sell his product and yells "You gonna need something for protection tonight? Uzi, Barretta. Look, on the cheap, cheap. Or a blade to cut your man throat. Whatever you need. We take any kind of payment" (Blum et al., 2014). Selling illegal weapons prior to the start of the purge violates what is considered law-abiding behavior.

Ritualism. Ritualists are nonconformists in terms of goals. They still have goals for success and prosperity but not ones that closely align with the American Dream. Ritualists realize that their strain stems from the inability to achieve the culturally outlined standards of economic success and thus scale down their own personal goals and aspirations (Lilly et al., 2019). They still, however, conform to the institutionalized means of achieving their goals, which in the Purge universe can include purge participation.

The ritualist examples involve the ideas of revenge and justice, which are not promoted in the American Dream. In *The Purge: Anarchy*, the main characters are fleeing the mercenaries and a group of collectors. Eva, the mother of the mother–

daughter duo, leads them to her co-workers house claiming she has a car they can borrow. While at the house, the co-worker's sister shoots her sister and husband because she found out they were having an affair (Blum et al., 2014). Purge participation for her was not a way to gain economic success but to enact revenge for the hurt she felt when uncovering the affair. She conformed to the institutionalized means (i.e., purge participation) provided by the government to achieve a means to an end that does not particularly align with the American Dream.

The second example focuses on Sergeant Leo Barnes, also in *The Purge: Anarchy*. Leo does not prescribe to the culturally dominant goals, but he does accept the purge as the institutionalized means to achieve his goal. Several years ago, Leo's son was killed in a drunk driving accident. The man who killed his son did not face any penalties due to a technicality (Blum et al., 2014). Leo decides to use the Purge as a way to get justice for his son. A few days before the purge, he disarms the man's security system so that he could slip in undetected during the purge (technically an innovative behavior). His actions are viewed as ritualism because as we learn about his character, he does not support the idea of the purge and only participates in violent actions (or attempts) when seeking justice. In the film *The Purge: Election Year*, Leo only engages in violent actions when protecting Senator Charlie Roan. When presented with the opportunity, he does not kill when it is not warranted (Blum et al., 2016). Leo's ultimate goals are not economic success or personal wealth demonstrating that he does not buy into the American Dream. He does, however, believe that the Purge can be used to his advantage to fulfill his own goals and desires.

Retreatism. The fourth mode of adaptation focuses on nonconformity in terms of both cultural goals and institutionalized means to achieve those goals. Retreatists reject the ideals associated with cultural success as well as the normative behaviors to gain success (Lilly et al., 2019). Merton (1968) describes retreatists as belonging to society but not being a part of it. Instead, retreatists engage in deviant behaviors, such as drug addiction or vagrancy, as a way to escape societal pressures and norms (Merton, 1968). In the Purge universe, homeless individuals exemplify reatreatists. Homeless encampments are strewn across the subway lines in *The Purge: Anarchy*. The homeless are attempting to wait out the purge by hiding below ground. They exemplify the part of society that does not subscribe to the American Dream or the purge.

Rebellion. Individuals that fall in this category reject the broader cultural goals imposed on all individuals by society. Instead of adjusting the pervasive, normative cultural goals to fit their own lives as the ritualists do, they fight to change the system (Lilly et al., 2019). The first rebels in the Purge universe timeline include the protestors outside the Park Hill Towers, the site of the first purge experiment.

Protestors exclaimed, "The NFFA knew that we, the impoverished, would stay if there was monetary gain. This is another way to keep the brown and black people down" (Blum et al., 2018). The citizens realize the imposition of socially structured capacities by the government and do not blame themselves for the failure to achieve economic success, but blame the system.

Rebels not only want to change the cultural goals but also the means to achieve the new goals. "The redistribution of wealth upward through killing has to stop. We must pick up arms. This year we will fight back!" is a proclamation by Carmelo Jones in *The Purge: Anarchy* (Blum et al., 2014). Carmelo Jones exemplifies how rebels seek to change the system through the rejection of broader cultural goals and institutionalized means. Throughout the film, Carmelo Jones displays underground videos to incite a revolution against the NFFA to end the purge. He also notes the inevitability of having to engage in violence during the purge by explaining change does not happen until the blood of the wealthy is shed (Blum et al., 2014). Jones is not the only character to adapt through rebellion. In *The Purge: Election Year*, a US Senator, Charlie Roan, campaigns for the presidency on the platform of eliminating the purge (Blum et al., 2016). Instead of purging, she seeks to change the system for a more equal society.

The Purge as a Market Economy

Messner and Rosenfeld (1997), concerned with the disproportionately high serious crime rate in the United States compared with other industrialized nations, set out to sociologically conceptualize what makes the American culture and society unique. They elaborated on the idea of anomie by arguing that the economy is interrelated with other social institutions in what they termed as institutional-anomie theory. When the economy is overemphasized in society, the balance among social institutions, which may have competing value systems, is disrupted and anomie and high crime rates follow (Messner & Rosenfeld, 2013). Anomic cultural pressure and crime are more likely to occur when the power dynamics are disrupted and economics dominates other noneconomic goals through two processes: socialization and social control (Messner & Rosenfeld, 1997). In the Purge universe, the purge becomes the main social institution. Through year-round marketing and product development, Americans are taught to believe that the success of all citizens depends upon involvement in the purge.

The idea of the purge is sold on a countrywide scale as a way to reduce crime and poverty in society. The NFFA capitalizes on the idea of the purge by creating a market economy for purging and safety. Big corporations make money by creating and selling high-tech security systems, which can only be purchased by middle- and upper-class citizens (Blum et al., 2013). Consequently, individuals who get jobs with those corporations have access to safety, to a certain extent. For example, in *The Purge*, security system salesman James Sandin has made a prosperous living from the purge market. The Sandins' neighbors take note that their economic prosperity is due to the neighbors purchasing the expensive security systems from James, making the Sandins the gossip of the community and later the target of their purge outrage (Blum et al., 2013). While the neighbors have every right to purge by killing the Sandin family, their motive is not related to economic success but rather hatred (Blum et al., 2013), which exemplifies the increase in anomie.

Socialization

Noneconomic goals set forth by the values important to other social institutions (such as family, education, and/or the political system) socialize individuals to respect social norms and law abidance (Messner & Rosenfeld, 1997). If noneconomic structures lose strength to properly socialize individuals, as anomie grows, deviant behaviors may emerge to participate in the dominant structure (i.e., economic success), as well as create a bigger demand for the market economy (Bernburg, 2002). For example, family places value on attachment between parent and child. Family, however, also places an emphasis on monetary success to provide for the family (Messner & Rosenfeld, 2013). The economic goal of providing food, housing, and education then becomes the dominating goal of the family, rather than closeness and engagement. Limited-opportunity families might have to turn to other means to reach their goals. Additionally, an increased labor market also creates a demand for childcare services, which continues to increase the need for more money (Messner & Rosenfeld, 2013).

Through the institutionalized means of purging, individuals are socialized to accept that engaging in crime for 12 hours once a year is beneficial to all. The idea of the purge coupled with economic success dominates the values of noneconomic institutions, such as family. For example, a teenager in *The Purge: Election Year* kills her parents so that she can go out and purge (Blum et al., 2016). While it is her right afforded to her by the NFFA, killing her parents does not align with the goal of family cohesion. The act of purging overpowers values associated with other social institutions. This act exemplifies how the purge has become part of the normative culture with an expectation that all should participate, even if it hurts and diminishes the roles of other social institutions.

Social Control

Social controls exert influence over an individual's behavior. When the goals of noneconomic institutions are strong, they bolster engagement in normative behavior. When economic success goals are given more credence than noneconomic realms of life, however, noneconomic institutions fail to govern behavior and "the result is relatively tenuous institutional engagement, weak social control, and high rates of crime" (Messner & Rosenfeld, 1997, p. 1397). Weakened social controls leave citizens engaging in any means necessary to achieve the American Dream while other aspects of social life are demoted. Participation in noneconomic roles is no longer the main focus. Rather, individuals seek heightened participation in the economic market, which may occur through legitimate or illegitimate means (Messner & Rosenfeld, 2006).

What happens when citizens begin to reject the idea of the purge? When other institutions start promoting competing values that challenge the social order associated with the purge, anomic pressures are created, which in turn weaken social controls (Messner & Rosenfeld, 2006). As more citizens rebel against the idea of the purge, more power dynamics are disrupted. In *The Purge: Election Year*, Charlie Roan finds support from a large constituency who is deviating away from the purge by supporting the banishing of the practice. By weakening social controls, citizens no longer view the purge as the only institutionalized means to gain and promote success and prosperity in the United States. This spurs the government to make drastic changes to ensure that other institutions, or people like Charlie Roan do not devalue the economic market. In order to maintain the status quo (i.e., the existing sociocultural conditions), the government removes immunity for high-ranking officials so that Charlie Roan can be legally assassinated and removed as a threat to the purge and NFFA control (Blum et al., 2016).

Lastly, while the purge can be viewed as an acceptable institutionalized means for achieving economic goals, it also creates an environment for alternative behavior that contradicts the purpose of the purge. The purpose of the purge is to allow individuals to release the beast one night a year so that people are law-abiding citizens the rest of the year. The growing competition among the lower class exacerbated by structural conditions (created by the government) promotes innovation over conformity. The interrelated value systems of noneconomic institutions begin to influence behavior and challenge the idea of the purge. The character Laney Rucker in *The Purge: Election Year* demonstrates how a change in values modifies her behavior (Blum et al., 2016). Once a hard-core purger, Laney now provides emergency medical services during purge night to help those in need.

Another character who rejects the idea of the purge in *The Purge: Election Year* is Dante Bishop and his followers. He, like Carmelo Jones in *The Purge: Anarchy*, views that the only way to end the purge is through violence against the NFFA's leadership (Blum et al., 2016). Thus, through the creation of violence as normative behavior to promote the American Dream more violent behavior deemed nonconformist manifests.

Conclusion

Commencing at the siren, any and all crime, including murder, will be legal for 12 continuous hours…Blessed be our New Founding Fathers and America. (Blum et al., 2014)

In an effort to maintain the status quo, the NFFA government engages in tactics to create structural obstacles for the lower classes to perpetuate a social hierarchy and economic competition for a healthy economic market. Using the framework of Merton's (1938) theory and Messner and Rosenfeld's (1997) institutional-anomie theory, we can understand how *The Purge* films depict normlessness, inequality, and social deviance. The Purge universe presents a society that allows citizens to release the beast in order to reduce crime and poverty rates. The government, however, perpetuates economic inequality by hiring mercenaries to reduce low-income communities, creating unattainable safety measures, and overemphasizing the values associated with the purge. The result is anomic pressure, strain, and deviant behavior.

According to Merton, societies that overemphasize the American Dream (i.e., economic success) will experience an imbalance of values with other social institutions. In the Purge universe, the imbalance of values led to rebellion (i.e., deviant behavior) against the NFFA and the practice of the purge (i.e., lack of engagement in crime during the purge). In nonfictional American society (i.e., real life), engagement in crime and delinquency exemplifies the imbalance of values. Comparing the different approaches between the fictional and nonfictional American societies demonstrates the need for a balance among social institutions and reduction in inequitable practices so that proper socialization and social controls exerted by various social institutions can reduce strains felt by citizens and bolster legitimate institutionalized norms.

Discussion Questions

1. Describe the American Dream in today's society. Do you think that it has changed or evolved since Merton first observed society and crime?
2. What parallels can you draw from the social structure represented in *The Purge* films with today's society?
3. How did Messner and Rosenfeld build upon Merton's theory of anomie?
4. Identify other popular culture characters that exemplify the different modes of adaptation and explain.

References

Bernburg, J. G. (2002). Anomie, Social Change and Crime: A Theoretical Examination of Institutional-Anomie Theory. *British Journal of Criminology, 42*, 729–742.

Blum, J., Bay, M., Form, A., Fuller, B., Lemercier, S. K. (Producers), & DeMonaco, J. (Director). (2013). *The Purge* [Motion Picture]. United States: Universal Pictures.

Blum, J., Bay, M., Form, A., Fuller, B., Lemercier, S. K. (Producers), & DeMonaco, J. (Director). (2014). *The Purge: Anarchy* [Motion Picture]. United States: Universal Pictures.

Blum, J., Bay, M., Form, A., Fuller, B., Lemercier, S. K. (Producers), & DeMonaco, J. (Director). (2016). *The Purge: Election Year* [Motion Picture]. United States: Universal Pictures.

Blum, J., Bay, M., Form, A., Fuller, B., Lemercier, S. K. (Producers), & McMurray, G. (Director). (2018). *The First Purge* [Motion Picture]. United States: Universal Pictures.

Lilly, J. R., Cullen, F. T., & Ball, R. A. (2019). *Criminological Theory: Context and Consequences* (7th ed.). Thousand Oaks, CA: Sage Publications.

Merton, R. (1938). Social Structure and Anomie. *American Sociological Review, 3*(5), 672–682.

Merton, R. (1957). Priorities in Scientific Discovery: A Chapter in the Sociology of Science. *American Sociological Review, 22*, 635–659.

Merton, R. (1959). Social Conformity, Deviation, and Opportunity Structures: A Comment on the Contributions of Dubin and Cloward. *American Sociological Review, 24*, 177–189.

Merton, R. K. (1968). *Social Theory and Social Structure*. New York: Free Press.

Messner, S. F., & Rosenfeld, R. (1997). Political Restraint of the Market and Levels of Criminal Homicide: A Cross-National Application of Institutional-Anomie Theory. *Social Forces, 75*(4), 1393–1416.

Messner, S. F., & Rosenfeld, R. (2006). The Present and Future of Institutional-Anomie Theory. In F. T. Cullen, J. P. Wright, & K. R. Blevins (Eds.), *Taking Stock: The Status of Criminological Theory* (Advances in Criminological Theory) (Vol. 15, pp. 127–148). New Brunswick, NJ: Transaction.

Messner, S. F., & Rosenfeld, R. (2013). *Crime and the American Dream* (5th ed.). Belmont, CA: Cengage Learning.

Rational Choice Theory and *Friends*

Rational Decision Making and *Friends*

6

Rachel Baumann

The origin of rational choice theory began with the philosophical theories of Cesare Beccaria and Jeremy Bentham—theories that would eventually assist in forming the classical school of criminology (Moran, 1996). The classical school of criminology focuses on the idea that people have free will and choose to either act according to societal rules or act against them (Moran, 1996). Since the formation of the classical school of criminology, criminologists have formed many different theories of crime that hold the assumption that humans have free will (Moran, 1996). Rational choice theory, as revived by Derek Cornish and Ronald Clarke, explains that people will mentally rationalize both the costs and benefits of their potential actions, seeking to maximize their pleasure and minimize their pain, in order to make decisions on how to ultimately act (McCarthy, Hagan, & Cohen, 1998). Additionally, Cornish and Clarke mention that while people consider the costs and benefits of their potential actions, "decisions are compromised by time, abilities, and the availability of relevant information," meaning that people have limited rationality and only have a vague understanding of the potential outcomes (McCarthy et al., 1998, p. 158).

Although Cornish and Clarke are recognized as the original designers of rational choice theory, other criminologists have either slightly altered the theory while maintaining the theory's core assumptions or have integrated concepts of the theory into their own (McCarthy et al., 1998). For example, Gary Becker's version of

R. Baumann (✉)
Saint Vincent College, Latrobe, PA, USA

© The Author(s) 2021
S. E. Daly (ed.), *Theories of Crime Through Popular Culture*,
https://doi.org/10.1007/978-3-030-54434-8_6

rational choice theory is focused on an economic viewpoint and claims that all people make decisions "'as if' they are aware of all possible outcomes," concluding that both offenders and nonoffenders use the same costs and benefits when making decisions (McCarthy et al., 1998). Another example is the idea of rational choice developed by Michael Gottfredson and Travis Hirschi, which claims that offenders have limited self-control and do not consider the future consequences and that these traits affect their ability to rationalize the costs of their actions properly (McCarthy et al., 1998).

This chapter focuses on the variation of rational choice theory developed by Bill McCarthy in 2002, who argues that this theory not only explains the thought processes of criminals but also showcases the very nature of human agency (Paternoster & Pogarsky, 2009). He describes four elements of "thoughtfully reflective decision making" that all humans experience when making decisions and explains how the process of thoughtfully reflective decision making varies depending on the individual and their state of being throughout their life (Paternoster & Pogarsky, 2009). The four elements of thoughtfully reflective decision making, hereinafter referred to as TRDM, are gathering information pertaining to the current situation, thinking about all potential courses of action and their consequences, making a decision on how to act, and reflecting on that decision in order to make better decisions in the future (Paternoster & Pogarsky, 2009).

There are numerous situations where the four elements of the TRDM process apply in the 1990s and 2000s television sitcom *Friends*, a show that follows six friends as they work together to get through the ups and downs of life. The show, although ending in 2004, continues to have a strong fan-following. The show's mass fan following comes from its willingness to tackle controversial topics and real-life scenarios. Throughout the show's ten seasons, the characters encounter countless situations where they face tough decisions that require them to gather information pertaining to their issue, think about their options, make decisions, and reflect on their decisions. Although most of the situations within the show do not pertain to criminal activity, they serve as good examples of situations that clearly follow the four elements of TRDM and help to clearly understand rational choice theory.

Ross' List

One of the most direct examples of decision making occurs in one of the earlier episodes, titled "The One with the List." The situation demonstrates a clear example of weighing costs and benefits within decision making. In this episode, Ross is dating a young girl named Julie. However, he discovers that his long-time crush, Rachel, has feelings for him. He now faces the decision to either stay with his girlfriend, Julie, or leave her for Rachel. Ross decides to create a pros and cons list for each girl in order to facilitate his decision making. By creating a pros and cons list for each girl, Ross is actively gathering and organizing all the information relevant to his situation, fulfilling the first element of the TRDM process. He then uses that list to consider all his options based on the information gathered, fulfilling the second element of the TRDM process. Although choosing Julia ultimately has the most pros and the least cons, Ross lets his emotions take over his decision making by saying, "She's not Rachel" (Crane & Kauffman, 1994–2004).

Ross ultimately chooses Rachel, fulfilling the third element of the TRDM process. However, he makes this decision based on his emotions rather than the gathered information, which McCarthy names as one of the extraneous factors that can influence decision making (Paternoster & Pogarsky, 2009). McCarthy claims that decisions made using "intuition, habit, emotions, or one's moral beliefs" requires no, or limited, cognitive work, which means an individual will use less reasoning and logic to make the decision (Paternoster & Pogarsky, 2009, p. 106). Ross then reflects on his decision, fulfilling element four of the TRDM process, when Rachel discovers his list of pros and cons and is hurt by the cons he has listed for her. Ross quickly regrets his decision to create the list and attempts to explain his actions to Rachel, who storms out of the room hurt and upset (Crane & Kauffman, 1994–2004). Ross reflects upon his decision, McCarthy would say, to "assess what went right and what went wrong" (Paternoster & Pogarsky, 2009, p. 105).

Joey's Bankruptcy and Stubbornness

In the episode titled, "The One Where Eddie Won't Go," audiences are provided with a great example of how decision making through emotions, rather than logic, can lead to poor results. Joey is fired from his acting role as Dr. Drake Ramoray, promptly leading the soap opera writers to kill his character. Estelle, Joey's acting agent, can only present Joey, who now needs a new acting job, with a role as a simple cab driver. Joey refuses to take such a small role, claiming that he will only accept larger roles after his experience acting as Dr. Drake Ramoray, one of the leading characters in the soap opera "Days of Our Lives." With no larger roles available and spending more than his new salary can afford, Joey accrues large amounts of debt (Crane & Kauffman, 1994–2004).

Joey's friend, Ross, discovers how much debt he now has and advises Joey to take whatever acting roles he can get to earn whatever money he can. Joey responds by gathering little information regarding his situation. He only thinks about his pride and how he will only accept larger acting jobs, completely disregarding the large amount of debt he has accumulated and the potential future consequences (Crane & Kauffman, 1994–2004). This is another example of someone limiting their rationality by letting emotions take over their decision making (Paternoster & Pogarsky, 2009).

With limited information gathering and rationality, Joey reduces his options for how to react to the situation. He ultimately chooses to continue his stubbornness and not accept any small acting roles, acting against Ross' suggestions to take whatever acting roles he could get. Eventually, men go to Joe's apartment and re-possess most of his possessions. Joey then admits to Ross that he has made a mistake, having reflected on his decision making and realizing what he has done after the consequences of his actions have come to fruition. Ross, feeling Joey has learned a lesson from the situation, agrees to buy one of Joey's repossessed items back for him: the large ceramic dog (Crane & Kauffman, 1994–2004).

Monica's Decision to Leave Richard

Another instance of rational choice theory occurs in the episode "The One with Barry and Mindy's Wedding," where viewers can see a clear example of logical decision making. In this episode, Monica and her boyfriend, Richard, discuss their future together. Monica admits to Richard that she wants to have children in the future. However, Richard, being significantly older than Monica, expresses reluctance to have any more children. He claims that he wants his future to focus on Monica and not raising more children. Monica, left heartbroken by this news, must now make a tough decision; either she can stay with Richard and accept not having any children or she can leave Richard and find someone else who wants the same things she does (Crane & Kauffman, 1994–2004).

Monica begins her decision-making process by gathering all the information regarding her situation, the first step of the TRDM process. She first chooses to explain to Richard how much she wants children, hoping he will change his mind. Richard, seeing Monica's indecisiveness, offers to have children with her if that will make her happy because he truly loves her. With this new information, Monica has several options for how to proceed with the situation and fulfills element two of TRDM by considering them all. She could agree to Richard's offer although she knew that is not what he truly wants, she could stay with Richard and choose to not have children, or she could leave Richard in search of somebody who also wants children. Although staying with Richard and having children with him is what she wants to choose, Monica considers Richard's feelings and does not want to force him to have children if he does not truly want them. She considers the fact that he has already had children with his former wife and has already endured the struggles of raising young children. Finally, she recognizes that Richard is older now and that forcing him to raise more young children with her now would not be fair to him. After gathering all her information and considering all her options, Monica ultimately chooses to leave Richard for a life of future children, fulfilling element three of TRDM. Although Monica loves Richard immensely, she recognizes that it would be unfair to ask him to have children with her if he truly does not want to (Crane & Kauffman, 1994–2004).

In the following episode, "The One with the Princess Leia Fantasy," viewers can see the final element of the TRDM process, Monica's reflection on her decision to leave Richard. As she thinks about her decision, Monica becomes depressed over losing Richard, the man she loves. However, regardless of how she feels, she still admits that she made the best choice for her situation (Crane & Kauffman, 1994–2004). McCarthy would consider Monica "deliberate, careful, and mindful" for coming to a logical conclusion rather than deciding through emotions (Paternoster & Pogarsky, 2009, p. 105). Rather than disregarding Richard's feelings and asking him to have children with her when that is not what he wants, just because she loves him and wants that future with him, she decides to logically consider the consequences and emotions of Richard as well. She does not limit her options or her rationality based on how she feels, but instead, she considers all of her options and chooses the best available option regardless of how it makes her feel (Crane & Kauffman, 1994–2004).

Ross and Rachel's Annulment

Revisiting the character of Ross, his battle for and with Rachel continues throughout the series and leads to them getting drunkenly married in Las Vegas. When choices need to be made in the aftermath of this incident, both emotions and logic influence the characters' decisions. In the episode titled "The One After Vegas," Rachel asks Ross to get the marriage annulled. Being divorced twice already, Ross hesitates to get the annulment, not wanting to have three failed marriages. Rachel demands the annulment, and Ross eventually agrees to get it. However, Ross performs limited information gathering by only focusing on the fact that he does not want a third failed marriage. With his limited information, Ross creates a situation where he now has few options. Ross, being ruled by his emotions rather than logic and rationality, chooses to not get the marriage annulled and simply tells Rachel that he did, leaving them secretly married (Crane & Kauffman, 1994–2004).

Of course, Rachel eventually learns the truth and becomes furious. Due to the prolonged amount of time after the marriage and accidentally informing the judge of their past relationship, the judge decides that she will not annul the marriage, and they must proceed through a full divorce process instead. Ross now reflects on his decision and realizes that by choosing to lie to Rachel and never actually getting the annulment, he finds himself in a worse situation than he would have been otherwise. His fears have come true, and he now has three true divorces rather than one annulment. Ross realizes that he made a poor decision by relying on his limited rationality and emotions rather than on logic and reasoning. Had Ross considered all the potential consequences and how his actions would make others feel, he would have allowed himself to have more options for reacting to his situation. Additionally, if he had not let his emotions affect his decision making, he could have made a logical choice of how to best handle the situation (Crane & Kauffman, 1994–2004).

Chandler and Rachel: Cheesecake Thieves

The show *Friends* does not include many examples of crime, but there are a couple of situations spread throughout the show's ten seasons. This example demonstrates how people seek the most reward and the least pain when making decisions and how they will select the criminal option if it appears the most beneficial. The characters Chandler and Rachel become cheesecake thieves in the episode "The One with All the Cheesecakes." Chandler accidentally receives a cheesecake at his front door meant for a woman in an apartment downstairs from his. Without looking at who the package is addressed to, Chandler opens and tastes the cheesecake. After tasting the delicious cheesecake, he decides to eat it, even though he realizes it is not intended for him. Rachel walks in on him eating the cheesecake, and Chandler coerces Rachel into tasting it. Rachel is amazed at how delicious it is and looks at the package to see where it came from only to find that it is not addressed to them. She scolds Chandler for taking something that does not belong to him, but Chandler explains his rationalization to Rachel. After gathering the information about his situation and observing his options, Chandler argues with Rachel that eating the cheesecake does not pose a problem. He came to the logical conclusion that their neighbor will call the bakery and claim she never got the cheesecake and that the bakery will send her another one. Choosing this option allows Chandler to maximize his pleasure by eating the delicious cheesecake but minimizes his pain by knowing that the neighbor will receive another cheesecake; he does not have to feel guilty. Rachel agrees with Chandler's logic and decides to share the cheesecake with him (Crane & Kauffman, 1994–2004).

The next day, Chandler and Rachel discover that a second cheesecake has arrived, but again to the wrong address. Rachel says they cannot eat the second cheesecake, and they attempt to take the cheesecake to its rightful owner. However, they find that the neighbor is not home. Chandler and Rachel then reason that the cheesecake cannot just sit in the hall and that they should watch it for their neighbor until she returns home. This choice ultimately causes Chandler and Rachel to not only eat the cheesecake but to fight over it. This situation shows that both Chandler and Rachel have limited rationality by not considering the neighbor lady's feelings or other potential consequences. They allow themselves to only gather information and create options of how to handle the situation that fulfill their selfish wants, choosing to neglect any information or options where they may feel guilty or cause themselves pain (Crane & Kauffman, 1994–2004).

The Mugging of Science Boy

One of the best examples of criminal decision making within this show occurs in the episode "The One with the Mugging." The episode begins with Ross and Phoebe walking down the street when a mugger approaches them. Ross begins to freak out and comply with the mugger's demands. However, this situation quickly becomes comedic when Phoebe recognizes the mugger as an old friend of hers. As Phoebe and the mugger chat, Ross looks dumbfounded. Later, when Ross and Phoebe meet Monica at the café that they frequent, Central Perk, Ross tells Monica about what happened. Phoebe explains how she knew the mugger from her days of living on the streets and how she used to also mug people for money. Ross and Monica look at her shocked. Phoebe defends her actions by saying that she needed the money for food, explaining that she did not grow up with any money as they did, and how she has had a hard life. Phoebe is explaining her rationality for why she would mug people; the benefit of eating outweighed any pains that came with mugging people. During her decision-making process, it was the best option for handling the situation she was in. The viewer can see that Phoebe recognizes her decision seems questionable due to her feeling that she must defend her actions to her friends. This is because Phoebe has now expanded the perspective of her limited rationality to include her friends' view of her. However, the show's audience can also see that she still stands by the decision she made due to how comfortable she seems by telling her friends these stories. She explains that she did what she had to do in her situation at that time, knowing what she knew then (Crane & Kauffman, 1994–2004).

Monica then explains to Phoebe that this situation was traumatizing for Ross because he was mugged as a kid when leaving the comic book store. Ross says the person who mugged him was a thug with a pipe who stole his backpack, which contained his own hand-written comic titled "Science Boy." When Ross leaves the café to get to work, Phoebe confides to Monica that the comic book store is where she used to mug people and that a pipe was her weapon of choice. Phoebe details how there was once a boy she mugged outside the comic book store with a backpack that had a "Geology Rocks" sticker, and Monica confirms that that boy was Ross. Phoebe is now made aware of an unforeseen pain that her decision has caused, not just for her but for Ross (Crane & Kauffman, 1994–2004).

With Phoebe now retroactively including Ross' feelings into her decision making and reflecting on her decision, element four of TRDM, she feels guilty and decides to tell Ross what she has discovered. Once she explains the situation to Ross and asks him for forgiveness, he ends up feeling hurt and humiliated. Phoebe tries to focus on the positive outlook of the situation by explaining how she never had any old memories with the group of friends and now they have an old memory together. By doing this, Phoebe offers Ross additional information and alternative rationality for this situation, hoping Ross will choose to view the situation from a milder perspective. Ross is not amused and leaves the café upset. Phoebe, feeling horrible for the decision she made in the past, decides to redeem herself now by presenting Ross with a box of her treasures she kept from her life on the streets. Ross is skeptical but listens to Phoebe as she removes the old copy of "Science Boy" from the box. Ross instantly becomes overjoyed from being reunited with this old, cherished item. Phoebe explains that she felt it was too important to get rid of, so she kept it for all those years. With this present, Ross chooses to let the past go and forgives Phoebe, focusing his choice on the good that came from the situation (Crane & Kauffman, 1994–2004).

Chandler the Doctor and Monica the Minister

Finally, in one of the last episodes of the series titled "The One with the Birth Mother," viewers watch as Chandler and Monica both process a difficult decision, achieve different conclusions, and need to explain their decision making to each other. Chandler and Monica wait on a list to adopt a baby because they cannot have children naturally due to health concerns. After waiting for a while, they finally receive a call saying that a birth mother would like to interview them as potential parents. Ecstatic, Chandler and Monica arrive at the meeting ready to impress the mother. However, they soon realize that she has mistaken them for another couple. There was a mistake with the identification numbers on the potential parent forms, and the birth mother believes Chandler is a doctor and Monica is a minister. Monica realizes the mistake but only considers her options with limited rationality. She senses that the birth mother respects them due to their occupations and knows that she wants a child more than anything else. So, making her choices through her emotions of wanting a child, Monica chooses to let the birth mother continue to believe the mistake (Crane & Kauffman, 1994–2004).

Chandler eventually becomes the voice of reason and convinces her that they must tell her the truth. Monica, reflecting on her decision and realizing that what she has done goes against her moral beliefs, decides that telling the birth mother the truth is the right thing to do. Although Monica acknowledges the best course of action, that action is too painful for her to do herself. So, Chandler chooses to tell the birth mother the truth alone, explaining how they only lied because they really want a baby to call their own. The birth mother, shocked by his honesty and moved by his genuine desire for a child, decides to still choose them as the parents for her child. This example shows how emotions can alter rational decision making, creating limited rationality within a person. Monica declined to consider the birth mother's feelings or the potential consequences for her actions at first. However, once Monica has the additional information to consider, provided by Chandler, and some time to reflect on her initial decision, she is able to realize the logic and reasoning she had been missing. This new mindset alters her decision, and Monica decides to choose another course of action by telling the birth mother the truth (Crane & Kauffman, 1994–2004).

Conclusion

The media presents many examples of rational choice theory that imitate real-world experiences. On the basis of the philosophies of Beccaria and Bentham, "human nature was predicated upon the search for pleasure and the avoidance of pain" (Hayward, 2007, p. 233). All human action is calculated to maximize pleasure and minimize pain (Hayward, 2007). Although emotions and moral beliefs can hinder rational decision making, humans logically process the information they know that pertains to a decision and choose the course of action with the best, most pleasurable, outcome (Paternoster & Pogarsky, 2009). In order to make such decisions, people gather information, think about the possible options they have, choose the best course of action, and reflect upon that decision to learn what went well and what went wrong for reference in later decision making (Paternoster & Pogarsky, 2009).

People use rational decision making in decisions both big and small in their everyday lives. The television show *Friends* explores the everyday lives of six individuals, all living their own lives, making numerous choices throughout the show, some big and some small. The show encounters silly topics, as well as serious ones, and viewers can relate to some of the characters' experiences. Therefore, the outcomes of these characters' decision-making processes could potentially occur in real-world scenarios as well. Knowing how people make decisions, using the TRDM process, for example, informs criminologists about how to potentially stop people from deciding to commit crimes and instead facilitate people to make law-abiding decisions.

Discussion Questions

1. What is rational choice theory? Who developed it? Where did it originate?
2. What is the TRDM process? Who developed it?
3. What are some of the extraneous factors that can cause limited rationality? How often do you think these factors are involved in real-world decision making? How do we avoid them?
4. After reading the chapter, watch one of the mentioned episodes of *Friends*. With the TRDM process in mind, consider what could have been different.
5. List the four elements of the TRDM process as though it were the best-case scenario. What was the worst-case scenario?
6. What would your TRDM process look like if you were in those situations? Would any of the limited rationality factors come into play?

References

Crane, D. (Producer), & Kauffman, M. (Producer). (1994–2004). *Friends* [Television Series]. Burbank, CA: NBC.

Hayward, K. (2007). Situational Crime Prevention and Its Discontents: Rational Choice Theory Versus the 'Culture of Now'. *Social Policy & Administration, 41*(3), 232–250.

McCarthy, B., Hagan, J., & Cohen, L. E. (1998). Uncertainty, Cooperation, and Crime: Understanding the Decision to Co-offend. *Social Forces, 77*(1), 155–176.

Moran, R. (1996). Bringing Rational Choice Theory Back to Reality. *The Journal of Criminal Law and Criminology (1973–), 86*(3), 1147–1160.

Paternoster, R., & Pogarsky, G. (2009). Rational Choice, Agency and Thoughtfully Reflective Decision Making: The Short and Long-term Consequences of Making Good Choices. *Journal of Quantitative Criminology, 2*, 103–127.

Opportunity Theories and *Super Mario Bros.*

7

Opportunities for Crime in the Mushroom Kingdom: Applying Rational Choice Perspective and Routine Activity Approach to *Super Mario Bros.*

Victoria A. Sytsma

Introduction

Mario Is a Murderer

Super Mario Bros. is a side-scrolling, 8-bit videogame and cultural juggernaut released on the Nintendo Entertainment System in 1985. According to the American edition of the *Super Mario Bros. Instruction Booklet*, Mario—the central protagonist of the game—is tasked with making his way through the Mushroom Kingdom to free the Mushroom People from a black-magic spell (Nintendo of America, Inc. [NAI], 1985). The spell was cast upon them by the Koopa, a tribe of magic turtles. To break the spell, Princess Toadstool—daughter of the Mushroom King—must be freed from her captor: Bowser, King of the Koopa.

As Mario moves through the environment *en route* to rescuing Princess Toadstool he must avoid pitfalls; he can collect coins and various power-ups; and he must avoid or attack enemies. In doing so, Mario commits hundreds of, what Cohen and Felson (1979, p. 589) referred to as, "direct-contact predatory violations". These crimes are conceptualized as consisting of direct physical contact between the offender and the target. Specifically, Mario commits thefts through the

V. A. Sytsma (✉)
Queen's University, Kingston, ON, Canada
e-mail: victoria.sytsma@queensu.ca

© The Author(s) 2021
S. E. Daly (ed.), *Theories of Crime Through Popular Culture*,
https://doi.org/10.1007/978-3-030-54434-8_7

69

gathering of gold coins, as well as assault and murder through the elimination of enemies.[1] It is not known who the victims of the coin theft are as there is no indication in the *Super Mario Bros. Instruction Booklet* who actually owns the coins: "Bonus Prizes...If Mario picks up 100 coins, he gets an extra life" (NAI, 1985, p. 7). Certain enemies, such as Little Goomba, are killed with one "stomp" (NAI, 1985, pp. 9–12). In contrast, enemies such as Koopa Troopa and Koopa Paratroopa require multiple "stomps" to be eliminated and thus are more likely to suffer an assault rather than be murdered.

The act of gathering power-ups cannot in and of itself be conceptualized as criminal. This is because power-ups are gifts from the Mushroom People. From the *Super Mario Bros. Instruction Booklet*: "If you come across mushrooms who have been turned into bricks or made invisible, they reward you by giving you a power boost" (NAI, 1985, p. 8). With that said, many coins and power-ups are difficult to reach as the Koopa and their followers (such as Little Goomba, a mushroom who chose to join the Koopa rather than maintain loyalty to the Mushroom Kingdom) often serve as guardians over desired rewards.

While this chapter makes the argument for *Super Mario Bros.* as an allegory of the opportunity theorist, it must be noted that because the Mushroom Kingdom has been overtaken by the Koopa, Mario is ostensibly moving through an occupied territory where crime and laws may be viewed differently than they would in a liberated or free territory. For the purpose of this book chapter, it is assumed that the Mushroom Kingdom maintains laws prohibiting theft, assault, and murder despite its occupation. The Koopa are acknowledged as soldiers of the Turtle Empire (see NAI, 1985, p. 10) in discussion of their routine activities, but the fact that *Super Mario Bros.* does not take place during peacetime in the Mushroom Kingdom is not belabored. Further, in the interest of length and simplicity, this chapter was written without consideration for other games from the Super Mario franchise. As such, while Mario's vocation is unknown, given his value system (e.g., he learned of the persecution of the Mushroom People and chose to come to their aid), he may be a fairly ordinary citizen turned vigilante—and some might perceive him to be a hero.

---

[1] Rather than assault and murder Mario may actually be engaging in cruelty to animals, depending on how one chooses to conceptualize the Koopa—which are not human, but are sometimes anthropomorphic in nature as in the case of Bowser.

Environmental Criminology

Early notions around deterrence laid the groundwork for subsequent theories concerned with rationality and ecology. In Cesare Beccaria's 1764 book, *An Essay on Crimes and Punishments*, Beccaria (1872) argued against the use of torture and death as a response to crime. Beccaria opined on more enlightened methods of crime prevention for the time and argued that the purpose of punishment should be to make a lasting impression on others while inflicting the least amount of pain on the offender. Beccaria's notions around influencing public perceptions form an early conceptualization of the concept of general deterrence. In Jeremy Bentham's, 1789 book, *An Introduction to the Principles of Morals and Legislation*, principles of deterrence were furthered through Bentham's argument that human behavior is driven by the need to maximize pleasure and minimize pain. Bentham (1789) suggested that efforts to control behavior should be developed around this pleasure-seeking drive.

Long after Beccaria and Bentham came twentieth-century criminological theories seeking to explain crime by way of identifying individual-level risk factors and societal-level "root causes" of crime. These "positive" (see Gottfredson & Hirschi, 1987) approaches proved unsatisfactory to some scholars. This is because despite strong social and economic conditions through the 1960s and 1970s, crime rates in North America were high. It is during this climate that opportunity theorists emerged with explanations for crime which combine the rational decision-making of deterrence theories with the notion that setting and environment can provide opportunity for crime. Felson and Clarke (1998) argued that criminological theory centered around the impact of ecological factors on crime avoids the pitfalls that come from attempting to empirically determine individual predictors of crime. Such pitfalls include the Sisyphean task of narrowing down the list of potential causes of crime. Felson and Clarke (1998) purported that the focus on setting provides an easier avenue for risk-factor identification, as setting-oriented theories rest on the principle that "easy or tempting opportunities entice people into criminal action" (p. 2). Such theories concerned with setting fall under the umbrella of *opportunity theories of crime* and include *rational choice perspective* and *routine activity approach*, as well as routine activity approach's nearest neighbor, *crime pattern theory*. Brantingham and Brantingham (1991) couch ecological theories within the field of *environmental criminology*, and Smith, Frazee, and Davison (2000) refer to the individual approaches that collectively make up the *opportunity theories of crime* as "intellectual cousins" (p. 490). Smith et al.'s sentiment is echoed by Jacques and Wright (2011), who use the term "theoretical siblings" (p. 738).

Rational Choice Perspective

One Player Game: Readiness

Rational choice perspective suggests that throughout our daily lives we set various objectives, such as acquiring money, moving through the community, or experiencing enjoyment. In determining how to meet such objectives individuals must weigh the costs and benefits associated with each available option for achieving a particular objective. In the case of criminal activity, when the reward for the criminal event is high and the risk is low, crime may occur. With that said, Derek Cornish and Ronald Clarke (1987) posited that decisions to offend are crime-specific and are the products of the interaction between characteristics of offence and of offender. In Clarke and Cornish's (1985) essay on modeling offender decision-making, the authors argued that crime involvement can be divided into various stages: *initial*, *continuance*, and *desistence*; and crime involvement should be framed differently from the *crime event*.

In the *initial* involvement stage there are two central decision points. First, the offender must accept his *readiness* to commit the specific offence. According to Clarke and Cornish (1985), the offender contemplates possible means of meeting objectives, as well as considers their willingness to engage in crime to meet objectives. Offending is the result of undergoing an evaluation process of the properties associated with the available courses of action and determining that committing an offence is the most desirable path (Cornish & Clarke, 1987). According to Clarke and Cornish (1985), the offender's decision to offend is influenced by their life experiences. Life experiences in turn are predicted by psychological, interpersonal, and socio-economic factors. Clarke and Cornish (1985) argued that such background factors are associated with exposure to particular challenges and opportunities, and these background factors influence how people respond to such challenges and opportunities. However, personal histories are moderated by situational elements. Further, the assessment process of the properties associated with the available courses of action to reach a particular goal may be quite cursory in nature and offenders may not be aware of the full range of activities that could satisfy their goals (Cornish & Clarke, 1987). They may be unaware of the ways in which availability of opportunity has restricted their choice, or unaware of the wide range of potential costs and benefits associated with each available option for achieving an objective. In other words, "the offender's decision-making processes will tend to display limited rather than normative rationality" (Cornish & Clarke, 1987, p. 942).

While it is clear that Mario accepts his readiness to commit crime, little is known about how his life experiences influence his willingness to resort to crime as a means of meeting objectives. The *Super Mario Bros. Instruction Booklet* provides very little background on Mario: "Mario, the hero of the story (maybe) hears about the Mushroom People's plight and sets out on a quest to free the Mushroom Princess from the evil Koopa and restore the fallen kingdom of the Mushroom people" (NAI, 1985, p. 2). It is unknown if Mario accepts his general readiness to commit crime upon hearing about the takeover of the Mushroom Kingdom, or if he contemplates this willingness to engage in criminality immediately prior to each crime event. We do however get a sense that despite his readiness to commit crime, he initially has a strong value system that centers around assisting those in need.

From the perspective of the player, who eventually learns various strategies for beating the game, it may be argued that Mario displays fairly normative rationality—after all, if he did not "steal" coins, he would not likely earn enough extra lives to make it to the end of the game (for every 100 coins collected Mario earns 1 additional life). However, from the perspective of Mario, who is experiencing the environment for the first time, he may not realize the implications of collecting coins—at least not at first. He may simply view the act of gathering them as a pleasurable activity (more on this below), and he is therefore displaying rather limited rationality. Once he realizes he can earn an extra life for every 100 coins, the decision-making process may lean toward more normative rationality and *continuance* is probable (see below for more on *continuance*). Ultimately, since we do not know what information Mario had about the Mushroom Kingdom prior to beginning his quest and we do not know the value of the coins beyond the Mushroom Kingdom, it is difficult to determine how bounded his rationality is with regard to his decisions to commit theft of gold coins.

The exploration of displays of rationality by a videogame character invites a particular paradox: is the videogame character merely an extension of the rational choices of the player, or can it be assumed that the character is driving the actions of those controlling him (at least to some degree)? For the purpose of this book chapter, I argue that from the perspective of the player, collecting power-ups and coins and destroying enemies is necessary in order to complete the game. Therefore, the amount of freedom the player has to project themselves onto the main character is limited. If the player is endeavoring to finish the game in its entirety, the player has little control over how Mario behaves in order to meet objectives. In other words, while committing "direct-contact predatory violations" is Mario's choice within his environment, it is scantly the player's choice if the player wants to complete the game—crime is necessary to avoid "Game Over". With that said separating the decisions of the character from those of the player does pose analytical and conceptual challenges for applying criminological theories to video games in general.

World 1-1: Choice-Structuring Properties

The second decision point in the *initial* involvement stage is the decision to commit the offence. The offender must first be presented with circumstances that create need and opportunity to commit an offence at the situational level. Clarke and Cornish (1985) theorized that at the situational level one's perception, experience, and processing of the available information contributes to the occurrence of the actual *crime event*. Cornish and Clarke (1987) termed those characteristics which make particular offences attractive to specific offenders, *choice-structuring properties*. This is because those properties which the offender considers relevant to their particular objectives—such as opportunity, costs, and benefits—help to structure the choice to offend.

Crime types are heterogeneous in their choice-structuring properties, particularly across goals. In order to achieve one's goals, the various available options are not exclusively criminal. Cornish and Clarke (1987) provided the example of driving while impaired. The options available to achieve the goal of getting home include the illegal option of driving while impaired, as well as many legal alternatives. Similarly, if the goal is to make money, there are nearly unlimited legal and illegal options to achieve this goal. It is because of this heterogeneity of choice-structuring properties that the potential for offending displacement is only present in very specific circumstances. Displacement to alternative offence types has the potential to occur only when those alternative offences share properties with the initial crime type, such as the shared goal of acquiring money. Even when various crime types share similar goals, displacement is not a certainty. As Cornish and Clarke (1987) noted, "some choice-structuring properties may have a more pivotal role to play in decisions concerning displacement. It is generally accepted, for example, that some offenders will not contemplate crimes which involve the use of violence" (p. 941).

During the course of the crime event the offender first selects a location and specific target based on factors such as ease of access to the location and target, level of guardianship, or the appeal of the target. For instance, the home selected for burglary might be especially affluent and located in a neighborhood the offender regularly frequents. The decision to engage in the crime event may change mid-crime commission as the external situation changes; for example, if a pedestrian passes by during a break-in, the offender may simply walk away (Clarke & Cornish, 1985). If the crime occurs and a reward is presented, positive reinforcement of the offending behavior will result in *continuance* (Clarke & Cornish, 1985). With continuation comes an improved and diversified offending skill set, possible enjoyment of the criminal lifestyle, and an expansion of interpersonal relationships with others who engage in criminality. *Continuance* is especially likely if offenders are arrested because an arrest decreases legitimate opportunities and expands the criminal peer group.

Mario has a number of objectives over the course of his journey. Mario's objectives can be divided into (i) situational and (ii) long term. Situational objectives include moving through the environment, gathering coins and power-ups, and surviving various interactions with the Koopa. Long-term objectives include acquiring enough coins to be granted an extra life and rescuing Princess Toadstool. Mario's situational objectives are largely intertwined with one another. While successfully moving though the environment often means avoiding physical barriers and pitfalls, it also means surviving various interactions with the Koopa. Further, surviving various interactions with the Koopa is more probable when power-ups, such as Fire Flower (a flower that gives Mario the ability to throw fireballs at enemies) have been acquired. The situational objective of gathering coins is also intertwined with the long-term objective of acquiring enough coins to be granted an extra life. The options available to Mario to meet objectives are sometimes diverse and sometimes limited; with the physical environment very often predicting whether or not Mario can meet his objectives with or without resorting to criminality.

Despite coin-collecting being a central objective, we do not know why Mario initially collects the first 100 coins. The initial collection of coins may be a pleasure-seeking behavior; however, it is unlikely any of his criminal behavior is *initially* driven by either hedonism or sadism given the information we have regarding Mario's value system: he learned of the persecution of the Mushroom People and chose to come to their aid. Alternatively, the coins may have value outside of the Mushroom Kingdom (monetary or otherwise) and Mario has an objective we are unaware of that requires coins or money to meet it. It could also be that Mario was informed of the value of coins in cultivating extra lives prior to beginning his quest. Regardless of the initial motivation to collect them, Mario will inevitably learn he can improve his odds of survival by collecting coins. Once he experiences the high-value reward of an extra life, *continuance* can be expected. In addition, Clarke and Cornish would predict that Mario will become quite skilled at collecting coins, and experience some satisfaction with the criminal lifestyle; thereby creating a pleasure-centered motivation that may not have been present at the outset.

The central *choice-structuring property* of coins at the situational level for Mario is likely ease of access. In many areas of the Mushroom Kingdom accessing coins poses very little personal risk to Mario. Coins are often visible to passersby, are unguarded, and, from Mario's perspective, they will prolong his life: low risk, and high reward over time. In other areas, the coins are less easily accessed. Coins may be hidden inside of bricks or well-guarded by an enemy. Attempting to access hidden or guarded targets poses a higher risk to personal safety, and may be considered low-reward for a number of reasons—such as Mario already having a large number of extra lives saved up, or the player controlling Mario being skilled enough that they believe they can complete the game without accumulating extra lives. Another reason why the collection of coins in less accessible areas may be considered high risk is the lengthy nature of the coin-collecting endeavor: it takes time to accumulate 100 coins and one difficult-to-reach area will not necessarily net the amount of coins needed to ensure an extra life. Unless the yield is certain to be large or enough to meet the 100-coin threshold, it may not be worth the risk.

The assault and murder of the Koopa and their followers possess differing choice-structuring properties depending on whether the Koopa pose a perceived threat to personal safety, or are perceived to be guardians of gold coins or power-ups. In the event that the Koopa are perceived to be a threat, Mario may choose to evade them or to subdue or kill them. The choice to subdue or kill them can depend on a number of factors. In some cases, getting close enough to the enemy to be able to kill or attack them can be riskier than evading an approaching enemy. For example, a pair of Koopa known as the Hammer Brothers pose a greater risk than Little Goomba because Hammer Brothers come in pairs, and they throw a weapon—if Mario were to risk getting close enough to kill one brother while the Koopa's hammer is in the air, even if Mario is successful, the hammer may fly back and strike him. Further, the other brother would still be nearby and continue to pose a threat.

Koopa Paratroopas are flying Koopa and may be perceived to pose greater risk than other types of Koopa because they are uniquely mobile. On the other hand, if Mario has acquired power-ups such as a Fire Flower, or Starman (giving him the power of invincibility), enemies pose very little, if any, risk. Despite power-ups the assault or murder of the Koopa may still be unattractive due to environmental factors, such as Mario's or the enemy's placement on a narrow platform or near a barrier that Mario could get trapped against. In the event that the Koopa are acting as guardians of gold coins or power-ups, Mario must weigh the value of the reward with both the enemy's abilities and the probability of being struck by the enemy. If the reward is considered quite valuable (such as a 1-up Mushroom which gives Mario an extra life), the guardian has few threatening attributes (such as flight, or weapon use), and the environment or terrain is easily traversed, the reward might outweigh the risk. Further, if the reward is less valuable but is not hidden (such as a coin or cluster of coins), and the guardian is less threatening, it may be worth the risk given that the reward over the long-term of coin-collecting is an extra life.

Thank You, Mario! Your Quest Is Over: Desistance

Finally, Clarke and Cornish (1985) posited that *desistance* occurs for a number of possible reasons. The offender may have an unpleasant experience, or they may have had a change in their circumstances, making their previous criminal lifestyle no longer feasible or desirable; such as marriage or increased police presence in their neighborhood of activity. Desistance does not necessarily mean desistance from crime generally, as the offender could move on to another crime type; nor does it necessarily mean desistance from the initial crime type permanently. They may return to the initial crime type as their circumstances continue to change.

Because Mario exists in a closed world in *Super Mario Bros.* we do not know how he would behave if he were able to rescue Princess Toadstool and exist freely in the Mushroom Kingdom or elsewhere. Those who have completed *Super Mario Bros.* know that once the game is completed and the player pushes button "B", Mario is put back to the beginning of the game and tasked with starting the quest again with an added degree of difficulty. Thus the likelihood of Mario's journey to permanent desistance from crime is unknown. That said, given the choice-structuring properties associated with Mario's general offending habits, an unpleasant experience leading to temporary or sporadic desistance from certain activities is likely. For example, if Mario (or the player controlling him) has been repeatedly injured or killed by Hammer Brothers during attempts to assault or murder them, he may elect to evade Hammer Brothers by jumping over or sprinting past when faced with them in the future.

Routine Activity Approach

Activity Spaces and the Routine Activities of the Mushroom Kingdom

Lawrence Cohen and Marcus Felson (1979, p. 588) presented the *routine activity approach* in their 1979 article titled, Social Change and Crime Rate Trends: A Routine Activity Approach. These theorists conceived of this approach in response to a documented "sociological paradox" that despite improving social and econo-mic conditions across the United States through the 1960s and 1970s, crime had increased dramatically. The routine activity approach is rooted in ecology in that the approach is concerned with how the spatial and temporal organization of social life facilitates criminal activities for those who have criminal inclinations. This approach is not concerned with why people may be inclined to commit crime, but rather the offender's proclivity toward crime is taken for granted. According to this approach, crimes take place when a *motivated offender*, a *suitable target*, and the *absence of a capable guardian* converge in space and time. If even one of the three elements that make up this theory is absent, crime can be avoided.

The concept of *routine activities* refers to, "recurrent and prevalent activities which provide for basic population and individual needs, whatever their biological or cultural origins. Thus routine activities would include formalized work, as well as the provision of standard food, shelter, sexual outlet, leisure, social interaction, learning and childrearing" (Cohen & Felson, 1979, p. 593). Cohen and Felson argued that post-WWII such routine activities shifted, keeping people outside of the home for longer hours, and with more desire and need for transportable consu-mer goods; thereby increasing the likelihood that the three elements of the routine activity approach will converge in space and time. While the routine activity appro-ach explains criminal events at the situational level, it also explains how macro-le-vel social change creates or eliminates opportunity. For instance, Cohen and Felson cited Patrick Colquhoun's (1800) Treatise on the Police of the Metropolis where Colquhoun attributed climbing crime rates in London to an increase in goods moving through London's various terminals and ports.

Brantingham and Brantingham (1993, 2008) added to the concept of *routine activities* their *crime pattern theory*. Crime pattern theory suggests that crime occurs when the *activity spaces* (e.g., home, work, shopping, entertainment, and the paths that join such "nodes") of motivated offenders and those of victims/tar-gets intersect. Further, crime will cluster at the intersection of multiple activity spaces, such as in places where shopping and entertainment districts overlap (Brantingham & Brantingham, 1993, 2008). As people engage in regular routine activities, they eventually cease to engage in a decision-making process, but rather adopt a default sequence. In the case of those who engage in crime, Brantingham and Brantingham (1993, 2008) referred to this guiding sequence as a *crime tem-plate*. Such crime templates are not static, and as sequences fail based on changing circumstances, the template is adjusted. Family and peers influence the forms such *guiding templates* take; and by aggregating offender crime templates, patterns of "typical" criminal processes emerge.

Before discussing the ways in which the routine activities of Mario and the Koopa intersect, it must first be established what their routine activities consist of. Again, little is known about Mario's background in *Super Mario Bros.* Across the Super Mario franchise, Mario's occupation ranges from carpenter to plumber to physician and more, but the *Super Mario Bros. Instruction Booklet* makes no mention of Mario's vocation or where he lives. What is known is that Mario endeavors to move through the various *activity spaces* of the Mushroom Kingdom to achieve the long-term goal of rescuing Princess Toadstool, with several situational objectives arising along the way.

In contrast, quite a bit is known about the prevalent activities of the Koopa. The Koopa are sometimes referred to as citizens of an empire in the *Super Mario Bros. Instruction Booklet* (see NAI, 1985, p. 10), and some characters Mario encounters in the *activity space* (such as green Koopa Troopa) are soldiers of the empire led by Bowser, King of the Koopa. Other characters encountered by Mario (such as Little Goomba) are not actually Koopa, but rather appear to be rebel insurgents of the Mushroom Kingdom who have joined the Koopa tribe. It is unclear if the Koopa have taken over the Mushroom Kingdom as an occupation or annexation, but it should be noted that Mario is moving through the environment after the central conflict between the Koopa and the Mushroom People has ended. Through their role as soldiers the routine activities of the Koopa and their followers consist of patrolling or guarding the ground or skies.[2] Mario's situational objectives of moving through the Mushroom Kingdom and gathering coins and power-ups create cause for him to regularly share activity space with the Koopa.

Mario's Friends as Handlers and the Rest of the "Two Triplets"

Motivated offenders are those who have "both criminal inclinations and the ability to carry out those inclinations" (Cohen & Felson, 1979, p. 590). In addition, the routine activity approach was meant to apply to a class of crimes Cohen and Felson (1979, p. 589) referred to as "direct-contact predatory violations". These crimes are conceptualized as consisting of direct physical contact between the offender and target. The target—which could be a person or object—may be either damaged or taken. Cohen and Felson (1979) identified high-priced goods that are both light and transportable (such as small electronics) as especially *suitable* targets, as well as people who go outside the home more often for work and social activities (such as young people and single adults). A *capable guardian* in this approach is someone

---

[2] As in the case of Lakitu, "the mysterious turtle who controls the clouds" (NAI, 1985, p. 12).

who protects targets. Capable guardians are not strictly police and security guards. These theorists posited that regular civilians fill the role of guardians regularly throughout their daily routine activities. In fact, Cohen and Felson (1979) noted that because guardianship is so commonplace and marked by the absence of crime, it often goes unnoticed. Felson (1986) later added to the theory the role of the *handler* who controls the offender. The notion of the handler draws on Hirschi's (1969) control theory and rests on the idea that various handlers in a society are in a position to exert informal social control over motivated offenders (Felson, 1986,1995). John Eck (1994,1995) added the term *place manager* to refer to those who monitor places.

Using these updates to the routine activity approach, Felson (1995, p. 55) presented the theory as "two triplets" consisting of three objects of supervision and three supervisors: *suitable targets* are protected by *guardians, motivated offenders* are controlled by *handlers,* and *amenable places* (those places where there is a potential for crime to occur) are supervised by *place managers.* Felson (1995) also added to the theory a description of varying levels of responsibility by each of the supervisor types. For instance, *personal responsibility* for targets, offenders, and places fall on owners of goods or property, or those directly responsible for other people, such as parents. *Assigned responsibility* refers to those specifically employed to monitor (such as a school principal or concierge). *Diffuse responsibility* refers to employees with more general assignment, and *general responsibility* refers to strangers or bystanders who have no specific connection to a target, offender, or place, but by virtue of their presence crime is prevented.

There are two suitable targets in *Super Mario Bros.*: (i) coins and (ii) those characters who are routinely occupying space in the Mushroom Kingdom. Though the Koopa and their followers are often targets, they also act as guardians over coins, as well as guardians over one another. Some guardians are more effective than others; with those characters who possess multiple abilities (such as the Hammer Brothers and Lakitu) likely serving as a greater deterrent for Mario (or the player) when he is seeking an opportunity to collect treasures or physically victimize others. In addition, Mario is the motivated offender and while the offender's proclivity toward crime is taken for granted in the *routine activity approach,* his motivations and readiness to commit crime have been discussed elsewhere in this chapter. Despite Mario moving through the environment alone, power-ups are gifts from the Mushroom People and the *Super Mario Bros. Instruction Booklet* does conceptualize these gift-givers as "Mario's Friends" (NAI, 1985, p. 8). The power-ups are likely given to increase the likelihood of Mario freeing the Mushroom People from the Koopa, but it could also be that Mario's friends are acting as handlers by showing support for him, thereby increasing informal social control (albeit the likelihood of this being the case is low).

Brantingham and Brantingham (1993, p. 17) posited, "Physical clusters of particular types of land use shape the movement and concentration of people, the awareness spaces of potential offenders, and the distributions of crime." Brantingham and Brantingham (2008) later referred to locations where large numbers of people tend to congregate as *crime generators*. Both the outdoor and indoor environments in the Mushroom Kingdom consist almost entirely of *amenable places*. Valuable goods are often in plain sight and characters are regularly moving about the space; thus, there are high concentrations of potential victims and targets. Again, just as the Koopa and their followers are often targets, they can also be described as place managers because of their routine guarding and patrolling activities. The Koopa can also be said to have *assigned responsibility* over goods and places because they are specifically employed to monitor such targets through their role as soldiers of Bowser's empire.

Policy Implications and Empirical Evidence

The policy implications born out of opportunity theory are numerous. For instance, in his 1971 book of the same name, C. Ray Jeffery conceived of the concept of *crime prevention through environmental design*, or CPTED. Jeffery (1971) was concerned with how the physical environment plays a role in learning via punishment and reward and posited that opportunity for crime, risk to the offender, and offender motivation can all be manipulated. Concurrent to Jeffery, in 1972 architect, Oscar Newman coined the term "defensible space" in his book, Defensible Space: Crime Prevention through Urban Design. Newman argued that crime and disorder can be curbed through urban design that reduces opportunity for such behavior. This urban design should include clear visibility of those walking through and using the space. The spaces people live and move through should also instill a sense of security in people so that they will interact with neighbors, take ownership over the area, and be more willing to intervene when they observe crime or disorder.

In Ronald Clarke's 1980 piece on *situational crime prevention*, he argued that understanding the offender's life circumstances and experiences contributes very little to developing actionable crime prevention strategies. Understanding the spatial and temporal distribution of specific crime types allows stakeholders to prevent crime through the development of setting manipulation tactics designed to "(i) reduce the physical opportunities for offending or (ii) increase the chances of an offender being caught" (Clarke, 1980, p. 139). Clarke (1983) described situational crime prevention as measures meant to reduce opportunities for crime, and increase the risks associated with committing crime. Such measures include various "target-hardening" initiatives, increased guardianship, and architecture designed with crime prevention in mind. Further, Cornish and Clarke (1987) noted that cataloguing choice-structuring properties of specific crime types can aid in crime prevention program development by allowing policy-makers to anticipate when displacement is possible. Clarke and Cornish (1985; Cornish & Clarke, 1986) also stressed the importance of developing crime-specific decision-making models given differences in motivation, techniques, and offender characteristics—and therefore differences in crime prevention strategies.

A number of modern policing innovations can be linked to principles of opportunity theories. Herman Goldstein proposed a then-radical approach to policing, known as problem-oriented policing (POP) in the late 1970s. Goldstein (1979) advocated for an approach to policing which starts with defining a particular crime problem and developing a thorough understanding of the crime problem through research, including analysis of the spatial and temporal trends of the crime type, victim and offender profiles, and the typical *modus operandi*. Once a crime problem is thoroughly understood, possible responses should be explored, with a novel response eventually being selected and executed. Eck and Spelman (1987) added to POP the "SARA" model, which stands for *scanning* to identify the crime problem; *analysis* to thoroughly understand the scope and nature of the problem; *responding* to the problem with a solution that is based on the knowledge gained during the analysis stage; and an *assessment* of the intervention to evaluate its impact on various outcomes of interest. A 2008 Campbell Systematic Review found POP to have a small but statistically significant impact on crime and disorder (Weisburd, Telep, Hinkle, & Eck, 2008).

Conceptually similar to POP is *hotspots policing*. Lawrence Sherman and David Weisburd (1995) discovered that increasing police officer presence in crime "hotspots" can produce reductions in disorder and crime calls for service. Police targeting of relatively small, high crime areas later become known as "hotspots policing" and the empirical evidence for such a policing innovation is fairly strong. For instance, a 2019 Campbell Systematic Review by Braga et al. concluded, "Hotspots policing generates statistically significant small reductions in overall crime and disorder in areas where the strategy is implemented. These crime control gains were evident across specific categories of crime outcomes including drug offenses, disorder offenses, property crimes, and violent crimes" (p. 2).

Finally, surveillance tools such as closed-circuit television cameras (CCTV) are theoretically supported by opportunity theories given the potential for deterrence that CCTV creates. A systematic review and meta-analysis on the effects of CCTV on crime by Piza, Welsh, Farrington, and Thomas (2019) found that while the mere presence of CCTV produces small crime reductions, when coupled with a diversity of interventions and active monitoring, effects are sizable.

Despite empirical evidence favoring a number of policy directions inspired by opportunity theories of crime, meta-analysis by Pratt, Cullen, Blevins, Daigle, and Madensen (2006) found that mean effect sizes of various indicators of deterrence theory on crime and deviance are rather small. While Pratt et al. (2006) found certainty of sanction to be a fairly well-supported dimension of deterrence theory in its ability to predict crime/deviance that predictive value was found to be crime-specific, with white-collar crimes having the strongest association with certainty. Pratt et al. (2006) recommended deterrence and rational choice theories are applied to specific crime types, rather than viewed as a general theory of crime. Pratt et al. (2006) also recommended deterrence and rational choice theories be integrated with other frameworks; particularly those that employ dimensions of informal social control and self-control similar to the integrated framework developed by Piquero and Tibbetts (1996). Piquero and Tibbetts' (1996) integrated theory combines deterrence principles with situational crime prevention and self-control. Piquero and Tibbetts (1996) found that low self-control impacts one's ability to perceive an activity as high risk (has the potential for sanction), and those with low self-control are more likely to derive pleasure from the activity.

Situational crime prevention is applicable to *Super Mario Bros.* Depending on how skilled the player is, there are many environmental elements that make targets less desirable due to guardianship, spatial barriers, and even temporality—moving forward at the wrong moment may result in missing the desired target, incurring damage to Mario, or even Mario's death. In an effort to prevent "direct-contact predatory violations", it is recommended that stakeholders such as Bowser, King of the Koopa, manipulate the physical space of the Mushroom Kingdom to reduce criminal opportunities and increase risk of apprehension of offenders. This includes adding narrow and difficult-to-reach platforms, removing loose coins from public spaces, and providing soldiers of the Turtle Empire with more clandestine patrol spaces. With that said while applying principles of situational crime prevention to a video game might keep game characters safer, the gameplay would surely suffer. Realistically, the physical spaces of *Super Mario Bros.* were carefully designed to provide game players with a fun and challenging platforming game that has endured for decades. Be he a murderer, thief, vigilante, or plumber, Mario remains the hero of the Mushroom Kingdom.

Discussion Questions

1. Using the example of bicycle theft on a college campus, brainstorm a situational crime prevention strategy that takes into consideration all three elements of routine activity approach (i.e., a motivated offender, a suitable target, and the absence of a capable guardian).

2. Cornish and Clarke termed those characteristics which make particular offences attractive to specific offenders, *choice-structuring properties*. If you were to find a duffle-bag containing cash near the library of a college campus (similar to Mario encountering gold coins throughout the Mushroom Kingdom), what choice-structuring properties of the duffle-bag are you likely to consider prior to making the choice to take the bag for yourself?

3. Brantingham and Brantingham's *crime pattern theory* suggests that crime occurs when the *activity spaces* of victims/targets and those of offenders intersect. What are some major activity spaces in your town or city? Are there locations where multiple activity spaces cluster, and what sorts of criminal activities are likely to take place within such activity spaces?

References

Beccaria, C. (1872). *An Essay on Crimes and Punishments* (New ed.). Albany: W.O. Little and Co.

Bentham, J. (1789). *An Introduction to the Principles of Morals and Legislation: Printed in the Year 1780, and Now First Published*. London: T. Payne.

Braga, A. A., Turchan, B., Papachristos, A. V., & Hureau, D. M. (2019). *Hot Spots Policing of Small Geographic Areas Effects on Crime*. Campbell Systematic Reviews. Oslo, Norway: Campbell Collaboration.

Brantingham, P. J., & Brantingham, P. L. (1991). *Environmental Criminology*. Prospect Heights, IL: Waveland Press.

Brantingham, P. J., & Brantingham, P. L. (2008). Crime Pattern Theory. In L. Mazerolle & R. Wortley (Eds.), *Environmental Criminology & Crime Analysis* (pp. 78–93). New York: Willan Publishing.

Brantingham, P. L., & Brantingham, P. J. (1993). Nodes, Paths and Edges: Considerations on the Complexity of Crime and the Physical Environment. *Journal of Environmental Psychology, 13*, 3–28.

Clarke, R. V. (1980). Situational Crime Prevention: Theory and Practice. *British Journal of Criminology, 20*, 136–147.

Clarke, R. V. (1983). Situational Crime Prevention: Its Theoretical Basis and Practical Scope. In M. Tonry & N. Morris (Eds.), *Crime and Justice* (Vol. 4, pp. 225–256). Chicago: University of Chicago Press.

Clarke, R. V., & Cornish, D. B. (1985). Modeling Offenders' Decisions: A Framework for Research and Policy. In M. Tonry & N. Morris (Eds.), *Crime and Justice* (Vol. 6, pp. 147–185). Chicago: University of Chicago Press.

Cohen, L., & Felson, M. (1979). Social Change and Crime Rate Trends: A Routine Activity Approach. *American Sociological Review, 44*, 588–608.

Colquhoun, P. (1800). *Treatise on the Police of the Metropolis*. London: Baldwin.

Cornish, D. B., & Clarke, R. V. (1986). Introduction. In D. B. Cornish & R. V. Clarke (Eds.), *The Reasoning Criminal: Rational Choice Perspectives on Offending* (pp. 1–13). New York: Springer-Verlag.

Cornish, D. B., & Clarke, R. V. (1987). Understanding Crime Displacement: An Application of Rational Choice Theory. *Criminology, 25*(4), 933–947.

Eck, J. E. (1994). *Drug Markets and Drug Places: A Case-Control Study of the Spatial Structure of Illicit Drug Dealing*. Doctoral dissertation, University of Maryland, College Park, MD.

Eck, J. E. (1995). A General Model of the Geography of Illicit Retail Market Places. In J. Eck & D. Weisburd (Eds.), *Crime and Place: Crime Prevention Studies* (Vol. 4, pp. 67–94). Monsey, NY: Criminal Justice Press.

Eck, J. E., & Spelman, W. (1987). *Problem Solving: Problem-Oriented Policing in Newport News*. Washington, DC: Police Executive Research Forum.

Felson, M. (1986). Routine Activities, Social Controls, Rational Decisions, and Criminal Outcomes. In D. Cornish & R. V. Clarke (Eds.), *The Reasoning Criminal* (pp. 119–112). New York: Springer-Verlag.

Felson, M. (1995). Those Who Discourage Crime. In J. Eck & D. Weisburd (Eds.), *Crime and Place: Crime Prevention Studies* (Vol. 4, pp. 53–66). Monsey, NY: Criminal Justice Press.

Felson, M., & Clarke, R. V. (1998). *Opportunity Makes the Thief: Practical Theory for Crime Prevention*. Police Research Series (Paper 98). London, UK: Policing and Reducing Crime Unit, Home Office.

Goldstein, H. (1979). Improving Policing: A Problem-Oriented Approach. *Crime and Delinquency, 25*, 236–258.

Gottfredson, M. R., & Hirschi, T. (Eds.). (1987). *Positive Criminology*. Beverly Hills, CA: Sage.

Hirschi, T. (1969). *Causes of Delinquency*. Berkeley, CA: University of California Press.

Jacques, S., & Wright, R. (2011). Informal Control and Illicit Drug Trade. *Criminology, 49*, 729–765.

Jeffery, C. R. (1971). *Crime Prevention Through Environmental Design*. Beverly Hills: Sage.

Newman, O. (1972). *Defensible Space: Crime Prevention Through Urban Design*. New York: Macmillan.

Nintendo of America, Inc. (1985). *Super Mario Bros. Instructional Booklet*. Redmond, WA: Nintendo.

Piquero, A. R., & Tibbetts, S. G. (1996). Specifying the Direct and Indirect Effects of Low Self-Control and Situational Factors in Offenders' Decision Making: Toward a More Complete Model of Rational Offending. *Justice Quarterly, 13*, 481–510.

Piza, E. L., Welsh, B. C., Farrington, D. P., & Thomas, A. L. (2019). CCTV Surveillance for Crime Prevention: A 40-Year Systematic Review with Meta-Analysis. *Criminology & Public Policy, 18*(1), 135–159.

Pratt, T. C., Cullen, F. T., Blevins, K. R., Daigle, L. E., & Madensen, T. D. (2006). The Empirical Status of Deterrence Theory: A Meta-Analysis. In F. T. Cullen, J. P. Wright, & K. R. Blevins (Eds.), *Taking Stock: The Status of Criminological Theory* (Vol. 15). New Brunswick, NJ: Transaction.

Sherman, L., & Weisburd, D. (1995). General Deterrent Effects of Police Patrol in Crime "Hot Spots": A Randomized, Controlled Trial. *Justice Quarterly, 12*(4), 625–648.

Smith, W. R., Frazee, S. G., & Davison, E. L. (2000). Furthering the Integration of Routine Activity and Social Disorganization Theories: Small Units of Analysis and the Study of Street Robbery as a Diffusion Process. *Criminology, 38*(2), 489–524.

Weisburd, D., Telep, C. W., Hinkle, J. C., & Eck, J. E. (2008). *The Effects of Problem-Oriented Policing on Crime and Disorder*. Campbell Systematic Reviews. Oslo, Norway: Campbell Collaboration.

Opportunity Theories and *The Bachelor*

8

The Bachelor Goes on a Date with Criminal Opportunity Theories

Cory Schnell

Introduction

Chemistry is defined as "the branch of science that deals with the identification of the substances of which matter is composed; the investigation of their properties and the ways in which they interact, combine, and change; and the use of these processes to form new substances" (Oxford, 2012). Outside of an educational context, when people refer to chemistry, they are likely discussing the dynamics of interpersonal relationships. This social conceptualization of chemistry examines the question—why do certain people get along and others do not? For example,

---

Sections from this chapter were adapted from a previous discussion of criminal opportunities theories I authored (see Schnell, 2017). While I tried to provide citations to any *Bachelor*-related facts provided, I had to rely more on my personal recollections of watching the show and other non-academic sources of information from the internet. A main source of this information is the *Bachelor Party* podcast. In addition, the analysis of *The Bachelor* is based upon me being a fan of the show, and I recognize there are likely other academic appraisals of the show with insightful analyses which I did not consult for this chapter.

444

C. Schnell (✉)
University of South Carolina, Columbia, SC, USA
e-mail: schnellc@mailbox.sc.edu

© The Author(s) 2021
S. E. Daly (ed.), *Theories of Crime Through Popular Culture*,
https://doi.org/10.1007/978-3-030-54434-8_8

why does Sarah always collaborate on projects with Jill at work? Why does Jim only throw the ball to Jordan during flag football games? The definition of social chemistry is almost identical to its academic counterpart, replacing particles with people to observe "the complex emotional or psychological interaction between two people" (Oxford, 2012). Social chemistry is crucial to understanding how people form connections beyond transactional social encounters (e.g. friendships, marriage, etc.). The change from particles to people is significant. People have agency and can act in surprising ways. Particles or matter can be more predictable; for instance, it is comparable to baking. There is a recipe for combining ingredients to form a new product which is more than the sum of its parts. You combine a specific mixture of eggs, flour, and other ingredients to create a batter that is baked to become a cake. With people, it can be more complicated. That is why the study of interpersonal chemistry is inexact. People can find it hard to describe and often revert to the infamous logic of Supreme Court Justice Potter Stewart in *Jacobellis v. Ohio (1964)* where he said of determining the definition of obscenity: "I know it when I see it".

The dynamics of social chemistry are essential to understand for dating or why certain individuals "couple up" and others do not. This chapter explores the concept of social chemistry by examining the reality TV dating show *The Bachelor*. Criminal opportunity theories that examine the chemistry for crime incidents to occur at specific places are used to inform this discussion. The analysis of chemistry is essential to understanding both *The Bachelor* and criminal opportunity theories. Both ask individuals to become "social chemists" or problem-solvers to determine individual's decision-making processes based upon unique situations. These theories are then applied to create a framework to understand why the lead suitor on *The Bachelor* selects certain contestants for dates throughout the show. This chapter is divided into three sections. The first section provides an overview of the television show *The Bachelor*. The second section features an introduction to criminal opportunity theories in criminology. The third section offers a preliminary framework that is influenced by criminal opportunity theories to evaluate the decision-making of suitors on *The Bachelor*. To borrow the immortal words of *The Bachelor's* host Chris Harrison, this will be the most dramatic chapter in this book!

The Bachelor: An Overview

The Bachelor is a reality TV dating show that premiered on the American Broadcasting Company (ABC) in 2002. Its premiere occurred around the same time other popular reality TV shows such as *Survivor* and *American Idol* helped revolutionize the landscape of American television in the twenty-first century. *The Bachelor* has spawned two other successful shows—*The Bachelorette* (2003 debut) and *Bachelor in Paradise* (2014 debut)—which offer variations on the same format created by *The Bachelor*. There have been several other spin-offs from the original show since its premiere (e.g. *Bachelor Pad, Listen to Your Heart*, etc.) and the franchise has also been exported to 37 countries around the world (Angelo, 2018). For the purpose of this chapter, *The Bachelor* and *The Bachelorette* are used interchangeably since they use the same format but just switch the sex of the lead suitor and contestants. Collectively, these two shows, as well as *Bachelor in Paradise*, and the discourse on social media which surround each show, form what is referred to as "Bachelor Nation" (see Kaufman, 2018). Despite mixed reviews from television critics over the years (see Metacritic, 2020), *The Bachelor* remains an enduring cultural phenomenon. Most contestants on the show today have grown up with *The Bachelor* being a fixture on television for almost their entire lives. The shows receive formidable ratings for ABC, especially amongst the coveted demographic of viewers aged 18–49 (see Porter, 2020). During the Covid-19 pandemic in spring 2020, President Trump repeatedly used the ratings of *The Bachelor* finale to provide a triumphant comparison point for the ratings of his daily press conferences by claiming they received similar numbers (Bump, 2020).

The premise of the show is one romantic lead suitor who dates anywhere between 20 and 30 contestants or available singles at the same time with the goal of finding someone to offer a marriage proposal by the end of the show. There are one-on-one and group dates each week where the suitor gets to learn more about each contestant. The field of contestants is whittled down each week with a tense rose ceremony where contestants are eliminated if they do not receive a rose from the suitor. Chris Harrison hosts the show and presides over the rose ceremonies. The show has begun to experiment with this format in recent years. One of the most apparent shifts is the reduction of screen time for Chris Harrison which gives the show more of a "fly on the wall" documentary-feel as opposed to a formally staged game show. The production design of the show is lavish, and the premise is mined for comedy although there is an earnest romanticism at the core of the show.

The production of *The Bachelor* extracted the DNA from the iconic romantic-comedies of film from the 1980s to 1990s such as *When Harry Met Sally* or *My Best Friend's Wedding* to create arguably the signature "rom-com" of both the reality TV and social media eras in the twenty-first century. Some *Bachelor* fans will ask as a personality litmus test about which half of the show they prefer (see Kaufman, 2018). The former being goofy (i.e. more "com") and the latter being more concerned with the relationships (i.e. more "rom"). Over time viewers start to grow attached to contestants as they learn more about each one through the serialized format of the show and just by proxy spending more time with them. This process simulates the way in which the lead starts to form connections with certain contestants or by which someone starts to fall in love. It is a genius design feature of the show. For the first few episodes, viewers can struggle to separate contestants. Was that Hannah B. or Hannah G. that was unable to give a coherent toast on a date? By halfway through the season viewers can feel like they are best friends with certain contestants and have strong opinions about who the lead should end up with. Each season is around 12 episodes long. For the most recent seasons, episodes are two hours long with finales that often span two nights and well over four hours. Being a member of Bachelor Nation requires investing a large amount of time.

One of the easiest ways to lure someone into Bachelor Nation shows is telling them you can view it as a sport. Each show is a contest. Someone wins at the end. People often watch the show in group atmospheres and drink alcohol in the same manner people do for sporting events. You root for certain contestants over other ones. If that does not work, you can simply say you get to watch people that range from the most attractive person at your high school to a supermodel travel around the world. One of the fine lines contestants must walk is between being competitive but not viewing the show as a contest (yes, I do see the irony here) because it is a *Bachelor* faux pas to say you "won" at the end of the show. Instead, your "journey" led you to love. There is a labyrinth of unwritten rules and jargon in which the show traffics, which I will highlight throughout the chapter. I wish this all was a joke but it is not. The show has existed in two general eras. The first era covered around the initial ten years the show (i.e. 2002–2012) aired when the contestants' primary objective appeared to be forming a relationship. Most of the contestants had careers, were older by modern TV standards (i.e. late 20s to late 30s), and their main motivation for being on the show was finding love. The show was more of a "rom" instead of a "com" during this era. The second era covers the last seven years (i.e. 2013–2020) when the contestants would be just as willing to use the show as a platform for their career interests. The contestants were younger and either viewed being on reality TV as a career or had jobs where being on the show could help their visibility through becoming an influencer on social media.

This was unavoidable during one of the latest cycles of *Bachelor* shows in 2019. On the 23rd season of *The Bachelor*, the lead, Colton Underwood, had no discernable job. He previously was on the practice squad of two NFL teams, ran his namesake charity, and loved dogs. His final four contestants included a former Miss North Carolina and an Instagram model while the woman he picked was appearing on her second reality TV dating show before the age of 24. Hannah Brown, a former Miss Alabama who appeared on Colton's season, was given the reigns of the

15th season of *The Bachelorette*. She ended up picking a man named Jed Wyatt, who explicitly told her he only came on the show to promote his music career and was later revealed to be dating someone up until the show started filming. They ended their engagement before the final episode of the season even aired. For the 24th season of the *Bachelor*, the production appeared to course correct by having Peter Weber, who is a pilot, as the lead suitor. Despite him having a well-defined career, "Pilot Pete" still provided a turbulent run as the lead, culminating with him breaking up with his fiancé, a 23-year-old model, before the show aired its finale. His mother Barb Weber would go on to become infamous in Bachelor Nation because of her aggressive disapproval of her son's most recent relationship with the show's runner-up Madison Prewett on the live after show. The newly formed couple broke up less than a week later. When these relationships do not last it leaves Bachelor Nation to ask: what went wrong? Viewers of *The Bachelor* often second guess the decisions of the lead and have a more objective view of the chemistry or lack of chemistry forming between people based on their vantage point from their couch at home. The next section of this chapter introduces criminal opportunity theories to provide a framework to further understand why the leads on *The Bachelor* select certain contestants.

Criminal Opportunity Theories

Marcus Felson's seminal book on criminal opportunity theories titled *Crime and Everyday Life* (2002) presents the metaphor "chemistry for crime" to describe how criminal opportunities influence crime (also see Felson & Eckert, 2016). While these theories have been applied to study other issues such as individual-level victimization rates (see Sampson & Wooldredge, 1987), they are most commonly used in place-based criminology to understand why certain places have more crime than others. Specifically, these theories are used for research on the distribution of crime at micro-places within cities which applies criminal opportunity theories to explain the spatial variability of patterns between these units of analysis (Weisburd, Groff, & Yang, 2012). The consideration of criminal opportunities in criminological theory is not entirely new (see Cloward & Ohlin, 1960; Sutherland, 1940), although contemporary scholarship has established the study of opportunity as a distinct theoretical approach within criminology (Eck & Weisburd, 1995). Opportunity theories are pragmatically focused on the situational emergence of crime events (i.e. foreground conditions) as opposed to other theoretical frameworks in criminology which are concerned with criminal dispositions (i.e. background conditions) such as strain or self-control theories (see Agnew, 1985; Gottfredson & Hirschi,

1990). In other words, these theories do not try to discover the factors which lead individuals to commit crime, they examine the factors which determine why they commit crime in a specific time and place. Three complementary criminal opportunity theories provide the foundation of this perspective: rational choice, routine activities, and crime pattern theory (Eck & Weisburd, 1995).

Rational Choice

Rational choice theory posits the act of committing a crime is inherently purposive and that an individual's participation in crime is the result of a cognitive decision-making process (Cornish &Clarke, 1986). This decision-making process can be limited or bounded to varying degrees of rationality but is nevertheless still a rational process (see Simon, 1972). This element of rational choice theory is one most fans of *The Bachelor* can easily embrace. The lead suitor makes decisions that follow an underlying logic to them but for other people it could appear difficult to understand why they are making certain decisions. Why did Peter pick Victoria F.? Why did he send home Kelley? In hindsight, people are even critical of their own decision-making processes, but in the moment, people make choices which appear rational to them. Historically, the earliest iteration of rational choice theory predates the founding of criminology as an academic discipline. Enlightenment scholars Cesare Beccaria (1764) and Jeremy Bentham (1789) proposed that individuals consciously choose to commit crimes and their decision-making processes can be influenced by the punishments associated with certain crimes. This scholarship also provided the foundation for deterrence theory in criminology (see Apel & Nagin, 2011). Becker (1968) introduced an influential choice model in economics which reinvigorated discourse and contemporary research on the subject throughout the social sciences (see Becker, 1993). In his contemporary expansion of the rational choice perspective in criminology, Clarke (1983) suggested that the decisions made during a crime event were primarily rooted in the offender's assessment of specific criminal opportunities.

Clarke and Cornish (1985) separate the decision-making process into various choices across different stages of criminal involvement. Clarke (1995, p. 10) suggests "a fundamental distinction be made between criminal involvement and crime events," with the former being "multi-stage and extend over substantial periods of time" and the latter being "frequently shorter processes, utilizing more circumscribed information largely related to immediate circumstances and situations." One reason people enjoy watching *The Bachelor* is because the viewer can try to imagine how they would react in this scenario and then provide critical analysis of the decisions by each person on the show. *Bachelor* leads make several key decisions at distinct stages of the process which lead them on a path to the final rose ceremony. One of the earliest impactful decisions is what contestant gets the first impression rose on the premiere episode. A later key decision is which four contestants the lead chooses to go on hometown dates. The lead's decisions during the first half of the show could be based on what contestants they have fun with, while their decision-making process later shifts more toward decisions about a life partner. For a potential criminal, the decision to hang out one night with friends that are involved in crime is only problematic because it could lead down a path where committing a crime is possible. The decision to go home and get a ski-mask because you want to commit a robbery is much more proximal to the actual commission of a crime.

Eck and Weisburd (1995) suggest "a rational choice perspective provides the basic rationale for defining places as important, since it suggests that offenders will select targets and define means to achieve their goals in a manner that can be explained" (p. 5). Cornish (1993) views rational choice as a meta-action theory because it specifically outlines how human decisions lead to crime outcomes. Offenders follow a situational progression that can be approximated through crime scripts (Cornish, 1994). This perspective also emphasizes adopting a crime specific prevention focus since scripts are unique for each offense (Clarke, 1983). Situational characteristics of locations can influence the available opportunities for crime through encouraging or discouraging actions of individuals at the micro-level (see Clarke & Cornish, 1985). For example, the presence of street lights could decrease the likelihood of a potential robber deciding to commit a crime while the presence of a bar on an adjacent street could increase the likelihood (see Roneck& Meier, 1991; Welsh & Farrington, 2008; Wright & Decker, 1997). A critique of rational choice theory is that it does not readily propose a model which is testable since decisions can always be interpreted to an extent as rational (Loughran, Paternoster, Chalfin, & Wilson, 2016; Parsons, 1951). This critique can be assuaged by offering hypotheses about offender behavior and crime events which opportunity theories explicitly address (Eck & Weisburd, 1995). The contemporary development of the rational choice perspective as an opportunity theory has also coincided with the emergence of situational crime prevention strategies. Through the targeting of the situational characteristics of locations, which facilitate the commission of specific crimes, crime control reductions can be achieved (Clarke, 1995).

Routine Activities

Routine activities theory offers a convenient approach to understand how the inter-action of individuals and certain locations results in the emergence of crime events. Routine activities are a general theory of crime which has been used to explain crimes ranging from street crime to white-collar crime (see Benson & Simpson, 2018). This theory suggests the spatial-temporal interaction of motivated offen-ders, suitable targets, and the absence of capable guardians are the prerequisite conditions or "chemistry" for crime events to occur (Cohen & Felson, 1979). The idea that a handful of components need to converge to create an opportunity is just as salient to understanding the chemistry for crime as it can be for the chemistry of dating on *The Bachelor*. This theory provides the foundation in the next section of this chapter for constructing a framework to consider why *Bachelor* leads select certain contestants. Routine activities theory builds on Hawley's (1950) investiga-tion of the spatial-temporal intersection of conditions which influenced the distri-bution of other social outcomes in neighborhoods. The theory was first introduced with a macro-level spatial analysis—exploring the factors associated with changes in national crime rates—but the theory can be applied across various units of ana-lysis (see Sampson & Wooldredge, 1987; Smith, Glave-Frazee, & Davison, 2000). Cohen and Felson (1979) initially used the theory to explain increases in predatory crime rates during the 1960s and 1970s in the United States. The authors found "the dispersion of activities away from households and families increases the op-portunity for crime and thus generates higher crime rates… as a byproduct of ch-anges in such variables as labor force participation and single-adult households" (p. 588). Today, routine activities theory is primarily explored using within city spatial units of analyses such as micro-places (see Weisburd et al., 2012).

The integration of routine activities and rational choice perspectives offers an enhanced comprehension of the situational characteristics at places which influ-ence crime events (Clarke & Felson, 1993). These two opportunity theories are helpful to unpack the decision-making of *Bachelor* leads as they survey their field of contestants. These theories suggest individuals make choices and respond to the ecological convergence of opportunity. On another hand, routine activities theory does not fit well with *The Bachelor* because one of the most novel facets of this theory is ignoring offender motivation. The theory assumes there will always be motivated offenders and leaves it to most other perspectives in criminology to ascertain why people want to commit crime. The motivation of contestants on *The Bachelor* is heavily considered within the decision-making process and the ele-ments of chemistry the lead uses to assess potential relationships. The culture of the show rewards contestants that are on the show for the "right reasons" or motivated to find love. For example, on the 11th season of *The Bachelorette*, Nick Viall, who finished second in the previous season, ruffled feathers of contestants when he was allowed back on the show by the lead Kaitlyn Bristowe because of their budding relationship before the show started filming. The other contestants protested Nick's addition because they felt he only wanted to be on television again (i.e. the wrong reasons). Viall would finish second again giving him the distinction of being the only person to finish second on two seasons of the show.

Conceptually, suitable targets are malleable depending on the specific crime category routine activities are used to explain. An important distinction can be found between property crimes and violent crimes because suitable targets switch from being objects, which are more closely associated with places, to people, which are more dynamic spatially. The concept of capable guardians or "guardianship" is primarily used to represent individuals which offer informal social control as opposed to sources of formal social control at place (i.e. police officers). According to Clarke and Felson (1993), "the most likely persons to prevent a crime are not policemen (who seldom are around to discover crimes in the act) but rather neighbors, friends, relatives, bystanders, or the owner of the property targeted" (p. 3). Guardianship as an indicator of informal social control at places can also be used to link routine activities theories to other place-based theories of crime (Braga & Clarke, 2014).

The interaction of these three components of routine activities can be illustrated using the problem analysis triangle (Eck, 1994). More importantly, the problem analysis triangle incorporates a controller for each of the three components of routine activities which can be used to prevent crime (Clarke & Eck, 2007; Eck & Clarke, 2003). Sampson, Eck, and Dunham (2010) have even proposed introducing a third layer of "super controllers" to fortify understanding of techniques for crime control at problem places. Since routine activities theory proposes the intersection of all three components is necessary for a crime event to occur this perspective suggests crime prevention efforts be focused on disrupting this convergence (Felson, 1987). The routine activities perspective provides a theoretical framework for problem-oriented policing and situational crime prevention strategies which have demonstrated effectiveness in reducing crime through targeting problem places within cities (Guerette & Bowers, 2009; Weisburd et al., 2010). Over the past 30 years, scholarship on routine activities (see Andresen & Farrell, 2015) has diversified to include tests of the theory (Messner & Blau, 1987), integration with disparate criminological theories (Franklin et al., 2012), and expansions to cyber-space which radically reconsider the concept of "place" (Reyns, 2013).

Crime Pattern Theory

Crime pattern theory investigates the distribution, movement, and interaction of criminal opportunities across time and space (Brantingham & Brantingham, 1991). Crime pattern theory expands upon the contributions of rational choice and routine activities theory through a broader understanding of the dynamic nature of criminal opportunities at places. Crime pattern theory is commonly associated with environmental criminology, which can be used interchangeably with criminal opportunity theories depending on the preference of the scholar. Rational choice theory outlines the decision-making processes of potential offenders. Routine activities theory demonstrates how these motivated, rational offenders interact with suitable targets experiencing no capable guardians at places for crime events to occur at a fixed point in time and space. Crime pattern theory offers an account of how each of these three components reached that specific point in time and space.

There is not a direct comparison with *The Bachelor* because the dating on the show unfolds in a controlled environment. *Bachelor in Paradise* does provide an exception because there is competition between multiple suitors and contestants which provides a more dynamic context. On season six of *Bachelor in Paradise*, one of the main feuds centered around Derek Peth, who previously was engaged to a fellow contestant on the show, arguing with a man named John Paul Jones over a potential guest appearance on Derek's podcast when the show ended filming. This petty feud made Tayshia Adams, who was considering both individuals to date, reject them because she viewed the conflict as reflecting poorly on their characters. If Derek did not run into a frisky John Paul Jones that night he might have been able to continue dating Tayshia. Dating outside of *The Bachelor* is easier to analyze using this opportunity theory. In other words, this theory is helpful to trace how two people get into a room (i.e. the chain of events) and continue to be involved in each other's lives to build a relationship. This theory can provide the backstory for the beginning of a relationship. Did two people meet because they had mutual friends at a party or did they randomly stumble upon each other at a book store? How did they end up there?

According to crime pattern theory, the relationship between crime and place can be understood through analyzing the spatial (i.e. where it occurred) and temporal (i.e. when it occurred) dimensions of crime events. This perspective can be considered a lifestyle theory of crime because it aims to unpack why crime events occur through understanding how crime is a function of everyday life (see Felson & Eckert, 2016). The offender's journey to crime demonstrates this idea; research suggests that individuals commit crimes in close proximity to where they live

(Bernasco, 2010; Phillips, 1980). The use of the word journey is evocative of *The Bachelor*. It is a common buzzword in Bachelor Nation parlance which could appear on a bingo board for a *Bachelor* drinking game because of its frequent usage. In the context of the show, one's journey is their personal voyage which leads them to love. An individual's daily routine could influence where they choose to commit crime. Eck and Weisburd (1995, p. 6) provide an insightful explanation of these findings:

> Just like other, non-offending individuals, offenders move among the spheres of home, school, work, shopping, and recreation. As they conduct their normal legitimate activities, they become aware of criminal opportunities. Thus, criminal opportunities that are not near the areas offenders routinely move through are unlikely to come to their attention. A given offender will be aware of only a subset of the possible targets available. Criminal opportunities found at places that come to the attention of offenders have an increased risk of becoming targets (Brantingham and Brantingham, 1993). While a few offenders may aggressively seek out uncharted areas, most will conduct their searches within the areas they become familiar with through noncriminal activities.

While the scope of crime pattern theory is much broader compared to the two other opportunity theories discussed in this section, empirical tests of this perspective are conceptually much more focused. Since crime pattern theory is not unified by a singular theory like routine activities, empirical tests can explore a wide range of hypotheses within the general framework of this opportunity perspective. This flexibility has resulted in a wide range of studies being conducted using crime pattern theory as the guiding theoretical construct. Tests of crime pattern theory hypotheses can be conceptualized as anything exploring the distribution, movement, and interaction of offenders and targets across time and space on crime. Over only the past few years, for example, analyses have examined the role of the accessibility of streets on burglary incidents (Johnson & Bowers, 2010), the influence of public transit on crime in cities (Groff & Lockwood, 2014), and drug markets as crime attractors at street corners (Taniguichi, Ratcliffe,& Taylor, 2011).

Applying Criminal Opportunity to *The Bachelor*

Before discussing the essential components to chemistry on *The Bachelor*, the broader environment in which the show unfolds must be addressed. On *The Bachelor* dating occurs in a quasi-laboratory setting. This presents a unique context to analyze relationships and chemistry—combined with the fact everyone is being recorded. In a predictable move, *Bachelor* producers during the Covid-19 pandemic suggested even the possibility of a *Bachelor: Quarantine* to adapt to a shut down in production (Wynne, 2020). This is not far-fetched because the show's production is already sequestered. Contestants all live together and are not allowed access to any personal devices, news from the outside world, or contract with friends or family. This reality distortion, which is of course the paradox of reality TV—to present the real world they must manipulate certain situations—extends to the concept of time. Between each rose ceremony, the viewers are constantly reminded a "week" has passed even though your intuitive sense of time (i.e. counting each time the sun goes up and down) tells you it is closer to three or four days used for filming. Even this simple observation of objective reality could be manipulated on these shows which might edit certain events out of order. The entire filming of the show is completed in around three months. This provides an additional layer of drama because the premise of the show asks that two people get engaged in a short period of time.

Contestants often are required to quit their jobs to join the sequestered production of the show. While the lead gets paid during filming the contestants do not receive compensation. Women that are cast have spent thousands of dollars to assemble the wardrobe of stylish dresses and evening wear which the show requires (Kaufman, 2018). The producers of the show do implicitly incentivize conflict, manipulate contestants' actions, and manufacture uncomfortable scenarios. During season 24, the producers arranged a date where one of the contestant's ex-boyfriends was the musical act. This woman had to slow dance on a stage with the lead while her ex-boyfriend awkwardly watched. These savvy production flourishes inspire the popular meme on social media which states "the devil works hard but the *Bachelor* producers work harder". A former *Bachelor*-producer helped create a fictionalized version of the show and how it is produced called *Unreal* where the Machiavellian producers continuously manipulated the contestants to extreme ends. Although this does occur (see Kaufman, 2018), the laboratory conditions of the show are still able to highlight some essential characteristics of chemistry and dating.

While every lead on *The Bachelor* has personal dating preferences, and decision-making processes can be difficult to model for individuals, there are some patterns that emerge across seasons which emphasize certain components of chemistry. Criminal opportunity informed this preliminary framework for understanding why certain contestants are selected throughout the show. Rational choice theory provides the basis for saying *Bachelor*'s have a decision-making process and routine activities theory offers a guideline for considering the convergence of key elements to determine why certain contestants are selected. *The Bachelor* lead is often reacting (i.e. rational choice) to the group of individuals (i.e. crime pattern theory) and specific actions or traits of individuals which emerge through these interactions (i.e. routine activities). There are four main categories fans of *The Bachelor* often consider when determining who the lead will select: *attractiveness, personality, lifestyle, and motivation.* Similar to routine activities theory, the interaction between these categories provides the potential chemistry for who stays and who is eliminated. It also is a similar set of criteria people might articulate in real life when dating. A key difference with routine activities theory is that all components are not required for a selection to be made. The key to crime prevention according to routine activities theory is removing or controlling one of the three elements of crime events of motivated offenders, suitable targets, and capable guardianship. While the removal of one of the components of *Bachelor* chemistry could hurt someone's case to stay, it does not necessarily preclude them from being selected. This role of chemistry is heightened on *The Bachelor* because it develops while the lead is dating around 20 other individuals which presents an effective counterfactual in the sample (i.e. the chemistry did not develop with them).

The category of *attractiveness* is subjective; each lead has a preference for the type of individual they are the most physically attracted to. One fascinating component of the show is observing which individuals separate themselves from the others because everyone on the show is objectively attractive. Each contestant tends to check off every box of the superficial standards of beauty which Western culture forward (i.e. fitness, fashion, jawlines, etc.). Viewers quickly realize that Bachelorette B prefers tall men or Bachelor A prefers brunettes. A pattern begins to emerge which could guide the analysis of the lead's decision-making process. *Personality* is one of the most elusive elements on *The Bachelor*. This is not necessarily a reflection of the contestants, which get the chance to shine on *Bachelor in Paradise*, but the editors who focus only on cliched conversations about romance. Certain personalities are bright enough to overcome this obstacle. Rachel Lindsay appeared on the 21st season of *The Bachelor* and stole the show with her intelligence, charisma, and wit. She would later go on to become the first African American lead of either *The Bachelor* or *Bachelorette*. Jason Tartick on the 14th season of *The Bachelorette* finished in third place but won over fans as the guy you would most want to be in your friend group or run for mayor of your town. He would later reveal he is friends with NFL player and legendary "fun hang" Rob Gronkowski, which further cemented his status.

Lifestyle is a crucial dimension because contestants often come from different backgrounds, a wide range of ages, and have very diverse life experiences. Since each season ends with a proposal, this component becomes important during the later stages of the show. During the 22nd season of *The Bachelor*, the lead Arie

Luyendyk Jr. connected with a contestant named Bekah Martinez. He would later learn she was only 22 years old while he was 36 years old. He made a point throughout the season of how he wanted to settle down and how much he loved going to sleep early, wearing cardigans, and sipping wine (i.e. old man things in his estimation). After Bekah was eliminated, she briefly disappeared, forcing her mom to file a missing person report, and was later found safely camping on a marijuana farm in Northern California. They had very different lifestyles. After he proposed to and broke up with Becca Kufrin, Arie Luyendyk went on to propose to Lauren Burnham who was much more reserved throughout the season which aligned better with his lifestyle. The couple is still together and has a child.

The final component is *motivation*. A reoccurring discussion on the show is either the lead or contestants are skeptical of someone's rationale for being on the show. Is it to find true love or become famous? The latter is defined in *Bachelor*-jargon as being "here for the wrong reasons." The show has a checkered history of people being there for the wrong reasons thus it is perceived as disrespectful to the lead and Bachelor Nation. Also, the lack of motivation for contestants to get engaged at the end of the show is a common reason a lead would eliminate a contestant. Motivation is not essential to routine activities theory because it is concerned with crime events instead of individual criminality. The concept of motivation is crucial to chemistry for *The Bachelor* because it reveals the willingness of a contestant to try in building a relationship.

Even when these four components converge it does not necessarily indicate chemistry or that this relationship will survive to the final rose ceremony. Each of these four components is just a key dimension to consider when appraising the decision-making process of the lead. Tyler Cameron was the runner-up on the 15th season of *The Bachelorette* but went on to win hearts all over America becoming a social media phenomenon. *The Bachelorette*, Hannah Brown, would remark that he was perfect, and as viewers we observed he checked all the boxes she previously outlined for a partner, but they still did not have that tangible chemistry. Hannah expressed she was worried he was *too* perfect and ultimately picked a man whose self-admitted greatest career achievement was writing a jingle for a small dog food company's commercial. *Bachelor* relationships are notorious for not lasting long beyond the show. That is why the rules of chemistry only apply to guessing who will advance on the show and not necessarily what relationship will last after the show. As of September 2020, for the final couples in *The Bachelor*, only 1 of 23 is married. Another 2 of the 23 are married to the runner-up of the show, which they switched over to in spectacular fashions after their season finale. For *The Bachelorette*, 5 of 15 couples are still married. The fact that most *Bachelor* relationships do not last, while a referendum on the show, does closely mirror the fact that crime is still a very rare occurrence. Weisburd's (2015) law of crime concentration finds that only about 4–6% of micro-places within cities account for 50% of the total crime incidents which indicates crime only happens in a small number of "hot spot" locations. Thus suggesting the chemistry for a lasting relationship from *The Bachelor* and crime might actually be more elusive than we assumed.

Conclusion

The concept of chemistry is central to *The Bachelor* and criminal opportunity theories. There is a very specific set of ingredients which produce the chemistry for a crime or a *Bachelor* relationship to occur. For crimes, according to routine activities theory, it is motivated offenders, suitable targets, and the lack of capable guardianship. While routine activities theories present all the elements and crime pattern theory considers how they interact, there is no clear-cut recipe for success on the *Bachelor*. These theories though are helpful to begin to identify specific elements of focus that could have an impact. The four components of attractiveness, lifestyle, personality, and motivation were identified as salient factors to evaluate the decision-making process for any lead on a *Bachelor* show. *The Bachelor* and any individual's personal dating experiences in general help highlight the importance of the concept of chemistry in the creation of a relationship. This chapter explained criminal opportunity theories then applied this perspective to propose how *The Bachelor* weighs factors to determine which contestants to select throughout the course of the show. There are certain limitations to this extension of criminal opportunity theories to *The Bachelor*, but overall it still provides an insightful framework to provide critical analysis of the show.

Discussion Questions

1. What are other components that should be considered to understand the decision-making process of lead suitors on *The Bachelor*? How are these similar or different to dating outside of *The Bachelor*?
2. How does opportunity influence interpersonal relationships? How would you define chemistry and how large of a role does it have in developing relationships?
3. How do criminal opportunity theories contrast with social disorganization theory which is the other predominant perspective in place-based criminology?

References

Agnew, R. (1985). A Revised Strain Theory of Delinquency. *Social Forces, 64*, 151–167.

Andresen, M. A., & Farrell, G. (2015). *The Criminal Act: The Role and Influence of Routine Activity Theory*. New York, NY: Palgrave MacMillan.

Angelo, M. (2018). The Bachelor Goes International. Will Bachelor Nation Follow? *The New York Times*. Retrieved from https://www.nytimes.com/2018/01/26/arts/television/the-bachelor-winter-games.html

Apel, R., & Nagin, D. S. (2011). General deterrence. In Tonry, M. (eds.), *The Oxford Handbook of Crime and Criminal Justice*. New York, NY: Oxford University Press, pp. 179–206.

Beccaria, C. (1764). *On Crimes and Punishments*. Seven Treasures Publications (reprinted in 2009).

Becker, G. S. (1968). Crime and Punishment: An Economic Approach. *Journal of Political Economy, 76*, 169–217.

Becker, G. S. (1993). Nobel Lecture: The Economic Way of Looking a Behavior. *Journal of Political Economy, 101*, 385–409.

Benson, M. L., & Simpson, S. S. (2018). *White-Collar Crime: An Opportunity Perspective* (3rd ed.). New York: Routledge.

Bentham, J. (1789). *An Introduction to the Principles of Morals and Legislation*. Oxford: Oxford University Press (reprinted in 1948).

Bernasco, W. (2010). A sentimental journey to crime: Effects of residential history on crime location choice. *Criminology, 48*, 389–416.

Braga, A. A., & Clarke, R. V. (2014). Explaining high-risk concentrations of crime in the city: Social disorganization, crime opportunities, and important next steps. *Journal of Research in Crime and Delinquency, 51*, 480–498.

Brantingham, P. J., & Brantingham, P. L. (1991). *Environmental Criminology*. Prospect Heights, IL: Waveland Press.

Bump, P. (2020). Trump Trains His Eye on Key Coronavirus Numbers: The Ratings of His Daily Briefings. *The Washington Post*. Retrieved from https://www.washingtonpost.com/politics/2020/04/10/trump-trains-his-eye-key-coronavirus-numbers-ratings-his-daily-briefings/

Clarke, R. V. (1983). Situational Crime Prevention: Its Theoretical Basis and Practical Scope. *Crime and Justice, 4*, 225–256.

Clarke, R. V. (1995). Situational Crime Prevention. *Crime and Justice, 19*, 91–150.

Clarke, R. V., & Cornish, D. B. (1985). Modeling Offender's Decisions: A Framework for Research and Policy. *Crime and Justice, 6*, 147–186.

Clarke, R. V., & Eck, J. (2007). *Understanding Risky Facilities - Problem-Oriented Guides for Police*. Problem-Solving Tools Series No. 6. Washington DC: National Institute of Justice.

Clarke, R.V., & Felson, M. (1993). Introduction: Criminology, routine activity, and rational choice. In Clarke, R.V. and Felson, M (eds.), *Routine Activity and Rational Choice - Advances in Criminological Theory*, Vol. 5. New Brunswick, NJ: Transaction Press, pp. 1–16.

Cloward, R. A., & Ohlin, L. E. (1960). *Delinquency and Opportunity: A Study of Delinquent Gangs*. Glencoe, IL: The Free Press.

Cohen, L.E., and Felson, M. (1979). Social change and crime rate trends: A routine activity approach. *American Sociological Review*, 44, 588–605.

Cornish, D. (1993). Theories of Action in Criminology: Learning Theory and Rational Choice Approaches. In R. V. Clarke & M. Felson (Eds.), *Routine Activity and Rational Choice: Advances in Criminological Theory* (Vol. 5, pp. 351–382). New Brunswick, NJ: Transaction Publishers.

Cornish, D. (1994). The Procedural Analysis of Offending and Its Relevance for Situational Prevention. In R. V. Clarke (Ed.), *Crime Prevention Studies* (Vol. 3, pp. 151–196). Monsey, NY: Criminal Justice Press.

Cornish, D. B., & Clarke, R. V. (1986). *The Reasoning Criminal*. New York, NY: Springer-Verlag.

Eck, J. E. (1994). *Drug Markets and Drug places: A Case-Control Study of the Special Structure of Illicit Drug Dealing*. Doctoral dissertation, University of Maryland, College Park.

Eck, J. E., & Weisburd, D. (1995). Crime Places in Crime Theory. In J. Eck & D. Weisburd (Eds.), *Crime and Place: Crime Prevention Studies* (Vol. 4, pp. 1–34). Monsey, NY: Criminal Justice Press.

Eck, J. E., & Clarke, R. V. (2003). Classifying common police problems: A routine activity approach. *Crime Prevention Studies, 16*, 7–39.

Felson, M. (1987). Routine activities and crime prevention in the developing metropolis. *Criminology, 25*, 911–932.

Felson, M., & Eckert, M. (2016). *Crime and Everyday Life*. Thousand Oaks, CA: Sage Publications.

Franklin, C. A., Franklin, T. W., Nobles, M. R., & Kercher, G. A. (2012). Assessing the effect of routine activity theory and self-control on property, personal, and sexual assault victimization. *Criminal Justice and Behavior, 39*, 1296–1315.

Gottfredson, M. R., & Hirschi, T. (1990). *A General Theory of Crime*. Palo Alto, CA: Stanford University Press.

Groff, E. R., & Lockwood, B. (2014). Criminogenic facilities and crime across street segments in Philadelphia: Uncovering evidence about the spatial extent of facility influence. *Journal of Research in Crime and Delinquency, 51*, 3277–3297.

Guerette, R. T., & Bowers, K. (2009). Assessing the Extent of Crime Displacement and Diffusion of Benefits: A Review of Situational Crime Prevention Evaluations. *Criminology, 47*, 1331–1368.

Kaufman, A. (2018). *Bachelor Nation: Inside the World of American's Favorite Guilty Pleasure*. New York: Penguin Random House.

Hawley, A. (1950). *Human Ecology: A Theory of Community Structure*. New York, NY: Ronald Press Company.

Johnson, S. D., & Bowers, K. J. (2010). Permeability and burglary risk: Are cul-de-sacs safer? *Journal of Quantitative Criminology, 26*, 89–111.

Loughran, T. A., Paternoster, R., Chalfin, A., & Wilson, T. (2016). Can Rational Choice be Considered a General Theory of Crime? Evidence from Individual-Level Panel Data. *Criminology, 54,* 86–112.

Messner, S. F., & Blau, J. R. (1987). Routine Leisure Activities and Rates of Crime: A Macro-Level Analysis. *Social Forces, 65,* 1035–1052.

Metacritic. (2020). Retrieved from https://www.metacritic.com/tv/the-bachelor

Oxford English Dictionary. (2012). Oxford: Oxford University Press.

Parsons, T. (1951). *Towards a General Theory of Action.* Cambridge, MA: Harvard University Press.

Phillips, P. D. (1980). Characteristics and typology of the journey to crime. In Georges-Abeyie, D.E. and Harries, K. (eds.), *Crime: A Spatial Perspective.* New York, NY: Columbia University Press.

Porter, R. (2020). 'The Bachelor' Premiere Scores 2-Year High with Digital Viewing. *The Hollywood Reporter.* Retrieved from https://www.hollywoodreporter.com/live-feed/bachelor-premiere-scores-2-year-high-digital-viewing-1281463

Reyns, B. W. (2013). Online routines and identity theft victimization: Further expanding routine activity theory beyond direct-contact offenses. *Journal of Research in Crime and Delinquency, 50,* 2216–2238.

Roneck, D., & Meier, P. (1991). Bar Blocks and Crime Revisited: Linking the Theory of Routine Activities to the Empiricism of "Hot Spots". *Criminology, 29,* 725–755.

Sampson, R., Eck, J. E., & Dunham, J. B. (2010). Super controllers and crime prevention: A routine activity explanation of crime prevention success and failure. *Security Journal, 23,* 37–51.

Sampson, R. J., & Wooldredge, J. D. (1987). Linking the micro- and macro-level dimensions of lifestyle-routine activity and opportunity models of predatory victimization. *Journal of Quantitative Criminology, 3,* 371–393.

Schnell, C. (2017). *Exploring the 'Criminology of Place' in Chicago: A Multi-level Analysis of the Spatial Variation in Violent Crime Across Micro-Places and Neighborhoods.* Dissertation submitted to Rutgers University, New Brunswick, NJ.

Simon, H. A. (1972). Theories of Bounded Rationality. In C. B. McGuire & R. Radner (Eds.), *Decisions and Organization* (pp. 161–176). North Holland, Amsterdam: North-Holland Publishing.

Smith, W. R., Glave-Frazee, S., & Davison, E. L. (2000). Furthering the integration of routine activities and social disorganization theories: Small units of analysis and the study of street robbery as a diffusion process. *Criminology, 38,* 489–524.

Sutherland, E. H. (1940). White-Collar Criminality. *American Sociological Review, 5,* 1–12.

Taniguchi, T. A., Ratcliffe, J. H., & Taylor, R. B. (2011). Gang set space, drug markets, and crime around drug corners in Camden. *Journal of Research in Crime and Delinquency, 48,* 327–363.

Weisburd, D., Groff, E. R., & Yang, S. (2012). *The Criminology of Place: Street Segments and Our Understanding of the Crime Problem.* New York, NY: Oxford University Press.

Weisburd, D., Telep, C. W., Hinkle, J. C., & Eck, J. E. (2010). Is problem-oriented policing effective in reducing crime and disorder? Findings from a Campbell systematic review. *Criminology & Public Policy, 9,* 139–172.

Weisburd, D. (2015). The law of crime concentration and the criminology of place. Criminology 53: 133–157.

Welsh, B., & Farrington, D. (2008). *Effects of Improved Street Lighting on Crime: A Systematic Review*. Oslo, Norway: The Campbell Collaboration.

Wright, R. T., & Decker, S. H. (1997). *Armed Robbers in Action: Stickups and Street Culture*. Boston, MA: Northeastern University Press.

Wynne, K. (2020). 'The Bachelor' Needs New Content So We Might Get a Quarantine Series. *Newsweek*. Retrieved from https://www.newsweek.com/bachelor-needs-new-content-so-we-might-get-quarantine-series-1499211

Routine Activity Theory and 13 Reasons Why

9

13 Reasons Why: Routine Activity Theory

Colton D. Robinson

Introduction

In the TV series *13 Reasons Why*, many situations relate to the criminological theory of routine activities. The show focuses on Hannah Baker who committed suicide and left 13 audio tapes for individuals whom she believed to play a role in her death. Episodes occur after her death while Clay Jensen, an acquaintance of hers, obtains the audiotapes, and flashbacks tell Hannah's story leading to her suicide.

Clay is one of the 13 individuals for whom Hannah recorded a tape detailing the reason he is involved in her suicide. Each tape contains information about a different person who had a part in her suicide. The series follows the 13 tapes in chronological order to gain knowledge on each character's part in the suicide. Each episode is a new tape with Hannah's story exposing another character and the reasons why that individual played a role in her suicide.

The following chapter will discuss how the scenarios in *13 Reasons Why* correlate with elements of routine activity theory to define deviant and criminal behaviors. The chapter will begin with a brief overview of routine activity theory. Following the overview of the theoretical components, the chapter elaborates on each episode introducing a new tape. For each recording, a scene will describe the deviant or criminal behavior which is displayed. That scene is then broken down to demonstrate the theoretical elements of routine activities that occur.

C. D. Robinson (✉)
Saint Vincent College, Latrobe, PA, USA

© The Author(s) 2021
S. E. Daly (ed.), *Theories of Crime Through Popular Culture*,
https://doi.org/10.1007/978-3-030-54434-8_9

Routine Activity Theory

Cohen and Felson (1979) developed routine activity theory. The theory is an extension of rational choice theory which asserts that criminal or deviant behaviors occur through the free choice of individuals who search for ways to avoid pain and gain pleasure. They suggest there are three main elements that lead to an occurrence of a crime. The elements include a motivated offender with deviant intentions, a suitable target, and a lack of capable guardianship (Cohen & Felson, 1979). The main idea suggests that crime is structured rather than a random act.

A motivated offender is an individual who is willing to commit a crime or deviant behavior with motivation to gain pleasure or to avoid pain. The second component is a suitable target. A suitable target refers to the perception of the motivated offender that there is vulnerability present. The more vulnerability, the more suitable the target becomes for the offender. Lastly, lack of guardianship means that no present physical person is capable of deterring the deviant behavior. Guardianship also refers to other forms of presence to deter criminal activity, such as surveillance cameras or alarms (Cohen & Felson, 1979).

Throughout the TV series, the three main elements of routine activity theory occur on multiple occasions. Below, the chapter will outline each episode to introduce new characters, describe relevant scenes, and support with research. The situations containing deviant or criminal behavior will be defined by the three components of the theory. Each scenario obtains a motivated offender, a suitable target, and a lack of capable guardianship.

Episode 1

Episode 1 began with Clay Jensen, one of Hannah Baker's classmates, obtaining the audiotapes with her stories explained by her. Clay started listening to the tapes on his father's boombox and then discovered the meaning behind the tapes. While Clay listened to the audiotapes, Hannah introduced Justin Foley. The first tape described why the character Justin belonged in her tapes and was a reason for her suicide (McCarthy, 2017).

Justin was a popular "jock" who was on multiple sports teams. Hannah agreed to go out on a date with Justin. The two teens met up late one night at a local playground. Hannah went down the playground slide and Justin proceeded to take a picture of Hannah on his phone while she was sliding down. The picture exposed underneath Hannah's dress, which Hannah was not aware of. Hannah and Justin started to make out, and Justin had the desire to go further by attempting to put his hands up her dress. Hannah did not consent, and she walked away while saying "Just get away from me." Justin was upset by the reaction of Hannah (McCarthy, 2017).

The following day at school, Justin was with his group of athletic friends who knew Justin was to go on a date with Hannah. Justin remained upset about the incident and wanted to impress his "jock" friends, so he showed them the picture revealing Hannah. Justin then proceeded to send the picture in a mass text to many of the other students attending Liberty High School. As a result of the picture, Hannah became labeled as "slut," "whore," "easy," and other profanities. This label was significant in her reasoning for committing suicide (McCarthy, 2017).

The situation with Justin above demonstrates the components of routine activity theory. The motivated offender in this situation was Justin. He became a motivated offender during the scene at the playground when he had the desire to continue further than kissing. Justin also became motivated when attempting to impress his friends. Justin wanted to avoid the pain of rejection and sent the picture in a mass text. The suitable target during this time was Hannah. She was vulnerable as she was nervous about her first date and was not aware that Justin had taken a picture which exposed parts of her body and would then be sent to others. Lack of capable guardianship is evident as there are no adults around during the time of the two teenagers spending time together. Justin and Hannah also met while it was dark outside. There is no capable guardianship as other individuals were not able to see the event due to the darkness, making it easier for Justin to portray the behavior of attempting to touch Hannah inappropriately without consent (McCarthy, 2017).

Behavior of this type, specifically sexual harassment, is a frequent occurrence within high schools. Fineran and Bennett (1999) studied gender and power issues of peer sexual harassment among teenagers, and in their survey of 1600 students, found that 87% of the girls and 71% of the boys experienced sexual harassment in grades 8–11. The sexual harassment included sexual jokes, sexual messages, spying on locker rooms and showers, and flashing. The categories of harassment which Hannah experienced from Justin would include the variables of pulling clothes off or down, forcing a sexual act more than kissing, as well as sexually explicit photographs without consent (Fineran & Bennett, 1999).

Hill and Kearl's (2011) AAUW report, *Crossing the Line: Sexual Harassment at School*, focused on the types of sexual harassment committed, the offender, and the victim. Although Hannah did not willingly "sext" the explicit picture of herself, the fact that the picture spread through a mass text message causes it to be considered "cyber-harassment." Similarly, Hill and Kearl (2011) argued that 36% of females have experienced cyber-harassment, noting three types of cyber-harassment that

Hannah experienced in the show. The types included "being sent unwelcome sexual comment, jokes, or having someone post them about or of you," "having someone spread unwelcome sexual rumors about you," and "being called gay or lesbian in a negative way." The percentage of girls were nearly always higher, except in the category of "being called gay or lesbian in a negative way." The report highlights the realities of the presentations in *13 Reasons Why*, demonstrating that many girls in high school may have experienced similar situations as Hannah.

Episode 2

The subject of the second tape shared information on character Jessica Davis. In the episode, Hannah became friends with Jessica as well as her friend Alex Standall. The three became best friends and did everything together. Over time, Alex and Jessica started a romantic relationship and spent less time with Hannah. When Alex broke up with Jessica, she became upset and blamed Hannah for their break-up, stating that Hannah was jealous. Jessica spread this idea to other peers in school. As a result, the idea that Hannah was jealous reinforced the thought that Hannah was a "slut" who wanted a relationship with Alex. While Clay was listening to this tape, Hannah's mother also found notes which suggested bullying of Hannah (McCarthy, 2017).

The deviant behavior explained by routine activity theory in this scenario is the concept of bullying. In the cycle of the theory's elements, Jessica becomes the motivated offender as she believes Hannah caused Alex to break up with her. Hannah becomes the suitable target with becoming jealous of the two starting a relationship and spending less time with her. Vulnerability is displayed because there is the excuse that Hannah sabotaged the relationship out of anger and jealousy, and other peers believe this was a possibility. During the time of the notes and rumors which caused the bullying behaviors toward Hannah, neither the principal nor teachers were present. No adults within the vicinity are the lack of capable guardianship of those who had the ability to stop the current behavior. The bullying and calling of names occurred in hallways and at the beginning of class before the teacher walked into the classroom. This lack of guardianship allowed Jessica and peers to conduct negative words to Hannah without an adult to enforce any repercussions (McCarthy, 2017).

Episode 3

Episode 3 explained Hannah's tape for why Alex is a cause of her death. During the episode, viewers are introduced to a new character, Bryce Walker. Bryce is a "jock" who is part of the same clique as Justin. Alex and Bryce discovered that Clay had possession of the tapes, and they did not want Clay to expose what they did on their tapes. Bryce bought alcohol from a gas station and challenged Clay and Alex to drink the alcohol, or else Bryce would not allow them to leave. Clay and Alex proceeded to drink the alcohol in fear of Bryce and his teammates (Shaver, 2017).

Bryce bought the alcohol for Alex and Clay to drink in order to threaten and show power over Clay and Alex, so the tapes were not exposed. Bryce becomes the motivated offender who bought the alcohol illegally to intimidate Clay from releasing information about the tapes. Alex and Clay both become suitable targets of threatening and bullying as they are coerced by Bryce and his fellow teammates, who are larger in physical stature, making Alex and Clay more inferior. There is a lack of capable guardianship portrayed in this scenario as there are no surveillance cameras. Bryce was not caught on camera in the gas station buying the alcohol nor were the boys seen drinking underage while in the alleyway (Shaver, 2017).

The television series glamorized underage drinking numerous times. Underage drinking has been associated with high school students, oftentimes in the context of parties. Edwards, Heeren, Hingson, and Rosenbloom (2009) highlighted the relationship between underage drinking and the respective odds of being in a motor vehicle crash, unintentionally injured, or engaging in a physical fight after drinking. The national sample consisted of 4021 "drinkers" and were broken down by their age of onset. The age groups were younger than 14, 14–15, 16–17, 18–20, and 21 and older. The results concluded that the earlier age of onset to start drinking, the greater the odds of being in physical fights, a motor vehicle crash, or an unintentional injury. This research comes to life in multiple episodes that include a car accident, physical fights, and injuries that all occur as a result of drinking.

Episode 4

Throughout episode 4, Hannah claimed that she heard camera clicks outside of her window in her bedroom. At school, she tells her friend Courtney Crimsen. Courtney agreed to stay with Hannah that night while her parents were not home. Courtney and Hannah stayed in Hannah's bedroom and while playing "Truth or Dare," the girls kissed and heard more camera clicks. Hannah advanced by shining a light out the window to discover that the individual who continuously stalked Hannah was Tyler Down. Tyler Down then spread the picture of the girls kissing around Liberty High School (Shaver, 2017).

The action of "stalking" is the deviant behavior explained by routine activity theory. The motivated offender is Tyler Down. His reasoning for following Hannah and taking these pictures is due to his love for Hannah and her kindness, his loneliness, and that he has to take pictures to catch people living life as part of the yearbook committee. Hannah and Courtney are both vulnerable targets in the episode as they cannot see who the stalker is while it is dark outside, as well as the fact that both girls are intoxicated. Hannah's parents are not home during this time which leads to a low level of guardianship (Shaver, 2017).

Stalking has become a prevalent subject in high school. This includes both during school hours and outside of school grounds. A study by Theriot identified "stalking" as inappropriate phone calls and e-mails, obsessively following the victim, continually visiting the victim's home or workplace, and theft of personal items. Tyler Down would fall into the category of following the victim, Hannah, around school as he would hide in the distance while watching her go from class to class. Tyler also visited Hannah's home multiple times, and this is when he snapped the photo of Hannah and Courtney together. Theriot (2008) explored the number of restraining orders against perpetrators who would be considered a "stalker" by this definition. The study found that for adolescent offenders of "stalking" there had been 757 restraining orders filed within a 10-month period (Theriot, 2008).

Episode 5

Episode 5 started with rumors about which individuals were in Tyler's picture. Courtney did not want the secret of her sexuality to be exposed, so she spread another rumor claiming it was Hannah and Laura, a classmate who had already come out as a lesbian. The episode continued as Clay took Courtney to Hannah's gravesite as a way to express to Courtney that she was selfish for caring about her sexuality more than Hannah needing her friend. Justin, Alex, and their other friend, Zach Dempsey, did not like Clay taking actions into his own hands by talking to those mentioned on Hannah's tapes. The group of Alex, Justin, and Zach stole Clay's bike while he was on his way home and forced him into their car. While in the car, the boys intimidated Clay by threatening him if he continued trying to handle things himself and speeding in the car until getting pulled over by a police officer (Alvarez, 2017).

Alex, Justin, and Zach became motivated offenders in the deviant behaviors of stealing Clay's bike and forcing him into their car. The three boys became motivated by the action of Clay taking Courtney to Hannah's grave site to get a reaction of regret out of her. Clay was the vulnerable target in this scene as he was riding his bike alone on the road and was no match for the three boys in the car. Until the police officer pulled the car over, there was no other sense of guardianship while it was dark outside and no other adults were present (Alvarez, 2017).

Episode 6

Two scenes in episode 6 relate to routine activity theory. The first scene occurred outside of the school when the character Montgomery was driving on school grounds and nearly ran into Alex with his car. Alex took a stand against Montgomery. The two boys engaged in a physical altercation on school grounds (Alvarez, 2017).

The deviant action of fighting at school is an example of routine activity theory. Both individuals act as motivated offenders in this situation. When Montgomery laughed at the fact that he almost ran his car into Alex, Alex started yelling at Montgomery. Montgomery then told Alex that Alex should be scared of Montgomery. At this point, Alex became infuriated and started the fight by pushing Montgomery away. Montgomery became mad at Alex and tackled him to the ground. They both became motivated by the act of hitting back at one another. The two boys ended up rolling on the ground until Montgomery fought his way on top of Alex when he repeatedly punched Alex in the face. Alex became the suitable target as he was not physically capable of assaulting Montgomery to the same extent as his body type was naturally smaller than and not as strong as Montgomery. Montgomery ended up contributing much more damage to Alex once Montgomery continued beating on Alex even after Alex was not able to fight back anymore. No school authority figures were at the scene of the fight, causing a lack of capable guardianship. No school authority figures were present until minutes after when Alex sustained injuries to his face and a gathering of students circled the fight. By that point, the damage had already been done (Alvarez, 2017).

The second incident which occurred in episode 6 included Hannah and Marcus Cole, the senior class president. Marcus and Hannah both participated in a Valentine's Day activity which matched the two as compatible with each other and agreed to go on a date. Marcus accepted a bet with his peers that he had the ability to "hook up" with Hannah while on their date. While on the date, Marcus sat on the same side of the booth as Hannah at the diner. Marcus attempted sexual assault as he grabbed Hannah's thigh and proceeded to put his hand underneath Hannah's dress until she screamed for him to get away from her (Alvarez, 2017).

The three components of the theory outlined in this scene include Marcus as the motivated offender by a bet he made with his friends. Hannah became a suitable target as she could not defend herself and froze. She was not able to move, and the only defense mechanism she was able to produce was yelling at him for touching her. No others were at the booth or were aware of the situation leading to no guardianship to witness the event taking place (Alvarez, 2017).

Episode 7

Midway through the season, Zach Dempsey played a significant role once again. Hannah recorded a tape explaining why Zach had a role in her killing herself. She elaborated that she rejected going on a date with Zach, so he advanced by decreasing her self-confidence by removing compliment notes written to her. Clay listened to the tape which explained what Zach had done to Hannah's confidence and wanted revenge. During a basketball game, while Zach was playing in the game, Clay went to the parking lot and keyed Zach's car (Araki, 2017).

Vandalism is a crime which has an impact on a victim. In the current situation, Clay becomes a motivated offender to commit vandalism to Zach's car out of anger and revenge. Zach became targeted while he is playing in the basketball game and Clay is not face-to-face with Zach in the parking lot. The explanation of lack of guardianship takes place as there are no authorities who were able to see Clay committing vandalism, in addition to the incident occurring outside the view of the cameras (Araki, 2017).

Vandalism is a crime many people have committed from a young age into adulthood by damaging the property of others. Vandalism could be as small throwing shoes over power lines to something as big as burning a car. Krivoshchekova, Kruzhkova, and Vorobyeva (2015) surveyed 1522 participants who have caused damage to public property at some point in their lives. Of the participants, 466 were of the young adult age group. The researchers explored motivations for why participants in this age group had committed vandalism. The most motivated individuals were explained as an "internally-oriented activity." Meaning that those who committed the act did not analyze or internalize the event or a conventional thought process. They are considered to be ready to take responsibility and that the act was opposite of their character (Krivoshchekova et al., 2015). Clay is an example of this when we observe his vandalism, as it seems that he did not internalize or analyze the situation and committed vandalism on Zach's car or consider the consequences. Clay took responsibility for his actions and could be viewed as "acting out of character."

Episode 8

Ryan Shaver was the next character who was revealed by Hannah's recorded tapes. Ryan was the inspiration for Hannah to write and present poems. Hannah produced one poem for a class which was a call for help but submitted it anonymously. Since the work was anonymous, Ryan stole Hannah's work not knowing it was hers and published it in the school magazine without her consent. Other peers then found the poem hilarious and made comments about the poem which offended Hannah (Araki, 2017).

Ryan became a motivated offender to steal the poem without consent, as he felt her expressions needed to be heard by others. Hannah was a target due to the reason that Ryan had a position with the school magazine to publish the poem. He had the power to publish the work without her consent, and she allowed Ryan to further the process since she submitted the piece anonymously. Guardianship was not available during this occurrence of the anonymously submitted poem. No one was able to step in to take the poem out of the magazine because there was no way of telling who the original author was or that it was stolen due to the anonymity (Araki, 2017).

Episode 9

The events in Episode 9 also contributed to Hannah's life coming to an end. The setting of the episode was a party at Jessica's house while her parents are out of town. Hannah was in a room upstairs at the party before Jessica and Justin stumbled into the same room. Hannah hid in the closet to avoid being seen. Justin had the intention of performing sexual acts with Jessica until she fell asleep due to her intoxication. Justin then let Jessica sleep on the bed while he left the room. Hannah then witnessed Bryce Walker come into the room and make his way over to the bed where Jessica slept. Bryce continued to press himself onto Jessica and removed her clothes. Bryce then proceeded to have sex with Jessica who was intoxicated and unconscious as Hannah witnessed the event still in hiding (Franklin, 2017).

Throughout this traumatic scene, Bryce was sexually motivated to commit the criminal act of raping Jessica. Jessica was both intoxicated and unconscious which proved her to be very vulnerable in this situation and made for an easy target. During Bryce forcing himself onto Jessica, Hannah was the only person present but found herself not able to move or reveal herself. Jessica's parents were gone for the weekend out of town, causing a lack of capable guardianship (Franklin, 2017).

An article explained the effects of direct as well as vicarious victimization. Vicarious victimization is defined as one experiencing trauma by witnessing the victimization of another person. The article explains that suicidal cognition and self-harm have a correlation with both direct and vicarious victimization. The article suggests that if one experiences being directly victimized or witnessing another person being victimized, they have a higher risk of suicidal ideations. Going through a traumatic event is seen as a predictor to self-harm in adolescence (Baldry & Winkel, 2003).

During this event, Jessica had been directly victimized by the offender, Bryce. Hannah was also victimized at this time. Hannah witnessed the heinous act which occurred to Jessica. Hannah could not move because she became so traumatized and was vicariously victimized herself (Franklin, 2017).

A National Institute of Justice study estimated that one-fifth to one-fourth of women are victims of completed or attempted rape while in high school and college. A link has been found between alcohol and sexual assault and rape. Often times, this is considered "party rape," which is a term defined for a distinct form of rape according to the U.S. Department of Justice. "Party rapes" are sexual assaults which take place off school grounds and involve the targeting of intoxicated women (Armstrong, Hamilton, & Sweeney, 2006).

Katz, Olin, Pazienza, and Rich (2014) found that 19% of women in undergraduate programs in college had been victim to attempted or completed sexual assault. Of the 19%, 83% of the women were under the influence of alcohol or drugs. Although the study focused on college undergraduates, it is suggested that the same rate is applied for females in high school (Katz et al., 2014). They also examined different responses of bystanders to friends or strangers who were at risk for party rape victimization. They found that empathetic concern was greater for females than males, especially if the bystander was considered friends with the potential party rape victim (Katz et al., 2014). This episode mirrors the study findings, as Hannah showed empathetic concern for Jessica as a bystander and as friends, this event had such an impact on Hannah that it played a role in her death.

Episode 10

The story of Sheri Holland explained the situation she caused and contributed to Hannah feeling guilt. After Hannah witnessed the rape of Jessica, she left the party, and Sheri offered Hannah a ride home. While driving home, the girls were in a minor accident which knocked down a stop sign. Sheri refused to call the police in fear that she would be held accountable; therefore, Sheri left Hannah who called the authorities. Moments later, there was a more substantial accident at the intersection as a result of the knocked down stop sign. The accident provoked the death of another student, Jeff Atkins, who was also traveling home from the party and was in the accident at the intersection (Franklin, 2017).

Fear of getting in trouble and being held accountable for knocking down a stop sign caused the motivation of Sheri not to contact the authorities. Jeff became a suitable target in the more substantial accident as he was not aware that a stop sign was missing from the intersection and miscommunication with another driver occurred. This allowed Jeff to become the victim of the crash, and he died due to Sheri's motivation to defiantly ignore the situation she caused. Sheri refused to notify the proper authorities because there were no other witnesses to take the role of guardianship (Franklin, 2017).

Episode 11

Clay finally reached the tape which Hannah recorded regarding his role in her death. Hannah expressed that Clay was not a reason as to why she committed suicide, but there was a need for him in the purpose of the story. The tape explained that Clay was the only true friend Hannah ever had. Hannah further claimed that although the tape talked about Clay, it was not his fault for her suicide. She then reported that the reason there was a tape dedicated to Clay was because he was not there the one time she needed him. The tape revealed a scene in which Hannah and Clay kissed. They then started to remove each other's clothes. Once Clay began to put his hands on Hannah, flashbacks occurred for her. Hannah started to vision Marcus touching her and felt the pain she had gone through previously. Hannah then threw Clay off of her and yelled at him to leave the room. Clay apologized and left. Clay did what Hannah told him to do, however, she actually wanted Clay to stay with her, so she did not feel this pain while alone. This scene caused Hannah to create the tape to explain that she thought he would always stay even when she forced him out. She stated that Clay did not pay attention to realize that she was hurting inside and needed someone there. After listening to the tape, he became overwhelmed with guilt and left school. Clay is with Tony, and Clay contemplated suicide himself by almost jumping off a cliff until Tony talked him into taking a step back and saving him (Yu, 2017).

Suicide is the deviant behavior described in this scene of episode 11. Clay plays the role of the motivated offender and the suitable target. Clay is motivated that he ruined Hannah's life and that she would still be living if he paid attention and believed her. He feels overwhelmed by much guilt and is motivated to take his own life. Clay also plays a suitable target as a result of his guilt. Clay mentally breaks down and feels like he is worthless and is emotionally unstable. A suitable target is one who allows the offender the opportunity to complete the deviant behavior. Clay allows his emotions to get the better of him and allows his guilt to take over. This allows him to become the target of himself as the motivated offender of taking his life. No guardians were in the vicinity as they were on top of a cliff, and they left school in the middle of the day, leading to no adults or anyone else who could prevent the potential suicide from happening (Franklin, 2017).

Episode 12

Possibly the most traumatic experience of Hannah transpired during the events of episode 12. Hannah was trusted by her parents to take a bank deposit to the bank for their local business. Hannah accidentally lost track of the deposit and understood that she furthered her parents' money problems with the store. Hannah felt as though she disappointed her parents and felt extremely guilty (Franklin, 2017).

Hannah decided to take a walk through the neighborhood to clear her head. She ultimately ended up at Bryce's house where he was hosting a small party while his parents were out of town. Hannah spent time in the hot tub with others including Bryce. The other peers started to leave and go inside the house. Hannah was the last person in the hot tub alone with Bryce. Once everyone left the outside area, and the two were alone, Bryce started to force himself on Hannah. Hannah attempted to resist his actions; however, Bryce was too powerful. Bryce continued by turning her over, restraining her hands so she could not fight back and pulled her underwear down. Bryce proceeded to have sexual intercourse with Hannah against her will, leaving her as another one of his rape victims (Franklin, 2017).

Bryce, once again, used the need for power as the primary motivation to commit a sexual offense. Hannah became vulnerable once she resisted but was overtaken by Bryce's strength. Hannah was a target who could not fight back against Bryce and ultimately became another sexually assaulted victim due to this reason. Bryce's parents could not serve as guardianship as they were out of town. The other individuals were not able to pose as guardians as they all left the party or went into the house. Bryce and Hannah were left alone outside in the dark. No one was in the vicinity to help Hannah during this traumatic experience (Franklin, 2017).

Episode 13

During the finale of Season 1 of *13 Reasons Why*, Hannah sought help one final time. Hannah wanted to get help and attempted to do so by seeing the school guidance counselor, Mr. Porter. Hannah entered Mr. Porter's office and ventured to gain help about the struggles in her life, including the incident leaving her a rape victim. Hannah did not explicitly explain the details of the rape or who forced themselves on her, rather, Hannah hinted at the event. Mr. Porter claimed to follow protocol by letting Hannah leave the office as he could not help without specific details (Alvarez, 2017).

Going to Mr. Porter was Hannah's last attempt at reaching out for someone to help her. Hannah felt as though she had no support from him or anyone else. This experience was Hannah's deciding factor on whether or not she went through with committing suicide or getting further help. With Mr. Porter's lack of support, Hannah later took her tapes to the post office to mail them to Tony. Hannah proceeded home, and during this time, she took her own life by slitting her wrists in the bathtub (Alvarez, 2017).

The motivation for Mr. Porter's decision to turn Hannah away was due to following the school's protocol for that situation. Hannah became more vulnerable than she had ever been before. Hannah felt no support and that there was no other way out of her pain besides causing her death. Neither Mr. Porter nor any other authority figure attempted to help Hannah in a time of need and did not show much guardianship for her (Alvarez, 2017).

Conclusion

Episode to episode, many characters excelled as the role of the offender, while many others portrayed the role of a suitable target when there was a lack of guardianship. Episodes throughout the series portrayed routine activity theory very well and held up when elements of the theory are explained to the situation. Episode 7 explained how Clay became a motivated offender as Zach was seen as a suitable target for Clay to vandalize Zach's car while no one proceeded within the vicinity. Episodes 9 and 12 have much evidence for the theory by explaining Bryce as the motivated offender to commit the criminal act of rape on the suitable targets of Jessica and Hannah while the parents of the home were out of town and there was a clear lack of guardianship during both occurrences.

Hannah Baker endured much pain while at Liberty High School which fundamentally provoked her into committing suicide. The series described many criminal or deviant behaviors explained by the three main elements of routine activity theory. Routine activity theory throughout *13 Reasons Why* focused on motivated offenders who were motivated to act deviantly, suitable targets who became victims, and the lack of capable guardianship. The three elements of the theory are a recipe for a crime or deviant act to occur, and throughout the series, the elements fusing together in various situations ultimately lead to the tragic scene of Hannah Baker taking her own life (Table 9.1).

Table 9.1 Episode guide and the three elements of routine activities theory

	Motivated offender	Suitable target	Lack of guardianship
Episode 1	Justin	Hannah	Alone together at the park at night
Episode 2	Jessica	Hannah	No school authority
Episode 3	Bryce	Clay and Alex	No cameras at the gas station
Episode 4	Tyler	Hannah and Courtney	Hannah's parents were not home
Episode 5	Alex, Justin, and Zach	Clay	Dark outside, no adults around
Episode 6	Montgomery and Marcus	Alex and Hannah	No others were at the same booth
Episode 7	Clay	Zach	Outside the view of the cameras
Episode 8	Ryan	Hannah	Poem was anonymous
Episode 9	Bryce	Jessica	Parents were out of town
Episode 10	Sheri	Jeff	No witnesses or authorities
Episode 11	Clay	Clay	No adults within the vicinity
Episode 12	Bryce	Hannah	Alone together at night
Episode 13	Mr. Porter	Hannah	No authority figure helped

Discussion Questions

1. Do you believe that if capable guardianship (teachers, parents, cameras, etc.) were present, there would be a reduction in the criminal or deviant behaviors which occurred in each episode? Why or why not?
2. Do you think routine activity theory accurately explains why deviant behaviors occurred throughout the series? Is there a different criminological theory that provides a better explanation as to why criminal and deviant behaviors were displayed throughout *13 Reasons Why*?
3. Describe a criminal act or deviant behavior you have committed or witnessed another person commit whether a real experience or seen in a TV show, movie, or video game. Can you use the three key elements of routine activity theory to explain why the behavior occurred? If so, please explain how the situation fulfilled the roles of a motivated offender, a suitable target, and lack of capable guardianship. If not, which elements were not present to support the theory in your scenario?

References

Alvarez, K. (Director). (2017). *13 Reasons Why* [Television Series]. Vallejo, CA: Netflix.

Araki, G. (Director). (2017). *13 Reasons Why* [Television Series]. Vallejo, CA: Netflix.

Armstrong, E. A., Hamilton, L., & Sweeney, B. (2006). Sexual Assault on Campus: A Multilevel, Integrative Approach to Party Rape. *Social Problems, 53*(4), 483–499.

Baldry, A. C., & Winkel, F. W. (2003). Direct and Vicarious Victimization at School and at Home as Risk Factors for Suicidal Cognition Among Italian Adolescents. *Journal of Adolescence, 26*(6), 703–716.

Cohen, L. E., & Felson, M. (1979). Social Change and Crime Rate Trends: A Routine Activity Approach. *American Sociological Review, 44*, 588–608.

Edwards, E., Heeren, T., Hingson, R. W., & Rosenbloom, D. (2009). Age of Drinking Onset and Injuries, Motor Vehicle Crashes, and Physical Fights After Drinking and When Not Drinking. *Alcoholism: Clinical and Experimental Research, 33*(5), 783–790.

Fineran, S., & Bennett, L. (1999). Gender and Power Issues of Peer Sexual Harassment Among Teenagers. *Journal of Interpersonal Violence, 14*(6), 626–641.

Franklin, C. (Director). (2017). *13 Reasons Why* [Television Series]. Vallejo, CA: Netflix.

Hill, C., & Kearl, H. (2011). *Crossing the Line: Sexual Harassment at School.* AAUW.

Katz, J., Olin, R., Pazienza, R., & Rich, H. (2014). That's What Friends Are For. *Journal of Interpersonal Violence, 30*(16), 2775–2792.

Krivoshchekova, M. S., Kruzhkova, O. V., & Vorobyeva, I. V. (2015). The Genesis of Vandalism: From Childhood to Adolescence. *Psychology in Russia: State of Art, 8*(1), 139–155.

McCarthy, T. (Director). (2017). *13 Reasons Why* [Television Series]. Vallejo, CA: Netflix.
Shaver, H. (Director). (2017). *13 Reasons Why* [Television Series]. Vallejo, CA: Netflix.
Theriot, M. T. (2008). Conceptual and Methodological Considerations for Assessment and Prevention of Adolescent Dating Violence and Stalking at School. *Children & Schools, 30*(4), 223–233.
Yu, J. (Producer). (2017). *13 Reasons Why* [Television Series]. Vallejo, CA: Netflix.

Self-Control Theory and *The Office*

10

"That's What She Said": Michael Scott and Self-Control Theory

Sarah E. Daly and Chad Painter

NBC's hit television show, *The Office*, aired from 2005 to 2013. *Rolling Stone* ranked it 48th on its list of 100 Great TV Shows of All-Time list and called it a "groundbreaking and original comedy" (Sheffield, 2016). Adapted from the original British series of the same name and style, its "mockumentary" approach chronicled the everyday hijinks of a mid-level paper company in Scranton, Pennsylvania. Portrayed by Steve Carell, Michael Gary Scott is the regional manager who often provided the main source of conflict in the show. He exhibited behaviors that were largely uncomfortable, absurd, and inappropriate, but at times may have been considered deviant or even criminal. His immaturity, impulsivity, and insensitivity created a working environment that some have considered uncomfortable at best and abusive at worst. The show's storylines often centered around Michael's antics, but the employees had their own foibles, problems, and arcs including Jim and Dwight's ongoing pranks, Angela's love triangles, Kelly and Ryan's tumultuous relationship, and Toby's inability to be anything more than the office's bland Human Resources representative. Although the show continued for two additional seasons after Carell's departure from the show, Michael Scott, "the World's Best Boss" remains the most iconic of the cast and "one of the most original characters of all time" (Jaremko-Greenwold, 2015).

S. E. Daly (✉) · C. Painter
Saint Vincent College, Latrobe, PA, USA
e-mail: sarah.daly@stvincent.edu

© The Author(s) 2021
S. E. Daly (ed.), *Theories of Crime Through Popular Culture*,
https://doi.org/10.1007/978-3-030-54434-8_10

Michael's unique personality, his childlike responses to conflict, and his compulsive need to be loved and accepted by his employees created problems for himself and those around him. These enduring behaviors and needs often have disastrous outcomes that made for 149 episodes of frustration, awkwardness, and hilarity. He gave Oscar ulcers, upset Angela with his ever "inappropriate" ideas, and disappointed or annoyed everyone in the office at one point or another. While Michael's choices and behaviors may shock viewers, those familiar with criminological theory must see a clear representation of Gottfredson and Hirschi's (1990) self-control theory (SCT).

Self-Control Theory: An Overview

Since its introduction in 1990, the theory has received notable attention from scholars and been the subject of much empirical testing and critique. Perhaps one of the most parsimonious of theories, researchers have used self-control theory (SCT) to explain a variety of criminal and deviant behaviors, including, but not limited to: driver aggression (Ellwanger & Pratt, 2014); corporate offending (Leeper Piquero, Schoepfer, & Langton, 2010); alcohol and substance abuse (Baker, 2010; Conner, Stein, & Longshore, 2008; Ford & Blumenstein, 2013; Jones, Lynam, & Piquero, 2015; Zavala & Kurtz, 2017); police misconduct (Donner, Fridell, & Jennings, 2016); and theft and delinquency (Chui & Chan, 2016). One of the theory's major strengths is its continued empirical measurement and support through decades of research.

One of the most important elements of the theory is that it does not only relate to or explain crime but also deviant or problematic behaviors that may not necessarily be considered illegal or criminal. As Gottfredson and Hirschi (1990) explained, "Crime is not an automatic or necessary consequence of self-control" (p. 91). Behaviors analogous to crime—imprudent, irresponsible actions—serve as a better measure of self-control, as it avoids the tautological issue of using engagement in crime to predict criminal activity. As Arneklev, Elis, and Medlicott (2006) found, "…if analogous behavior measures include illegal activities, they are stronger predictors of crime than are attitudinal indicators of low self-control…When stripped of illegal behavior, Imprudent (Analogous) Behavior is not as efficacious in predicting crime, yet is still significant" (p. 47). It could be argued that nearly all of Michael's behaviors that served as the foundation for storylines on *The Office* could be considered analogous to crime if not illegal. These imprudent, yet hilarious, antics serve as the foundation for this chapter and its relation to SCT.

Gottfredson and Hirschi identify parenting or child-rearing as the most influential factors in the development of self-control. They note, "all of the characteristics associated with low self-control tend to show themselves in the absence of nurturance, discipline, or training" (Gottfredson & Hirschi, 1990, p. 95). They continue by asserting that parents can help to develop and support higher levels of self-control by monitoring children, recognizing bad behaviors, and punishing them. When children experience this, they learn delayed gratification, empathy, independence, and patience. Unfortunately, we know relatively little about Michael Scott's family, although there are quick allusions to his resentment of his stepfather, Jeff, his strained relationship with his nana, Barbara, and unnamed siblings. Yet, we can speculate that there may have been issues of attachment, attention, or punishment that may have affected Michael's development.

Despite its parsimony and popularity, SCT, however, is not without its critiques and weaknesses. In one of the earliest published criticisms of the theory, Barlow (1991) states that "Gottfredson and Hirschi never provide an operational definition of specifying a basis for distinguishing degrees of self-control" (p. 241). However, in 1993, Grasmick, Tittle, Bursik, and Arneklev created a scale by which researchers could measure self-control. By conceptualizing six tenets of the theory and operationalizing them through a 24-question survey, they attempted to address one of the primary criticisms of the theory.

Based on Gottfredson and Hirschi's (1990) early work, Grasmick, Tittle, Bursik, and Arneklev (1993) asserted that the scale measures low self-control as "a single unidimensional latent trait" (p. 9). The authors, however, concluded that "contrary results [suggest] the theory needs expansion, refinement, and elaboration before it can explain crime to the degree Gottfredson and Hirschi imply...[their] formulation constitutes an important innovation, but it requires additional theoretical work" (Grasmick et al., 1993, p. 26). These researchers and, later, Higgins (2007) further developed Gottfredson and Hirschi's (1990) original theory by elaborating self-control theory and classifying behaviors into six different constructs.[1] We use these constructs to offer an overview of self-control theory and demonstrate Michael Scott's low self-control as exhibited through imprudent, irresponsible, and even deviant and criminal behavior.

---

[1] The Grasmick Scale was then used as a measurement tool in subsequent research studies (e.g., Grasmick et al., 1993), but through quantitative analysis and validity testing, Higgins (2007) found that the original Grasmick scale does not have construct validity and that items 2, 6, 9, 12, 13, 19, 20, and 22 (see Table 10.1) should be omitted from the scale to improve the use of the Grasmick Scale as a measure of self-control.

Table 10.1 Grasmick's scale with Higgins' revisions

Item number	Construct	Survey question
1	Impulsivity	I often act on the spur of the moment without stopping to think
2		*I don't devote much thought and effort to preparing for the future*
3		I often do whatever brings me pleasure here and now, even at the cost of some distant goal
4		I'm more concerned with what happens to me in the short run than in the long run
5	Simple tasks	I frequently try to avoid projects that I know will be difficult
6		*When things get complicated, I tend to quit or withdraw*
7		The things in life that are easiest to do bring me the most pleasure
8		I dislike really hard tasks that stretch my abilities to the limit
9	Risk-seeking	I like to test myself every now and then by doing something a little risky
10		Sometimes I will take a risk just for the fun of it
11		I sometimes find it exciting to do things for which I might get in trouble
12		*Excitement and adventure are more important to me than security*
13	Physical activities	*If I had a choice, I would almost always rather do something physical than something mental*
14		I almost always feel better when I am on the move than when I am sitting and thinking
15		I like to get out and do things more than I like to read or contemplate ideas
16		I seem to have more energy and a greater need for activity than most other people my age
17	Self-centered	I try to look out for myself first, even if it means making things difficult for other people
18		I'm not very sympathetic to other people when they are having problems
19		*If things I do upset people, it's their problem, not mine*
20		*I will try to get the things I want even when I know it's causing problems for other people*
21	Temper	I lose my temper pretty easily
22		*Often, when I'm angry at people I feel more like hurting them than talking to them about why I'm angry*
23		When I'm really angry, other people better stay away from me
24		When I have a serious disagreement with someone, it's usually hard for me to talk to them without getting upset

Note: Items in italics are ones that were removed from the original scale and thus not included as a part of the organization of this chapter

Applying Self-Control Theory to Michael Scott

To provide readers with a thorough examination and application of the theory, this chapter is organized based on the six constructs and uses items from the scale for each to present specific examples of Michael's behavior. These items, present in bold and in quotes, can acquaint readers and students with the elements of the theory while also observing the questions from the Grasmick and Higgins scales. For each, we offer the outlandish, comical, and perhaps cringe-worthy antics, while also applying the notion of self-control theory at work in high- and low-cost situations (see also Seipel & Eifler, 2010). We hope this supports the notion "that low self-control in combination with opportunity to commit crime [at the office] is a (perhaps *the*) primary cause of criminal behavior" (Grasmick et al., 1993, p. 6).

Impulsivity

First, impulsivity relates to the tendency to act quickly without consideration of consequences. As Gottfredson and Hirschi (1990) explain, "The impulsive or short-sighted person fails to consider the negative or painful consequences of his acts" (p. 95). Ignoring the notion of consequences and punishment allows or encourages people to engage in crime or behaviors analogous to crime because they would be less fearful of the outcomes.

Michael's behavior often reflects impulsivity and a lack of planning or forethought. He planned several events and activities quickly and whimsically, often with unsuccessful or disastrous results (see, for example, Michael Scott's Dunder Mifflin Scranton Meredith Palmer Memorial Celebrity Rabies Awareness Fun Run Pro-Am Race for the Cure; the raid at the Utica Branch; and Michael's original plan to propose to Holly). While often hilarious, his lack of concern for details, consequences, and logical thinking led to some of the most memorable episodes of the series and the most cringe-worthy.

I often act on the spur of the moment without stopping to think.

In Season 7, Episode 7, "Christening," Michael attended the baptism of Jim and Pam's first child, Cece. At the reception in the church hall, he was overcome with awe at a teenage girl's explanation of the volunteer work that her youth group planned to do in Quimixto, Mexico. As he stood in line to shake their hands as they boarded the bus, he impulsively decided to join the group and leave with them.

Despite being warned by nearly everyone (except Andy Bernard who rushed to join him when he saw that Erin was impressed), he argued that it was not irresponsible, because he had never been so sure about anything in his life. As the bus pulled away, he began to realize the ramifications of what he had done, and after only 45 minutes on the road, he demanded to be let off the bus, exclaiming that he has already given back to society and that now is the time for him to take.

Had Michael stopped to consider his actions at the time, he would have realized that he had no luggage or supplies, that the trip required months of manual labor, and that he did not know anyone on the trip, save for Andy. Yet, despite his coworkers' protests, he left for Mexico only to change his mind shortly thereafter.

Similarly, when he decided to open "The Michael Scott Paper Company" in Season 5, Episode 21, he did not stop to think about the many obstacles that he would face in a dying industry. Both Pam and Oscar attempted to explain the challenges he would face, and Michael heard from his potential replacement that management jobs were scarce. Even in light of this reality, Michael pressed on in his goal without thinking.

One might argue that he did, in fact, plan for the company by hiring a team, securing an office space, and organizing meetings and events to promote the company, but he lacked the insight and the skills to do this effectively or realize his own shortcomings in the process. Despite his best efforts, his actions seemed more like an attempt to recreate his position at Dunder Mifflin and exact revenge on his former company rather than legitimate attempts to start and successfully run a small business.

I often do whatever brings me pleasure here and now, even at the cost of some distant goal.

Similarly, in what may be one of the most uncomfortable episodes of the series, Michael faced the consequences of a terrible promise he made ten years earlier. In Season 6, Episode 12, we learn that when he met a group of third graders, he promised them that he would pay for their college tuition if they finished high school. When the time came to face this group of students, affectionately known as "Scott's Tots," to tell them that he could not pay, he explained to the camera crew, "I have made some empty promises in my life, but hands down, that was the most generous" (Season 6, Episode 12, Timestamp: 5:14). Though he made the promise before the beginning of the show, it is clear that this is an example of his impulsivity and his overwhelming need to be liked. An ongoing theme throughout the show, Michael once tellingly explained that he has a constant need to be praised. To satisfy this need to be liked and praised, he made this promise to the students, likely knowing full well that he would not have the financial means to do it. This promise brought him pleasure at the time, though it clearly led to discomfort, disappointment, and financial distress for the students years later. Even with ten years to plan, renege on his promise, or find another way to help the students, he could not bring himself to admit his mistake, because his immediate pleasure and gratification were the most important goal.

I'm more concerned with what happens to me in the short run than in the long run.

In Season 5 Episode 10, Michael is forced to make a decision that raises tensions within the office. The accounting department had found a budget surplus, and he must spend the money or risk losing it in the next year. Two teams formed, each suggesting that Michael purchase different items for the office. Pressure from both sides to either purchase a new copier or a new set of office chairs overwhelmed Michael, and multiple employees attempted to swindle Michael in furtherance of their agenda. After Jim invited him to lunch and Pam flattered him on his appearance, Michael called David Wallace, CFO of Dunder Mifflin, for advice. David informed Michael that managers who finished under budget can return the surplus and receive a bonus check. Michael tried to hide this information and decided that the office does not need any new items. Michael's employees quickly realized what had happened, and he then placed the burden of deciding on everyone else. If they could not reach a decision, he would keep the bonus.

Disregarding the potential of a decision being reached, Michael purchased an expensive fur coat from Burlington Coat Factory using his credit card, anticipating that he would receive the bonus check. Michael was surprised when shortly after, the employees came to him with their decision to buy a new copier. Michael could not return the coat because animal rights activists threw fake blood on him as he exited the store. Michael displayed an extreme need for instant gratification; no long-term consequence was considered during his decision-making process.

Simple Tasks

Next, Gottfredson and Hirschi (1990) argue that criminal acts "provide easy or simple gratification of desires" (p. 89). Because those with low self-control often "lack diligence, tenacity, or persistence in the course of action," (p. 89), they generally prefer simple tasks and generally dislike more complex or difficult undertakings. They may avoid responsibilities that they know will be hard for them or quit when those tasks require additional work or commitment.

Michael Scott was many things, but the average viewer would likely not consider him to be astute or a complex thinker. The vast majority of his foibles on *The Office* are exceedingly simple tasks or a result of Michael attempting to avoid complex or difficult tasks. Though many required thoughtful reflection, higher-order thinking, and keen insight or knowledge, this was often far beyond his abilities. Some may argue that his strong sales record may be an indication of a certain skill set, such as an intuitive ability to read people and relate to them. However, viewers rarely observe him undertaking responsibilities or tasks that may be difficult, complicated, or unpleasant. Rather, we see him delegate the most unpleasant tasks to others or avoid them altogether. This section highlights moments that demonstrate his aversion to the complexity and his tendency to figuratively—and sometimes literally—run away from his problems.

I frequently try to avoid projects that I know will be difficult.

Early in the show (Season 1, Episode 3), Jan, Michael's corporate superior, informed him that he must make changes to the employees' insurance plan. He delegated the responsibility to Dwight, who was always eager to assume an administrative role because Michael recognized that any changes would be unpleasant news for his employees.

In various episodes and scenes throughout the show, Michael avoided completing tasks or being productive. Instead, he preferred to amuse himself and his colleagues or distract himself with activities that entertained him more. Perhaps one of the best examples of his avoidance was in Season 2, Episode 6, when he found multiple ways to avoid signing timecards, purchase orders, and expense reports. Though these were not intellectually difficult tasks, he found it hard to concentrate, instead choosing to tap on his mug and sing, practice his signatures (ironically, not on the forms he was supposed to be signing), and engage in a fight with Dwight at the local dojo.

Additionally, when Michael returned from his Jamaican vacation in Season 3, Episode 11, he was upset when he learned that the yearly inventory review had not been completed because of his absence. He then stated, "I specifically went on vacation so I would miss it" (Season 3, Episode 11 4:07). He then went on to say that "inventory is boring. In the islands, they don't make you do stuff like take inventory. Why do you think so many businesses move to the Caymans?" (Season 3, Episode 11 4:10).

The things in life that are easiest to do bring me the most pleasure.

The moments in which Michael seems happiest are those that require or demonstrate little skill or planning. From his failed jokes (e.g., "Buddha my bread," "what's updog") to his lackluster improvisation, he enjoys attempting humor but fails to note the nuances and skill involved in successful comedy. Yet, he still finds immense amusement and pleasure in trying, all while thinking of himself as hilarious. Other examples of his almost childlike interest in simple activities include Tube City, the maze for gerbils he wanted to construct in his office (Season 6, Episode 10), his enthusiasm for elementary-level magic tricks (Season 3, Episode 18; Season 7, Episode 1), and his easy distraction while playing Connect Four with Toby (Season 7, Episode 2).

Combined with his obvious dislike of difficult tasks, it is clear that Michael values simplicity and ease in his life.

I dislike really hard tasks that stretch my abilities to the limit.

The previously listed responses and examples demonstrate Michael's preference for easy tasks and his disdain for difficult ones. Perhaps most telling is Jim's interpretation of Michael's behavior. In Season 6, Episode 3, Jim offered a pie chart to explain his conclusions after studying Michael for years. He noted that one section in green—more than half of the chart—shows that he spends most of his time procrastinating while the remaining section in yellow represents the time Michael spends distracting others. There is a tiny section in red marked "critical thinking," but Jim explained that he enlarged the section so that viewers would be able to see it.

Those who knew Michael best, and often suffered as a result of his contempt for difficult tasks, recognized that he rarely attempted to improve himself or enhance his abilities. While he developed as a character over the course of seven seasons, he remained fairly rigid in his limited social, professional, and personal life, wreaking havoc on his employees with his childish and stubborn behavior.

Risk-Seeking

Gottfredson and Hirschi (1990) explain that "people lacking self-control…tend to be adventuresome, active, and physical" because "criminal acts…involve danger, speed, agility, deception, or power" (p. 89). Breaking the law or engaging in behaviors analogous to crime is often based on the desire for thrills or excitement. Those who are cautious or guarded are less likely to engage in risky activities. Michael frequently engaged in daring, dangerous, or risky behavior often because he failed to consider the consequences, or he simply wanted to do what was most appealing to him. These often made those around him uncomfortable or had disastrous outcomes that left the employees, the company executives, or his romantic partners uncomfortable or disappointed. While his impulsive, risky behavior frustrated most people in his life, they provided hours of hilarity for viewers.

Sometimes I will take a risk just for the fun of it.

After Dwight found a half-smoked joint in the parking lot and began an investigation, Michael revealed that he attended an Alicia Keys concert and smoked what he called a "clove cigarette." Although he likely did not realize the potential for drug-testing at work, he explained that he smoked what they were passing around because "everyone in the aisle was doing it" and he was intrigued by a girl with a lip ring (Season 2, Episode 20, 8:05).

The vast majority of Michael's attention and energy is focused on his desire to have fun and make the workplace enjoyable for his employees as well. His near-constant reliance on games (Murder Mystery, the Survivor challenge on beach day), costumes (his sumo/fat suit, his jazzercise outfit from the "Let's Get Ethical" seminar), and showmanship is always a risk (and typically one that fails, as it always falls short in accomplishing what needs to be done), but it satisfies his desire to have fun and amuse himself, even if it comes at the cost of alienating, distracting, or bothering others.

I sometimes find it exciting to do things for which I might get in trouble.

Perhaps the most iconic artifact of The Office and Michael Scott is the retort, "That's what she said." Used 45 times in the series, it is Michael's way of making even the most innocent of statements sexual. In Season 2, Episode 2, when he was chastised by upper management for his inappropriate comments at the workplace, Michael announced that his "comedy" was over and there would be no more jokes in the office. Jim asked him if that included "That's what she said," and Michael said that it did. Jim responded by goading him with easy setups for the joke while Jan and the corporate attorney observed. Despite his bosses in the room and the very clear expectation that he should improve his behavior, he took a risk and shouted, "That's what she said," knowing full well that he would likely get into trouble for his response, particularly because his bosses were standing next to him. He exhibited self-control for a fleeting moment here before allowing the fun and humor of the situation to outweigh the consequences.

When Phyllis was flashed in the parking lot before work (Season 3, Episode 21), employees were concerned and comforting her. When Michael arrived at work and learned of the incident, he began to laugh, lacking any concern for the severity of the situation. Shortly after, he made an inappropriate gesture toward Phyllis, mimicking what he perceived the flasher to have done. Even in the most serious of circumstances, Michael risked potential disciplinary actions to make a distasteful joke at Phyllis's expense.

Physical Activities

Gottfredson and Hirsch (1990) posited that "people lacking self-control need not possess or value cognitive or academic skills" (p. 89). The show frequently alludes to the fact that Michael is not overwhelmingly intelligent or cerebral (e.g., "spider face," "explain this to me like I'm five," "I'm a little 'stitious'"). This physical activity element of self-control theory is not specifically related to a preference for physicality alone, but rather relative to a disdain for cognitive engagement. Yet, instead of focusing on Michael's insinuated stupidity, many of the episodes of *The Office* involve physical comedy. Thus, Michael Scott's physicality creates humorous situations, but they often arise as a result of his avoidance for a negative or unpleasant situation. It is often clear that he does not enjoy critical thinking or reflective silence; instead, he wants to be up and moving around, finding physical activities to be the most fun. It obviously serves as a distraction for him, but his physicality is his preferred method of addressing any number of issues.

I almost always get better when I am on the move than when I am sitting and thinking.

In Season 4, Episode 7, Michael was not invited to the wilderness retreat with Ryan and other members of the company, so he decided to create his own retreat. Dwight drove Michael "deep into the Pennsylvania wilderness" (4:15) to spend time alone surviving in the "wild." Michael was motivated; he built a shelter, searched for food, and even documented the trip. Yet, Dwight kept a close eye on him, fearing that he would not survive on his own. Luckily, Dwight's supervision saved Michael's life after Michael almost consumed poisonous mushrooms. Michael's reaction to not being invited to the retreat affected him more while he was thinking about it in the office. The idea to participate in his own retreat was a physical activity that diverted the negative outcomes into positive experiences in his own mind.

Another fitting example occurred in the Season 4 opener. The first scene showed Michael claiming that the upcoming year will be "very good," citing his relationship with Jan and the return of certain employees to the office. When he pulled into the parking lot, however, he struck Meredith Palmer with his car. Once in the hospital, Meredith found out she had been exposed to rabies in the past. Rather than admitting fault or rationally thinking of a way he could have amended the situation, he decided that he actually helped Meredith, concluding that she would have contracted rabies had she not been struck by his car. Michael then created the "Michael Scott's Dunder Mifflin Scranton Meredith Palmer Memorial Celebrity Rabies Awareness Pro-Am Fun Run Race for The Cure," a race intended to raise awareness for rabies. After thinking about the situation, Michael could not handle being at fault for the accident and again resorted to physical activity in an attempt to correct the situation.

I like to get out and do things more than I like to read or contemplate ideas.

As a result of Michael physically disciplining his nephew who he had hired, in Season 7, Episode 2, Michael was forced to receive six hours of counseling to avoid being fired. When Michael found out that the counseling would be administered by Toby Flenderson, his nemesis in Human Resources, he implied that he would rather be fired. After Toby's numerous attempts at getting through to Michael, he finally gets him to speak a bit about his childhood. Michael began to recall some of his experiences as a child and spoke of the experiences aloud to Toby. Michael then realized he was opening to Toby and became enraged, pleading his discontent for Toby and spilling insults.

The notion of revisiting childhood experiences and sharing them with Toby caused Michael to act out aggressively. The setting of a quiet room where ideas are discussed and experiences are shared made Michael uncomfortable, increasing his anxiety and imprudent behavior.

I seem to have more energy and a greater need for activity than most other people my age.

Michael started dating Pam's mother, Helene, after Jim and Pam's wedding. In Season 6, Episode 9, on Helene's birthday, Michael organized a birthday lunch for Helene and invited Jim and Pam. Still concerned about the relationship, Pam decided to attend lunch, feeling that she could not miss her mother's birthday celebration.

At the table, Pam engaged her mother, asking if she would be claiming a lesser age for her birthday once again. Helene stated that she was "sticking with 49," (Season 6, Episode 9, 7:07) and Pam exclaimed that that was the ninth year in a row. After learning Helene's actual age, 58, Michael asked about several activities typically engaged in by younger people, gauging if Helene was too old to do them. When she rejected every idea Michael presented, Michael immediately ended the relationship while still at lunch. He cited several factors that led to the decision, all that related to the age difference. Michael felt that his energy level and need for activity, which was seemingly high for his age, well exceeded that of Helene and he deemed it necessary to end the relationship immediately.

Self-Centered

Perhaps one of Michael's most notable qualities is his self-centeredness. He frequently engages in behaviors that hurt or harm others because his primary concern is for his own well-being. In many cases, he is a disappointing person and even unlikeable. Michael is often only concerned with what makes him happy or protects his own self-interests, even if it has negative consequences for those he considers his best friends. This supports Gottfredson and Hirschi's (1990) assertion that "people with low self-control tend to be self-centered, indifferent, or insensitive to the suffering and needs of others." His employees regularly voiced their disdain for Michael's actions and shared their discomfort with him, and we know that his behaviors negatively affected his employees.

> *I try to look out for myself first, even if it means making things difficult for other people.*

In Season 2 Episode 4, "the temp" Ryan Howard accidentally started a fire in the kitchen setting off the alarm, Angela and Dwight attempted to evacuate the employees in an orderly way. However, Michael quickly ran by the others to ensure his own safety. He physically pushed Jim, who subsequently bumped into Pam and Oscar, and hallway footage showed him running from the building. He rationalized this behavior by explaining that although women and children should be saved or evacuated first, he does not employ children and—to treat women in the workplace equally—he is avoiding a lawsuit by not treating them preferentially.

Besides, in an attempt to correct his own mistake of sharing gossip about Stanley's infidelity, he attempted to spread rumors about everyone in the office (Season 6, Episode 1). While one might argue that he was trying to help Stanley, their conversation indicated that Michael was essentially trying to remain in Stanley's good graces and ensure, as always, that he was well-liked. In doing so, he spread hurtful rumors, particularly about his employees' sexuality, eating habits, personal relationships, and employment status. By trying to save his reputation and friendship with Stanley, he made life increasingly difficult for the rest of his employees that day.

Both the warehouse and the office employees had to complete safety training. When the warehouse crew suggested that their job was more dangerous, Michael wanted to prove them wrong. He determined that depression is one of the dangers of working in an office, and with Michael's lack of visual aids during his safety training, he decided to do a demonstration. Michael had planned to jump off the roof of the office after stating the "cold, hard facts of depression" (Season 3, Episode 19, 10:43). He wanted the fake suicide to make the warehouse workers believe that the office jobs are dangerous but hope that they realize they should have been nicer to Michael. The employees soon realized the danger of his proposed stunt and offered calming words to talk him off the roof. His desire to make a statement and benefit himself puts the other employees in emotional distress.

I'm not very sympathetic to other people when they are having problems.

In more childlike behavior, Michael always had a thoroughly vested interest in everyone celebrating and acknowledging his birthday (March 15). However, in Season 2, Episode 19, Michael's birthday celebrations were dampened by the possibility of Kevin having skin cancer. While everyone anxiously awaited the results from the doctor, Michael and Dwight attempted to create a birthday celebration with donuts, baloney and ketchup subs, and birthday festivities. Michael saw that Kevin's fear and everyone's concern was dampening the mood, and after a failed attempt to send him home for the day, he brought everyone to the skating rink. Though he claimed it was to distract Kevin, the preplanned decorations and Michael's affinity for skating tell us that the party was for his amusement, not Kevin's benefit. Even in the face of potentially devastating news, Michael could not be sympathetic to Kevin's situation, and instead, he focused on his birthday and enjoyment.

Temper

While emotions such as frustration or irritation are typically situational rather than indicative of personality traits, the response to these feelings may be the impetus for crimes for those with self-control. They may react with violent or vicious responses to stimuli that incite these feelings, as "people with low self-control tend to have minimal tolerance for frustration" (Gottfredson & Hirschi, 1990, p. 90). Michael frequently exhibited behaviors that were childlike in his ability to address stress or negative circumstances. His coping mechanisms often involved physical violence, pouting, or verbally lashing out at others. While his anger issues may not have been as severe as Andy Bernard's (which required anger management classes due to punching a hole in the wall), they still created an often-hostile environment and situations in which Michael's anger was palpable.

I lose my temper pretty easily.

In the summer leading up to the Season 7 premiere, Michael hired his nephew, Luke, as an assistant for the office. Michael constantly received negative feedback from other employees about Luke's job performance, including failure to deliver to customers, incorrect coffee orders, and an overall lack of motivation. However, Michael dismissed the complaints to protect his nephew and keep him employed with the company. After a while, Michael's temper grew short, and after Luke continued to distract others during a meeting, Michael pulled him aside. When Michael attempted to peacefully resolve the situation, Luke continued to mock Michael, treating the conversation as a joke. Michael finally lost control and began spanking Luke against his will in front of everyone in the office. His quick loss of control of his temper caused him to react physically. He was subsequently disciplined for his actions and forced to engage in counseling with Toby.

Michael was upset when others referred to Gabe as "the boss," but when he was invited to a viewing party at Gabe's apartment, Michael reluctantly accepted the invitation (Season 7, Episode 8). Several times at the party, Michael vocally shared his disdain for Gabe; once he criticized Gabe using pizza dough for making pigs-in-a-blanket, and again when Gabe continued to turn the television volume down. Michael clearly disliked Gabe, but instead of avoiding him, he turned off the cable and ruined the party for everyone. His temper not only affected Gabe but everyone else in addition.

When I'm really angry, other people better stay away from me.

Michael's unfortunate miscommunication with Ryan convinced him that he was invited to New York City for the launch party, celebrating the launch of Dunder Mifflin's new website. Once he realized his mistake halfway to New York, he returned to the office and rearranged the previously organized party to his own liking and decided to order pizza. When it arrived, Michael presented a coupon, claiming that he was entitled to receive all of the pizza at 50% off. When the delivery boy stated that the coupon only applies to orders of two pizzas, (Michael ordered eight) Michael expressed extreme disapproval and forced the boy into the break room.

After making the boy wait for several hours, Michael called the pizza shop and demanded that he receive his order at the discounted price and additional pizza for the inconvenience, which sounded eerily similar to demands of ransom for the boy. Michael eventually paid for the pizza and freed the boy after he realized that he was, in fact, committing the crime of kidnapping, reckless endangerment, false imprisonment, or child abuse. Michael's lack of self-control caused him to act impulsively as a result of the anger he felt and essentially kidnap a minor.

Michael also made the office feel his anger when the other employees did not take him seriously during his "Prison Mike" display. After discovering an employee was formerly in prison and hearing others compare the office to a prison, Michael gave a presentation, playing the role of a former convict. After the employees overwhelmed him with questions to discredit his performance, he left the meeting and locked the employees in the room. Michael's anger made him trap the employees in the room, and he justified his behaviors by noting, "They are such babies. I am going to leave them in there until they can appreciate what it's like to have freedom" (Season 3, Episode 9 17:41).

When I have a serious disagreement with someone, it's usually hard for me to talk calmly about it without getting upset.

At the start of Season 5, Episode 9, members of the office were in the conference room eating brownies. Ryan questioned Kelly as to why she was taking two, but she informed him that she was taking one to Toby. Michael overheard the conversation, laughed, and stated that she should "send it to him in Costa Rica," (Season 5, Episode 9, 0:35) failing to realize that Toby had moved back to Scranton after a six-month stay in Costa Rica. Michael continued to treat comments regarding Toby as a joke genuinely believing he never returned.

Jim then asked Michael to go back to Toby's desk to see if he was there. When Michael discovered that Toby had actually returned, and when he was greeted, Michael looked at him and screamed, "No! God! No, God, please no! No! No! Nooooo!" (Season 5, Episode 9, 1:27). Michael was extremely upset with Toby's presence and immediately began screaming, showing a lack of control.

Conclusion

While fans of the show would argue that Michael Scott is one of the most oddly lovable, iconic characters in television history, he undoubtedly has his flaws. In nearly every episode, he demonstrated that he lacks self-control. His self-centeredness, short temper, lack of concern for others, and avoidance of critical thinking may create hilarious scenes for viewers, but they also demonstrate a pattern of behaviors analogous to crime and sometimes, actual crimes.

Like Michael Scott, SCT is also flawed and criticized. More empirical testing and conceptualization are needed, but the application of the theory allows students of criminology to consider how Michael's behavior highlights the six elements of the theory: impulsivity, simple tasks, risk-seeking, physical activity, self-centered, and temper. Yet, its parsimony and easy application allow criminologists to understand how self-control can affect crime and deviant behavior and consider how parenting and development can lead to juvenile adult and adult crimes. Perhaps with time, further research, and more testing of the instruments, SCT might become the biggest thing yet. *That's what she said.*

Discussion Questions

1. For fans of *The Office*, are there other characters who may have similar or contrasting characteristics? Compare them to Michael and identify ways in which they have more or less self-control.
2. What individual factors or characteristics can serve moderating factors, or those that would inhibit the negative effects of low self-control? Does Michael ever exhibit any of these?
3. What strategies or interventions would you use to address these behaviors? How can the criminal justice system address self-control to reduce offending?

References

Arneklev, B. J., Elis, F., & Medlicott, S. (2006). Testing the General Theory of Crime: Comparing the effects of "imprudent behavior" and an attitudinal indicator of "low self-control." *Western Criminology Review, 7*(3), 41–55.

Baker, J. O. (2010). The Expression of Low Self-Control as Problematic Drinking in Adolescents: An Integrated Control Perspective. *Journal of Criminal Justice, 38*(3), 237–244.

Barlow, H. D. (1991). Review Essay: Explaining Crimes and Analogous Acts, or the Unrestrained Will Grab at Pleasure Whenever They Can. *The Journal of Criminal Law & Criminology, 82*(1), 229–242.

Chui, W. H., & Chan, H. C. (2016). The Gendered Analysis of Self-Control on Theft and Violent Delinquency: An Examination of the Hong Kong Adolescent Population. *Crime and Delinquency, 62*(12), 1648–1677.

Conner, B. T., Stein, J. A., & Longshore, D. (2008). Examining Self-Control as a Multidimensional Predictor of Crime and Drug Use in Adolescents with Criminal Histories. *Journal of Behavioral Health Services and Research, 36*(2), 137–149.

Donner, C. M., Fridell, L. A., & Jennings, W. G. (2016). The Relationship Between Self-Control and Police Misconduct: A Multi-Agency Study of First-Line Police Supervisors. *Criminal Justice and Behavior, 43*(7), 841–862.

Ellwanger, S. J., & Pratt, T. C. (2014). Self-Control, Negative Affect, and Young Driver Aggression: An Assessment of Competing Theoretical Claims. *International Journal of Offender Therapy and Comparative Criminology, 58*(1), 85–106.

Ford, J. A., & Blumenstein, L. (2013). Self-Control and Substance Use Among College Students. *Journal of Drug Issues, 43*(1), 56–68.

Grasmick, H. G., Tittle, C. R., Bursik, R. J., & Arneklev, B. J. (1993). Testing the Core Empirical Implications of Gottfredson and Hirschi's General Theory of Crime. *Journal of Research in Crime and Delinquency, 30*, 5–29.

Gottfredson, M. R., & Hirschi, T. (1990). *A general theory of crime.* Stanford, CA: Stanford University Press.

Higgins, G. E. (2007). Examining the Original Grasmick Scale: A Rasch Model Approach. *Criminal Justice and Behavior, 34*(2), 157–178.

Jaremko-Greenwold, A. (2015, March 24). Why Michael Scott Is One of the Most Original Characters of All Time. *Indie Wire.* Retrieved from https://www.indiewire.com/2015/03/the-office-10-years-later-why-michael-scott-is-one-of-the-most-original-characters-of-all-time-248114/

Jones, S., Lynam, D. R., & Piquero, A. R. (2015). Substance Use, Personality, and Inhibitors: Testing Hirschi's Predictions About the Reconceptualization of Self-Control. *Crime & Delinquency, 61*(4), 538–558.

Leeper Piquero, N., Schoepfer, A., & Langton, L. (2010). Complete Out of Control or the Desire to Be in Complete Control? How Low Self-Control and the Desire for Control Relate to Corporate Offending. *Crime & Delinquency, 56*(4), 627–647.

Seipel, C., & Eifler, S. (2010). Opportunity, Rational Choice, and Self-Control: On the Interaction of Person and Situation in a General Theory of Crime. *Crime & Delinquency, 56*(2), 167–197.

Sheffield, R. (2016, September 21). 100 Greatest TV Shows of All Time. *Rolling Stone.* Retrieved from https://www.rollingstone.com/tv/tv-lists/100-greatest-tv-shows-of-all-time-105998/eastbound-and-down-106484/

Zavala, E., & Kurtz, D. L. (2017). Using Gottfredson and Hirschi's A General Theory of Crime to Explain Problematic Alcohol Consumption by Police Officers: A Test of Self-Control as Self-Regulation. *Journal of Drug Issues, 47*(3), 505–522.

For Further Reading

Hirschi, T., & Gottfredson, M. R. (2000). In Defense of Self-Control. *Theoretical Criminology, 4*(1), 55–69.

Episodes

Health Care (Season 1, Episode 3)

Daniels, G., Kaling, M., Lieberstein, P. (Writers), & Whittingham, K. (Director). (2005). Health Care [Television Series Episode]. In G. Daniels, R. Gervais, H. Klein, S. Merchant, & B. Silverman (Executive Producers), *The Office*. Los Angeles, CA: National Broadcasting Company.

Sexual Harassment (Season 2, Episode 2)

Daniels, G., Novak, B. J. (Writers), & Kwapis, K. (Director). (2005). Sexual Harassment [Television Series Episode]. In G. Daniels, R. Gervais, H. Klein, S. Merchant, & B. Silverman (Executive Producers), *The Office*. Los Angeles, CA: National Broadcasting Company.

The Fire (Season 2, Episode 4)

Daniels, G., Novak, B. J. (Writers), & Kwapis, K. (Director). (2005). The Fire [Television Series Episode]. In G. Daniels, R. Gervais, H. Klein, S. Merchant, & B. Silverman (Executive Producers), *The Office*. Los Angeles, CA: National Broadcasting Company.

The Fight (Season 2, Episode 6)

Stupnitsky, G., Eisenberg, L. (Writers), & Kawpis, K. (Director). (2005). The Fight [Television Series Episode]. In G. Daniels, R. Gervais, H. Klein, S. Merchant, & B. Silverman (Executive Producers), *The Office*. Los Angeles, CA: National Broadcasting Company.

Michael's Birthday (Season 2, Episode 19)

Daniels, G., Eisenberg, L., Stupnitsky, G. (Writers), & Whittingham, K. (Director). (2006). Michael's Birthday [Television Series Episode]. In G. Daniels, R. Gervais, H. Klein, S. Merchant, & B. Silverman (Executive Producers), *The Office*. Los Angeles, CA: National Broadcasting Company.

Drug Testing (Season 2, Episode 20)

Daniels, G., Celotta, J. (Writers), & Daniels, G. (Director). (2006). Drug Testing [Television Series Episode]. In G. Daniels, R. Gervais, H. Klein, S. Merchant, & B. Silverman (Executive Producers), *The Office*. Los Angeles, CA: National Broadcasting Company.

The Convict (Season 3, Episode 9)

Daniels, G., Gervais, R., Merchant, S. (Writers), & Blitz, J. (Director). (2007). The Convict [Television Series Episode]. In G. Daniels, R. Gervais, H. Klein, K. Kwapis, & B. Silverman (Executive Producers), *The Office*. Los Angeles, CA: National Broadcasting Company.

Back from Vacation (Season 3, Episode 11)
Daniels, G., Spitzer, J. (Writers), & Farino, J. (Director). (2007). Back from Vacation [Television Episode]. In G. Daniels, R. Gervais, S. Merchant (Executive Producers), *The Office*. Los Angeles, CA: National Broadcasting Company.

Women's Appreciation (Season 3, Episode 21)
Daniels, G., Eisenberg, L., Stupnitsky, G. (Writers), & Gates, T. (Director). (2007). Women's Appreciation [Television Episode]. In G. Daniels, R. Gervais, S. Merchant (Executive Producers), *The Office*. Los Angeles, CA: National Broadcasting Company.

Beach Games (Season 3, Episode 22)
Daniels, G., Celotta, J. (Writers), & Ramis, H. (Director). (2007). Beach Games [Television Series Episode]. In G. Daniels, R. Gervais, & S. Merchant (Executive Producers), *The Office*. Los Angeles, CA: National Broadcasting Company.

Fun Run (Season 4, Episode 1)
Daniels, G. (Writer), & Daniels, G. (Producer). (2007). Fun Run [Television Series Episode]. In G. Daniels, R. Gervais, H. Klein, S. Merchant, & B. Silverman (Executive Producers), *The Office*. Los Angeles, CA: National Broadcasting Company.

Money (Season 4, Episode 4)
Daniels, G., Lieberstein, P. (Writers), & Lieberstein, P. (Director). (2007). Money [Television Series Episode]. In G. Daniels, R. Gervais, H. Klein, S. Merchant, & B. Silverman (Executive Producers), *The Office*. Los Angeles, CA: National Broadcasting Company.

Local Ad (Season 4, Episode 5)
Daniels, G., Novak, B. J. (Writers), & Reitman, J. (Director). (2007). Local Ad [Television Series Episode]. In G. Daniels, R. Gervais, H. Klein, S. Merchant, & B. Silverman (Executive Producers), *The Office*. Los Angeles, CA: National Broadcasting Company.

Branch Wars (Season 4, Episode 6)
Daniels, G., Kaling, M. (Writers), & Whedon, J. (Director). (2007). Branch Wars [Television Series Episode]. In G. Daniels, R. Gervais, H. Klein, S. Merchant, & B. Silverman (Executive Producers), *The Office*. Los Angeles, CA: National Broadcasting Company.

Survivor Man (Season 4, Episode 7)
Carell, S., Daniel, G. (Writers), & Feig, P. (Director). (2007). Survivor Man [Television Series Episode]. In G. Daniels, R. Gervais, H. Klein, S. Merchant, & B. Silverman (Executive Producers), *The Office*. Los Angeles, CA: National Broadcasting Company.

Weight Loss Part II (Season 5, Episode 2)
Daniels, G., Eisenberg, L., Stupnitsky, G. (Writers), & Feig, P. (Director). (2008). Weight Loss Part II [Television Series Episode]. In G. Daniels, R. Gervais, P. Liberstein, S. Merchant, & B. Silverman (Executive Producers), *The Office*. Los Angeles, CA: National Broadcasting Company.

Business Ethics (Season 5, Episode 3)

Daniels, G., Koh, R. (Writers), & Blitz, J. (Director). (2008). Business Ethics [Television Series Episode]. In G. Daniels, R. Gervais, H. Klein, P. Lieberstein, S. Merchant, & B. Silverman (Executive Producers), *The Office*. Los Angeles, CA: National Broadcasting Company.

Frame Toby (Season 5, Episode 9)

Daniels, G., Kaling, M. (Writers), & Reitman, J. (Director). (2008). Frame Toby [Television Series Episode]. In J. Celotta, G. Daniels, R. Gervais, H. Klein, P. Lieberstein, S. Merchant, & B. Silverman (Executive Producers), *The Office*. Los Angeles, CA: National Broadcasting Company.

The Surplus (Season 5, Episode 10)

Daniels, G., Eisenberg, L., & Stupnitsky, G. (Writers), & Feig, P. (Director). (2008). The Surplus [Television Series Episode]. In J. Celotta, G. Daniels, R. Gervais, H. Klein, P. Lieberstein, S. Merchant, & B. Silverman (Executive Producers), *The Office*. Los Angeles, CA: National Broadcasting Company.

Michael Scott Paper Company (Season 5, Episode 23)

Daniels, G., Spitzer, J. (Writers), & Stupnitsky, G. (Director). (2009). Michael Scott Paper Company [Television Series Episode]. In J. Celotta, G. Daniels, R. Gervais, H. Klein, P. Lieberstein, S. Merchant, & B. Silverman (Executive Producers), *The Office*. Los Angeles, CA: National Broadcasting Company.

Gossip (Season 6, Episode 1)

Daniels, G., Lieberstein, P. (Writers), & Liberstein, P. (Director). (2009). Gossip [Television Series Episode]. In G. Daniels, R. Gervais, H. Klein, P. Lieberstein, S. Merchant, & B. Silverman (Executive Producers), *The Office*. Los Angeles, CA: National Broadcasting Company.

The Promotion (Season 6, Episode 3)

Celotta, J., Daniels, G. (Writers), & Celotta, J. (Director). (2009). The Promotion [Television Series Episode]. In G. Daniels, R. Gervais, H. Klein, P. Lieberstein, S. Merchant, & B. Silverman (Executive Producers), *The Office*. Los Angeles, CA: National Broadcasting Company.

Double Date (Season 6, Episode 9)

Daniels, G., Grandy, C. (Writers), & Gordon, S. (Director). (2009). Double Date [Television Series Episode]. In G. Daniels, R. Gervais, H. Klein, P. Lieberstein, S. Merchant, & B. Silverman (Executive Producers), *The Office*. Los Angeles, CA: National Broadcasting Company.

Murder (Season 6, Episode 10)
Chun, D., Daniels, G. (Writers), & Daniels, G. (Director). (2009). Murder [Television Series Episode]. In G. Daniels, R. Gervais, H. Klein, P. Lieberstein, S. Merchant, & B. Silverman (Executive Producers), *The Office*. Los Angeles, CA: National Broadcasting Company.

Scott's Tots (Season 6, Episode 12)
Daniels, G., Eisenberg, L., & Stupnitsky, G. (Writers), & Novak, B. J. (Director). (2009). Scott's Tots [Television Series Episode]. In G. Daniels, R. Gervais, H. Klein, P. Lieberstein, S. Merchant, & B. Silverman (Executive Producers), *The Office*. Los Angeles, CA: National Broadcasting Company.

Nepotism (Season 7, Episode 1)
Chun, D., Daniels, G. (Writers), & Blitz, J. (Director). (2010). Nepotism [Television Series Episode]. In G. Daniels, R. Gervais, H. Klein, P. Liebersterin, S. Merchant, & B. Silverman (Executive Producers), *The Office*. Los Angeles, CA: National Broadcasting Company.

Counseling (Season 7, Episode 2)
Daniels, G., Novak, B. J. (Writers), & Blitz, J. (Director). (2010). Counseling [Television Series Episode]. In G. Daniels, R. Gervais, H. Klein, P. Lieberstein, S. Merchant, & B. Silverman (Executive Producers), *The Office*. Los Angeles, CA: National Broadcasting Company.

Christening (Season 7, Episode 7)
Daniels, G., Ocko, P. (Writers), & Hardcastle, A. (Director). (2010). Christening [Television Series Episode]. In G. Daniels, R. Gervais, H. Klein, P. Lieberstein, S. Merchant, & B. Silverman (Executive Producers), *The Office*. Los Angeles, CA: National Broadcasting Company.

Viewing Party (Season 7, Episode 8)
Daniels, G., Vitti, J. (Writers), & Whittingham, K. (Director). (2010). Viewing Party [Television Series Episode]. In G. Daniels, R. Gervais, H. Klein, P. Lieberstein, S. Merchant, & B. Silverman (Executive Producers), *The Office*. Los Angeles, CA: National Broadcasting Company.

Collective Efficacy Theory and *Mister Rogers' Neighborhood*

11

Strong Communities and Neighborhoods: Collective
Efficacy and Mister Rogers' Neighborhood of Make-
Believe

Dana Winters and Kristopher Kell

Launched nationally in 1968, *Mister Rogers' Neighborhood* helped children to express their feelings, accept differences, and learn what it meant to be good neighbors. Guided by the foundational importance of childhood and the desire to present children and families with a high-quality and developmental option for television programming, Fred Rogers worked to bring concepts of kindness, compassion, and cooperation into countless households over 30 years and nearly 900 episodes.

While many were introduced to Fred Rogers through *Mister Rogers' Neighborhood*, Fred Rogers often wrote and spoke publicly about the needs of communities and families in support of children. The ideas frequently found within his public speeches for adult audiences often mirrored the ideas that he presented to children through his television program. He was not afraid to challenge adults to create a world where children had the best opportunity to grow to be competent, confident, and caring human beings. He often would talk about the need for radical kindness and compassion in our world, and call communities to action for the benefit of all people. In what would become his final commencement address, given in May 2002 at Dartmouth University, Fred offered these words to the graduates, calling them to support their neighbors and world throughout the many challenges they faced:

D. Winters (✉) · K. Kell
Saint Vincent College, Latrobe, PA, USA
e-mail: dana.winters@stvincent.edu

© The Author(s) 2021
S. E. Daly (ed.), *Theories of Crime Through Popular Culture*,
https://doi.org/10.1007/978-3-030-54434-8_11

You don't ever have to do anything sensational for people to love you. When I say, "It's you I like," I'm talking about that part of you that knows that life is far more than anything you can ever see or hear or touch … that deep part of you that allows you to stand for those things without which humankind cannot survive: love that conquers hate, peace that rises triumphant over war, and justice that proves more powerful than greed. So, in all that you do in all of your life, I wish you the strength and the grace to make those choices which will allow you and your neighbor to become the best of whoever you are. (Rogers, 2002)

It is in this sentiment, so common to many of Fred's messages through the program and his public service, that we see the deep commitment Fred had to embrace each person's role within a community to work together for social benefit. He asks the graduates to make choices not only with individual need in mind but with the needs of entire communities and neighborhoods. This focus on communal good and the role of communities in creating societies of mutual aid and care is also found within Fred's messaging on *Mister Rogers' Neighborhood*, especially through the Neighborhood of Make-Believe.

It is in this Neighborhood of Make-Believe where we see citizens of all forms, ages, faces, ethnicities, and genders working together to build a community based on trust, social cohesion, and collective efficacy. The conflict was a normal part of the Neighborhood, and viewers watched as the citizens worked together to address issues like food insecurity, anger, destruction of property, and environmental damage. Each group of week-long episodes included a conflict or story where citizens of the Neighborhood worked together for the benefit of the communal need, often displaying many foundational elements of collective efficacy such as group dynamics, attachment to the community, informal social control, and the coordination across communities to address the needs of others. Viewers not only saw the benefits of collective efficacy through community action, but also the incivilities (typically from Lady Elaine) that are possible when the collective breaks down and how internal social control can restore order through kinship and friendship (Armstrong, Katz, & Schnebly, 2015; Kasarda & Janowitz, 1974).

A Brief Introduction to Collective Efficacy

The theory of collective efficacy proposes that through social learning and social influence, a group of people can set and achieve a collective goal (Bandura, 1997; Souza, 2014). By influencing the behavior and actions of group members, it is possible to unite the community in ways that make a collective goal achievable (Souza, 2014). Within criminology, the most commonly studied goals are the prevention of crime or increasing neighborhood safety; however, collective efficacy can also be focused on goals such as mutual aid and generally improving the community (Armstrong et al., 2015; Swatt, Uchida, Varano & Solomon, 2013).

Two main factors influence a group's ability to exercise collective efficacy: skill and belief (Bandura, 1997, 2000). In any community, different members will have different abilities and skills. Collective efficacy requires that members combine these skills and work together. Of course, these skills must be relevant to the task at hand; it would be difficult for someone with no experience in organizing to facilitate a neighborhood watch or food drive on their own, but it would be doable in collaboration with persons with relevant experience (Souza, 2014). In a similar vein, collective efficacy requires belief, namely, the belief that a proposed goal can really be met. If group members disagree on the reality of a goal, it will be impossible for them to collaborate to make that goal a reality (Souza, 2014).

Social Control and Community Attachment

While skill and belief are core to the successful implementation of collective efficacy, these factors are further influenced by social control (Souza, 2014: Sampson, Raudenbush, & Earls, 1997). This kind of control is a motivating force that encourages people to prioritize community goals without being externally forced to do so. It can be something as small as volunteering to supervise a group of neighborhood children playing on the street, to intervening in an emergency to save the life of another community member (Sampson, 1998). Social control utilizes kinship, friendship, and other interpersonal bonds to control behavior within a community (Sampson et al., 1997). Often, social control is exercised to address issues (like truancy or loitering) that would often fall under the jurisdiction of government or law enforcement agencies (Sampson et al., 1997). Social control-based interventions can be reactive to a current issue or can proactively prevent an issue by reinforcing pro-social behaviors and values (Hoffman, 2003; Sampson et al., 1997). While social control is often related to community policing, it isn't limited to combating anti-social behavior. Members of the community can use their bonds to aid each other and improve the happiness and overall well-being of the community through the sharing of resources, time, and knowledge (Wickes & Hipp, 2018). While social control often takes the form of direct commands, requests, or suggestions from friends and fellow community members, it can also be exercised through less direct methods (Wickes & Hipp, 2018). This more informal social control is the kind of control that tends to be most present in instances of collective efficacy (Souza, 2014).

Informal social control relies upon the same bonds and relationships as formal or regular social control but is the definition, less direct and overt (Wickes & Hipp, 2018). It relies on an individual coopting the values or goals of friends and members of his or her community. Valuing a bond with another person may lead an individual to adopt some of the beliefs that person holds, and can make said individual more receptive to ideas and concerns from persons they are bonded to (Hoffman, 2003; Wickes & Hipp, 2018). Not only does informal social control make collective efficacy possible, but it also brings a community closer together by uniting them in common goals. Perhaps more importantly, people who have internalized common goals are more likely to share resources, knowledge, and time with other members of the community who need aid (Wickes & Hipp, 2018). As community values and goals are internalized by the individual, they will act to fulfill those goals.

Interpersonal attachment serves as a driving force for informal (and formal) social control, and consequently collective efficacy at large. Attachment motivates people to care about each other and demands a person care about the safety, needs, and goals of the people they are attached to. Furthermore, bonds with members inside one's own community correspond with attachment to the community as a whole (Sampson, 1998). These bonds have multiple benefits. People with strong community attachment report lower levels of perceived violence (Armstrong et al., 2015). Additionally, having multiple attachments within the same community generally makes a person more willing to exercise social control and influence the behaviors of their friends and acquaintances (Armstrong et al., 2015). In a community that lacks attachment, people are far less likely to reach out to or help people that they do not know (Sampson et al., 1997).

Factors Influencing Collective Efficacy, Social Control, and Attachment

Given that interpersonal and community attachment play such a strong role in the foundations of collective efficacy, it follows that factors that damage interpersonal trust and attachment make it far more difficult for collective efficacy to take place (Sampson et al., 1997). Unsurprisingly, racial/ethnic discrimination, class separation, and economic stratification within a community impact a community's ability to come together and severely damage trust and attachment between community members (Kasarda & Janowitz, 1974). Economic stratification across communities tends to result in significantly different life experiences. For example, members of higher economic classes tend to live further away from their friendship or kinship groups, often resulting in attachments spanning multiple communities, rather than focusing on one community, where social control can be exercised (Sampson, 1998). This can result in people from different economic classes, even those living in the same community, facing considerably different challenges and struggles in their everyday lives. These different experiences may lead to a lower likelihood of informal social control and collective efficacy due to a lack of collective action and experience within the community (Sampson et al., 1997).

One final factor influencing collective efficacy is the length of residency (Kasarda & Janowitz, 1974). To form effective bonds and attachments, an individual must live in the community. Consequently, communities with high rates of residential instability are far less likely to achieve levels of community attachment and informal social control that make collective efficacy possible (Kasarda & Janowitz, 1974; Sampson, 1998). Without interpersonal relationships and attachments, it is far less likely that community attachment can be built. Since community attachment is vital to the activation of both formal and informal social control, it is less likely that collective efficacy can take effect (Bandura, 1997, 2000). At the heart of any effective community effort are the bonds, friendships, kinships, and other interpersonal relationships that turn strangers into neighbors.

Mister Rogers' Neighborhood as a Center of Collective Efficacy

Radical for his time, Fred Rogers was committed to communicating with children, through television, about topics that many adults worried were too controversial and difficult for children to truly understand. Through its time on air, *Mister Rogers' Neighborhood* covered topics such as divorce, death, racial injustice, food insecurity, mad feelings, unkindness, and more. In addressing all of these concepts, viewers were comforted by Fred's direct approach in talking with his "television neighbors," visits to see how others in the "neighborhood" were thinking and addressing these topics, and by daily trips to the "Neighborhood of Make-Believe," a land of imagination where anything was possible. In each episode, Mister Rogers would welcome his television neighbors into the Neighborhood of Make-Believe for 10–12 minutes of the 30-minute episode. The Neighborhood of Make-Believe was yet another way of addressing the very real inside lives of children and the ever-changing outside worlds around them. Many of the most difficult subjects, such as shame, guilt, self-confidence, and difference were captured through conversations and on-goings of the Neighborhood of Make-Believe.

Within the Neighborhood of Make-Believe, viewers were privy to the inner workings of a community, with differences, conflicts, individual needs, and communal goals. Trips to the Neighborhood often displayed many foundational elements of collective efficacy such as group dynamics, attachment to the community, informal social control, and the coordination across communities to address the needs of others. To demonstrate these foundational elements of collective efficacy found within the Neighborhood of Make-Believe, this chapter discusses two week-long story arcs spread across five episodes, each, within the Neighborhood. Each arc within the Neighborhood of Make-Believe applies to a larger theme discussed throughout the full episodes of *Mister Rogers' Neighborhood* for that week. This chapter uses each of those arcs to demonstrate collective efficacy and discuss how children were taught and shown how to function in a productive society.

Food Insecurity in the Neighborhood

In 1984, Fred Rogers devoted one of his "theme weeks" of episodes to discussing food and hunger. As he describes to his television neighbors how some people and animals do not have enough food to eat, he spent the week visiting with people around his neighborhood who make or provide food for communities. This included a trip to an applesauce manufacturer, Chef Brockett's bakery, a vegetable soup factory, and a visit to Mr. Costa's home to make pasta. Within the Neighborhood of Make-Believe, television viewers were invited by Mister Rogers to imagine what could happen in a community where there is not enough food.

In the first episode of this week (Rogers & Lally, 1984a), we follow the trolley to the Neighborhood of Make-Believe where X the Owl is waiting patiently, and at times impatiently, for the delivery of seeds for his new garden. After Mr. McFeely helps X the Owl to plant the seeds, they wait for them to grow by playing hide and seek and trying to be patient. While viewers have not been introduced to the conflict for this week, the episode shows neighbors coming together to wait for the planting of the seeds. It is evident, even for a first-time viewer, that the citizens of the Neighborhood of Make-Believe all have a deep attachment to their community and to one another. They support each other individually but do so in a way that benefits the community, as well (Sampson, 1998).

As the week moves on, viewers are introduced to the conflict in the second episode of the week (Rogers & Lally, 1984b). As the segment opens, Queen Sara talks to Lady Aberlin about her "Hunger Project" and how helpful X the Owl's "speedy seeds" could be to the work she is doing. X the Owl's seeds have begun to sprout vegetables and he invites his neighborhood friends to dinner to eat his new vegetables. After X the Owl, Henrietta, and Bob Dog exit, viewers see a goat stealing X the Owl's vegetables from his garden. When X the Owl discovers that the plants are gone, he gets very upset. Lady Aberlin, Henrietta, and Bob Dog all vow to help X the Owl find who has taken the plants. They come together as a community to help X the Owl, a symbol of their community attachment, which indicates that those with higher levels of community attachment are more likely to reach out to help people within their community, even without the direct individual benefit (Sampson, 1998).

As the scene continues, Lady Elaine talks with Betty Okonak Templeton and Lady Aberlin, telling them that her entire garden in Southwood is gone and has been stolen. When Lady Aberlin tells them that X the Owl's garden has also been stolen, they all decide to meet at the Castle to "make some plans." Betty Okonak Templeton responds by saying, "I would certainly be interested in participating. I mean there's hardly been a time in history that I can remember that plants and gardens were in jeopardy. And those are things that folks like us that really care about the finer things of life can hardly afford to let go unchecked. Don't you agree?" Betty's concern is for her community, and in seeing that there could be an issue affecting all its citizens. She indicates the importance of that community, and her own desire to protect it. On the way back to the castle, Lady Aberlin talks with Bob Dog who is taking his turn "guarding X's garden." This is the first example of informal social control within this specific story arc in the Neighborhood of Make-Believe. Identifying a potential problem that could affect the community, as a whole, the neighbors work together to protect one another and the Neighborhood. This indicator of collective efficacy is a product of the neighbors operating interdependently within a social system toward a common goal (Bandura, 1997, 2000), in this case, the protection of the community.

The collective efficacy and informal social control evidenced by the community coming together willingly without individual motivating factors continues in the third episode of the week (Rogers & Lally, 1984c), where the citizens of the Neighborhood of Make-Believe work together to guard their community. When viewers arrive in the Neighborhood of Make-Believe, King Friday is talking with Lady Aberlin, Bob Dog, and Handyman Negri, who are serving as garden guards seeking to catch the vegetable thief. Disguised in capes and false noses, the guards are ordered by King Friday to guard the gardens and "if anyone should come to take part of any part of any garden" the guards are to report back immediately. King Friday provides an example of a formal leader within a community who works to support the internal social control. This internal social control takes shape both directly and indirectly, as the group comes together independently of a third party (direct informal social control) and then gains the support of the governmental authority in King Friday, who works to create supports for them to continue their work in protecting the Neighborhood (indirect informal social control) (Swatt, Varano, Uchida, & Solomon, 2013).

As they monitor the Neighborhood, guarding the various gardens, Bob Dog and Lady Aberlin discover the old goat from Northwood stealing from a garden near Daniel's clock. Together, they confront him, asking him if it is his garden and telling him that he should not be taking the plants. The goat responds that Northwood doesn't have any food—which surprises both Bob Dog and Lady Aberlin. They ask him how that can be and why he was stealing, and he tells them that he didn't think that anyone would help him. They respond by telling him they will all go to the castle and "make a plan together." Even when faced with an external threat, the neighbors seek to "make a plan together," rather than addressing the issue individually.

At the Castle, the "Garden Guards" report that "the one who has been taking the food is one who has no food where he lives." King Friday is surprised by this and asks the old goat about the situation. The old goat says that he didn't think anyone would help so he had been taking plants from the Neighborhood of Make-Believe to Northwood to feed the hungry people there. When analyzing the community dynamics of old goat's response, it may be that Northwood community's informal social control lacks the same level of activation as what is found in the Neighborhood of Make-Believe (Sampson et al., 1997). The old goat felt compelled to individually seek food during the shortage in Northwood instead of establishing a communal effort to respond to the crisis. It could be that his community lacks the trust and solidarity to activate the high levels of informal social control, which are evident within the Neighborhood of Make-Believe (Sampson et al., 1997). King Friday responds to the old goat by saying, "Of course we will help! I declare an all-out effort!" and commands the garden guards to plant as many seeds as possible to help during this emergency. When the goat questions why they would do this, Queen Sara tells him that the people of Northwood would do the same for them—and they only need to ask for help and they shall receive it. This is a comment that exemplifies community trust, solidarity, and mutuality, all examples of high levels of attachment to the community, informal social control, and collective efficacy (Sampson et al., 1997).

As the story continues to unfold in the fourth episode of the week (Rogers & Lally, 1984d), the Neighborhood of Make-Believe is full of sprouting plants, where the speedy seeds have produced a full harvest. Talking with the old goat, Lady Aberlin says, "All of us in the neighborhood are happy to help." They all look at the gardens and talk about how happy they are to help the citizens of Northwood. They have named the project the "All-Out Effort for Northwood" and every person in the

Neighborhood of Make-Believe is working together to provide food for the citizens of Northwood. Even Daniel plants a can of vegetable soup, hoping that it will grow additional cans of vegetable soup to be able to give to Northwood. In this episode, in particular, viewers see the true meaning of action across an entire community. As internal social control grows within a community, even the youngest or most vulnerable members of a community can provide for the internal social efforts which contribute to collective efficacy (Hoffman, 2003; Souza, 2014). Daniel Striped Tiger, one of the youngest members of the Neighborhood of Make-Believe is an example of that. He wants so much to contribute to the effort in any way that he can. After learning that his cans will not grow as the many plants have grown, he tells his neighbors that he will, instead, give of his friendship to the citizens of Northwood.

In the final episode of the arc (Rogers & Lally, 1984e), Lady Aberlin, Bob Dog, and Handyman Negri are packaging food in the Neighborhood of Make-Believe to send to Northwood when Lady Aberlin says, "I'd like to meet those people from Northwood. They're really smart to want us to send seeds and plants so they can grow their own food." King Friday calls everyone to the castle and congratulates and thanks them for their effort in supporting Northwood.

In working toward a goal for those outside of their neighborhood, the citizens of the Neighborhood of Make-Believe have not only provided help and service but have created opportunities for internal capacity-building for another community. As collective efficacy strengthens, these elements have the power to affect other like communities and plant seeds of collective efficacy across other communities, as well (Sampson, 1998; Swatt et al., 2013). Across this story arc, viewers see examples of strong community attachment, kinship/friendship ties in working together to protect and help others, informal social control in the guarding of community members' gardens, and true collective efficacy in the solidarity across citizens to provide for their own community and a neighboring community. The citizens of the Neighborhood of Make-Believe exhibit a strong belief in the power of their collective effort to protect their community and to provide for the needs of others (Bandura, 2000).

Deviance and Anger in the Neighborhood of Make-Believe

In 1995, *Mister Rogers' Neighborhood* devoted a week to understanding and managing mad feelings for children. These episodes included Mister Rogers sharing his own ways of managing his anger, such as allowing his emotion to come through the songs he would play on the piano. The week paid special care to show viewers how to deal with anger in ways that do not hurt ourselves or anyone else. The week's story arc within the Neighborhood of Make-Believe echoed this theme. In the first episode (Rogers & Walsh, 1995a), the viewers see that Lady Elaine is struggling to draw Grandpere's Tower and is getting progressively angrier with every attempt. Her area is littered with ill-fated attempts to draw, and she is openly frustrated with her inability to draw well. As she gets angrier, she gets more vocal about that anger. Others in the Neighborhood, including Henrietta, express that they are afraid of Lady Elaine's anger. Finally, Lady Elaine retreats to the top of her home, the Museum-Go-Round, where she proceeds to spin around and around with increasing speed. This adds to the fear for the citizens of the Neighborhood of Make-Believe, who wonder what she might do next. As Lady Elaine gets angrier, those close to her in the Neighborhood fear that she may do something harmful to herself or others as a response to her anger. Their fear is based on previous incidents of incivility and mistrust between the community and Lady Elaine when she has reacted to her anger and strong feelings in ways that have caused feelings of discomfort for the citizens of the Neighborhood of Make-Believe.

As the second episode of this week (Rogers & Walsh, 1995b) ventures to the Neighborhood of Make-Believe, viewers find Queen Sara and Bob Troll talking about how Lady Elaine will not listen to anyone in the Neighborhood about her anger. Fearing that there could be an act of personal violence within the Neighborhood, the citizens begin to collectively work to mitigate the effects on the community through activating their collective efficacy (Sampson et al., 1997). Bob Troll, in wanting to help his neighbor, draws a beautiful picture of Grandpere's Tower for Lady Elaine. He and Mayor Maggie, who is visiting from neighboring Westwood in an attempt to help the Neighborhood to manage Lady Elaine's behavior, take the drawing to Lady Elaine and try to reason with her. The drawing makes her even angrier. Instead of talking about her feelings and relying on her neighbors and community for the help they are trying to provide, Lady Elaine uses her boomerang-toomerang-zoomerang (a magical boomerang) to turn Grandpere's Tower upside down. Everyone becomes more upset by this behavior, and Mayor Maggie expresses to the citizens of the Neighborhood of Make-Believe that, "Something must be done!" As the third episode opens (Rogers & Walsh, 1995c), Mayor Maggie from Westwood and King Friday are talking together about what can be done with Lady Elaine. She brings Assistant Mayor Aber from Westwood to help with Grandpere's needs, showing community solidarity and friendship to community members who have been affected by the act. King Friday expresses, "This unruly behavior must be curtailed!" and tells Mayor Maggie that he will talk with Lady Elaine. When King Friday intervenes, as the "government" official of the Neighborhood of Make-Believe, he recognizes and joins in the informal social control response that other neighbors had taken to promote order and safety within the community (Sampson et al., 1997). Instead of activating a formal response that would supersede the informal response of the neighbors, King Friday joins with other community members in planning to talk with Lady Elaine about her behavior. However, when King Friday arrives to talk with Lady Elaine and she will not talk with him, he responds with, "It looks like I might need to muster an army!" While King Friday did not "muster an army," had he followed through with this decree, the informal social control of the community would have been instantly replaced with external action. While the external action may have increased the protection of the Neighborhood, it would not have contributed to the collective efficacy that is a strong symbol of the Neighborhood of Make-Believe (Sampson et al., 1997).

As this episode continues, Ana Platypus is crying and afraid of what is happening in the Neighborhood of Make-Believe. When talking with Assistant Mayor Aber, she says, "she (Lady Elaine) is our neighbor, what if she would do it to us?" To this, Assistant Mayor Aber responds, "All of the grownups here and in Westwood are going to keep trying to help." Aber reinforces the strong informal social control and kinship ties of the neighborhood to Ana by telling her that everyone in her own community and a neighboring community is working together to help. This is especially important for Ana, who as a child, feels helpless in this situation. While she does not recognize the collective efficacy within this setting, she recognizes that she is safe within her community because of the shared action they take (Sampson et al., 1997).

The fourth episode of the arc (Rogers & Walsh, 1995d) shows the neighbors still working together to find a solution for Lady Elaine's anger and subsequent behavior. King Friday and Lady Aberlin talk about Lady Elaine, and Lady Aberlin asks, "Do you suppose she would listen if she could get over the mad that she feels?" To this thought, Lady Aberlin asks Daniel to borrow his pounding board to see if Lady Elaine could use it to let go of her anger—and do something else with her mad feelings. At this time, a long-time friend of Lady Elaine's, Betty Okonak Templeton comes to visit to see if she can help her. Bringing flour, oil, and salt to make play clay that Lady Elaine can use to pound and build, Betty convinces Lady Elaine to accept help from her neighbors in managing her anger. As Mister Rogers finishes the week of the program devoted to mad feelings (Rogers & Walsh, 1995e), Lady Elaine and Betty Okonak Templeton continue to spend time together in hopes that they can manage Lady Elaine's anger and restore order to the Neighborhood of Make-Believe. As Daniel and Lady Aberlin continue to work together, King Friday arrives and summons Lady Elaine to tell her that her "neighbors are worried about her" and she admits that she is worried about herself, too—and that she is very upset. She presents a clay tower that she has created for the Neighborhood of Make

Believe as an apology and uses her boomerang-toomerang-zoomerang to turn Grandpere's Tower right. The successful restoration to peace and calm within the Neighborhood of Make-Believe would not have been possible without the collective action of the many citizens of the Neighborhood. The community worked together to support one another and to respond to the incivility of one of their community members. They self-policed their community in a way that transcends the individual need for protection.

Conclusion

Across both of these story arcs, viewers see examples of the many factors associated with collective efficacy: group dynamics, kinship/friendship, attachment to the community, and informal social control. While the typical viewers of *Mister Rogers' Neighborhood*, three- to five-year-old children, certainly could not identify these components, they learned valuable lessons concerning community action, working together, and care for others. The examples of communities coming together to protect and help others are indicators of collective efficacy, which "is an important neighborhood-level process that functions as an intermediary between neighborhood conditions and disorder" (Swatt et al., 2013, p. 2). It is through these strong social networks that disorder and violence are prevented and values of communal action and harmony are promoted (Swatt et al., 2013). These concepts are foundational for children, who will play an increasingly more active role in the informal social control and collective efficacy of their communities and neighborhoods. Showing children the importance of community and the contribution each person makes to the collective becomes the building blocks of productive neighborhoods and future adults who value collective efficacy in building strong communities.

Discussion Questions

1. As the meaning of "community" continues to evolve due to a more global world, what are the implications on collective efficacy for groups whose citizens may not be geographically close to one another?
2. What are other possible communal responses to people like the old goat from Northwood who steal or commit other crimes out of necessity?

3. Are there any other children's shows that showcase collective efficacy? Any adult oriented programs? How do these programs contribute to understandings of collective efficacy?

References

Armstrong, T. A., Katz, C. M., & Schnebly, S. M. (2015). The Relationship Between Citizen Perceptions of Collective Efficacy and Neighborhood Violent Crime. *Crime and Delinquency, 6*(1), 121–142.

Bandura, A. (1997). *Self-Efficacy: The Exercise of Control.* New York: Freeman.

Bandura, A. (2000). Exercise of Human Agency Through Collective Efficacy. *American Psychological Society, 9*(3), 75–78.

Hoffman, J. P. (2003). A Contextual Analysis of Differential Association, Social Control, and Strain Theories of Delinquency. *Social Forces, 81*(3), 753–785.

Kasarda, J. D., & Janowitz, M. (1974). Community Attachment in Mass Society. *American Sociological Review, 39*(3), 328–339.

Rogers, F. (2002, May). *Commencement Address.* Dartmouth University.

Rogers, F. (Writer), & Lally, P. (Director). (1984a, November 19). Episode #1536 (Season 15, Episode 11) [TV Series Episode]. In F. Rogers (Executive Producer), *Mister Rogers' Neighborhood.* Family Communications, Inc.

Rogers, F. (Writer), & Lally, P. (Director). (1984b, November 20). Episode #1537 (Season 15, Episode 12) [TV Series Episode]. In F. Rogers (Executive Producer), *Mister Rogers' Neighborhood.* Family Communications, Inc.

Rogers, F. (Writer), & Lally, P. (Director). (1984c, November 21). Episode #1538 (Season 15, Episode 13) [TV Series Episode]. In F. Rogers (Executive Producer), *Mister Rogers' Neighborhood.* Family Communications, Inc.

Rogers, F. (Writer), & Lally, P. (Director). (1984d, November 22). Episode #1539 (Season 15, Episode 14) [TV Series Episode]. In F. Rogers (Executive Producer), *Mister Rogers' Neighborhood.* Family Communications, Inc.

Rogers, F. (Writer), & Lally, P. (Director). (1984e, November 23). Episode #1540 (Season 15, Episode 15) [TV Series Episode]. In F. Rogers (Executive Producer), *Mister Rogers' Neighborhood.* Family Communications, Inc.

Rogers, F. (Writer), & Walsh, B. (Director). (1995a, October 16). Episode #1691 (Season 22, Episode 11) [TV Series Episode]. In F. Rogers (Executive Producer), *Mister Rogers' Neighborhood.* Family Communications, Inc.

Rogers, F. (Writer), & Walsh, B. (Director). (1995b, October 17). Episode #1692 (Season 22, Episode 12) [TV Series Episode]. In F. Rogers (Executive Producer), *Mister Rogers' Neighborhood.* Family Communications, Inc.

Rogers, F. (Writer), & Walsh, B. (Director). (1995c, October 18). Episode #1693 (Season 22, Episode 13) [TV Series Episode]. In F. Rogers (Executive Producer), *Mister Rogers' Neighborhood.* Family Communications, Inc.

Rogers, F. (Writer), & Walsh, B. (Director). (1995d, October 19). Episode #1694 (Season 22, Episode 14) [TV Series Episode]. In F. Rogers (Executive Producer), *Mister Rogers' Neighborhood*. Family Communications, Inc.

Rogers, F. (Writer), & Walsh, B. (Director). (1995e, October 20). Episode #1695 (Season 22, Episode 15) [TV Series Episode]. In F. Rogers (Executive Producer), *Mister Rogers' Neighborhood*. Family Communications, Inc.

Sampson, R. J. (1998). Local Friendship Ties and Community Attachment in Mass Society: A Multilevel Systemic Model. *American Sociological Review, 5*(5), 766–779.

Sampson, R. J., Raudenbush, S. W., & Earls, F. (1997). Neighborhoods and Violent Crime: A Multilevel Study of Collective Efficacy. *Science, 227*(5328), 918–924.

Souza, R. (2014). Collective Efficacy. In T. L. Thompson (Ed.), *SAGE Reference Encyclopedia of Health Communication* (pp. 204–205). Thousand Oaks, CA: SAGE Publications Inc.

Swatt, M. L., Uchida, C. D., Varano, S. P., & Solomon, S. E. (2013). Fear of Crime, Incivilities, and Collective Efficacy in Four Miami Neighborhoods. *Journal of Criminal Justice, 41*, 1–11.

Wickes, R., & Hipp, J. R. (2018). The Spatial and Temporal Dynamics of Neighborhood Informal Social Control and Crime. *Social Forces, 97*(1), 277–308.

Life-Course Theory and *Romance*

12

At the Movies: Representation of Life-Course Criminology and Desistance in Romance Films

Lauren Humby

Idealistic heteronormative notions of love, romance, and relationships dominate movie narratives. Boy meets girl. Boy and girl fall in love. Boy and girl live happily ever after. While this may appear harmless, these films have the potential to deliver powerful rhetoric messages that lead viewers to adopt unhealthy and unrealistic ideas of love and romance. Films depicting love between a sweet, naïve, and innocent heroine and the mysterious, deviant bad boy have been labeled particularly harmful. These movies follow a reverse Cinderella narrative in which the quintessential, criminally inclined bad boy transforms into a law-abiding citizen after he falls in love with the heroine. Since hetero-romantic love is the principal storyline in many of these movies, it is often cited as the reason for the fated bad boy's transformation. While these movies may cultivate and reinforce toxic ideas about love and relationships, this may not be due to a film's misrepresentation, but rather a lack of consideration regarding life-course criminology and desistance.

L. Humby (✉)
University of Southern Queensland, Toowoomba, QLD, Australia
e-mail: lauren.humby@usq.edu.au

© The Author(s) 2021
S. E. Daly (ed.), *Theories of Crime Through Popular Culture*,
https://doi.org/10.1007/978-3-030-54434-8_12

Life-Course Criminology and Desistance

Theories of crime and criminal behavior provide a critical foundation in criminology. They provide knowledge regarding why crime occurs, why it varies, factors that increase or decrease criminality, and the sorts of interventions that could be useful in reducing and preventing crime (Akers, Sellers, & Jennings, 2016; Burke, 2018; Garland, 1990; Hayes & Prenzler, 2019; White, Haines, & Asquith, 2017). For decades, criminological theories focused on identifying why an offender *starts* to commit a crime. The majority of these theories were static and aimed to identify which individual characteristics elicited criminal behavior. They considered criminality to be innate and something that offenders have little to no control over (e.g. Lombroso, 2006 [1876]). Over time, it became evident that human behavior changes according to circumstance and multiple causal factors can influence offending behavior. This finding led to the development of several dynamic theories of crime, including life-course criminology. Adapted from Elder's (1985) life course perspective, life-course criminology recognizes that as individuals age, they experience transitions in life, which can act as turning points and redirect criminal trajectories (Sampson & Laub, 1993; Thornberry, 1997). Research examining transitions over the life course seeks to explain why offenders *start* committing a crime, why they *persist* or continue to commit a crime, and why they *desist* or stop.

Desistance is a fundamental concept within life-course criminology. The concept of desistance has been defined many times in the literature. While the literal meaning of desistance is "to stop," applying this definition to criminality is problematic. No offender commits crime constantly; thus, cessation from offending happens often, albeit temporarily (Maruna, 2001). Criminologists have attempted to quantify the period required to determine desistance; however, this has led to disagreement in the literature. While some suggest one year is sufficient to determine desistance, others suggest that desistance can only be truly measured when an offender dies (Maruna, Immarigeon, & LeBel, 2013; Warr, 1998).

Laub and Sampson (2001) respond to these definitional issues by distinguishing between termination, the time at which criminal activity stops, and desistance, the process that causes and supports the termination. Defining desistance as a process acknowledges that offenders can reoffend and desist simultaneously by reducing the frequency, severity, and variety of offenses (Le Blanc & Loeber, 1998). There has been much research dedicated to identifying the factors that contribute to desistance. Although theories within life-course criminology are founded on the same basic assumptions, "their theoretical constructs vary" (Center for Criminology and Public Policy Research [CCPPR], 2003, p. 104). As such, there is not one universally accepted theory of life-course criminology or desistance (CCPPR, 2003). Most theories, however, fit into one of the three broad categories: ontogenetic, sociogenetic, and narrative theories. Ontogenetic theories are maturational theories of crime which posit that age predicts criminality. Sociogenetic theories expand on this idea, however suggest that it is not age itself that increases the likelihood of criminal behaviour, but rather the social processes associated with age. Narrative theories acknowledge the impact of age and social processes, however, posit that a cognitive shift from offender to non-offender is needed for desistance.

Ontogenetic Theories

The age-crime curve is a well-known and consistently demonstrated phenomenon widely accepted by criminologists. Longitudinal studies of crime over the life course consistently show that criminal behavior peaks in adolescence and declines with age (Glueck & Glueck, 1930, 1937, 1950; Quetelet 1984 [1831]). One of the first to examine the relationship between age and crime was Adolphe Quetelet who found that crime peaked for men in their late teens to mid-twenties and declined thereafter. He argued that "with age [a] man's physical strength and passions develop" and "their energy afterwards diminishes" (Quetelet 1984 [1831], pp. 54–56).

Glueck and Glueck (1937) also studied the effect of age on crime, however, unsatisfied that age could be considered the only factor, developed a theory of maturational reform, which posits that as individuals age they mature, physically, psychologically, and socially. Subsequent research on desistance has made numerous attempts to elaborate on the maturational theory of desistance by dissecting the processes of maturation to identify which contributed to a reduction in crime.

Sociogenetic Theories

Perhaps the most notable contemporary study to dissect the processes of maturation is that of Sampson and Laub (1993, 2009). Their age-graded life-course theory is a sociogenetic theory which suggests that "individual behavior is mediated over time through interactions with age-graded institutions" (Laub, Sampson, & Sweeten, 2006). It hypothesizes that strong attachments to others and commitments to conventional social institutions (e.g. school, family, work, marriage) produce social capital, which reduces offending behavior due to an individual's desire to maintain these relationships (Hirschi, 1969; Matza, 1964; Sampson & Laub, 1993).

Therefore, those who do not develop social bonds are more likely to participate in the crime, while those who invest in social institutions and build prosocial relationships are less prone to criminal behavior. Sociogenetic theories also suggest that relationships with others reduce crime and deviancy as a result of the informal social controls they provide (Hirschi, 1969; Matza, 1964; Sampson & Laub, 1993). While sociogenetic theories explain how biological and social processes impact desistance, they fail to recognize psychological factors.

Narrative Theories

Maruna's (2001) narrative theory of desistance addresses this gap by explaining crime and criminal behavior through individual differences in cognitive processes. Maruna (2001) claims an offender's self-identity, or narrative, impacts desistance more than age or environmental factors associated with age. Through an analysis of autobiographical narratives of 20 active offenders (persisters) and 30 desisting offenders, Maruna found that offender narratives could predict the likelihood of future offending behavior. The self-constructed stories of those who persisted with crime followed a condemnation script in which offenders described themselves as victims of circumstance. The narratives of desisters, on the other hand, followed a redemption script, in which they constructed a story to redeem themselves of their criminal past and alluded to a meaningful future. Since Maruna's (2001) initial research, additional studies have supported his theory and have shown that desistance is often precipitated by a cognitive shift, transformation or turning point that involves a reshaping of the individual's identity that is in line with a conventional lifestyle (Giordano, Cernkovich, & Rudolph, 2002; Laub & Sampson, 2001; LeBel, Burnett, Maruna, & Bushway, 2008; Rumgay, 2004).

The Power of Film

Movies are a popular medium in today's society. They are not only a form of entertainment and escapism, but also educational (Walt Disney, 1948, as cited in Van Riper, 2014). While this can be beneficial, movies also have the potential to distort our perceptions and realities. One genre that is often criticized for cultivating and endorsing rhetoric beliefs, attitudes, and behaviors is the teen romance genre. Research suggests that behind their light-hearted and fluffy romantic narratives lie powerful archetypes that engender unrealistic expectations and serve to cultivate and reinforce popular cultural myths such as "love at first sight," "love conquers all," and "love is all you need" (Chia & Gunther, 2006; Galician, 2004; Galloway, Engstrom, & Emmers-Sommer, 2015; Hefner & Wilson, 2013; Holmes, 2007; Johnson, 2007; Kile, 1992; Martin & Kazyak, 2009; Parry, 2018, Tanner, Haddock, Zimmerman, & Lund, 2003; Todd, 2013; Ward & Friedman, 2006). Content analyses show that many romance films utilize reverse Cinderella rescue narratives, in which the heroine saves the stereotypical bad boy from a future life of crime. Rescue narratives such as these are often criticized for their propensity to romanticize aggressive and criminal behavior. It is suggested that they reinforce the idea that "love transforms and elevates people to better versions of themselves" (Zwier, 2012, p. 42) and "any problems of character, misunderstandings or incompatible goals" can be resolved through love (Hubbard, 1985, p. 122; see also Franiuk & Scherr, 2013; Martin & Kazyak, 2009; Parry, 2018).

Film Summaries

Step Up follows the life of Tyler Gage, a street kid who gets into trouble trespassing with his friends and damaging property of the Maryland School of Arts. When caught by a security guard, Tyler receives 200 hours of community service which he has to serve by cleaning the Maryland School of Arts every day after school. While doing his community service, Tyler meets Nora, a dance student who is preparing for her senior showcase. After Nora's dance partner suffers from a sprained ankle, Nora must find a new partner for her showcase. After no suitable dance partner is found in the school, Tyler offers to help. Although Nora is skeptical at first, she eventually accepts Tyler's help. Through the course of the movie, Tyler and Nora grow closer, and Tyler begins to spend more time with Nora than with his deviant friends Mac and Skinny. By the end of the movie, Tyler performs with Nora and is accepted into the Maryland School of Arts as a transfer student. Tyler and Nora celebrate with a kiss (Feig, Gibgot, Shankman, Wachsberger, & Fletcher, 2006).

A Walk to Remember tells the similar story of Landon Carter, a popular and rebellious, 17-year-old senior, who receives community service after a prank goes wrong and a fellow student is seriously injured. While fulfilling his community service, Landon gets to know Jamie, the town preacher's daughter and social outcast who spends her time helping others. While Landon and his friends initially ridicule Jamie, as Landon spends more time with Jamie as a result of his community service, he begins to fall for her which culminates in an off-script kiss in the school play. Their kiss leads to an unlikely love that grows as Landon helps Jamie tick off her bucket list. Then, Jamie shocks Landon by telling him she has leukemia and has stopped responding to treatments. Although heartbroken by the news and upset that Jamie had lied by omission, Landon supports her through her treatment. The two are wed and soon after Jamie passes away. In the final scenes of the film, Landon is accepted into medical school (Di Novi & Lowry, 2002).

Representations of Life-Course Criminology in Romance Films

While these films may appear to promote unrealistic ideas about the transformational power of love, further analysis of these films through the lens of life-course criminology reveals that these films do not necessarily cultivate and reinforce unrealistic ideas about love and romance. For decades, research has examined whether movie depictions of crime and violence influence crime rates, with many finding a positive link between deviant behavior and media exposure (Anderson et al., 2003; Bandura, Ross, & Ross, 1961; Berkowitz, Corwin, & Heironimus, 1963; Lövaas, 1961). While it has been suggested that crime and violence are gratuitously depicted in the film, particularly those targeted toward adolescents (Coyne, Callister, & Robinson, 2010), from a criminological point of view, films that feature male teens engaging in crime and deviancy are more likely to be an accurate representation of teen culture than those that do not.

Empirical data on crime consistently shows an age-crime curve, which suggests offending behavior peaks for young men between the ages of 15 and 19 (Farrington, 1986; Sampson & Laub, 2003). While it could (and has) be argued that films, such as *Step Up* and *A Walk to Remember*, romanticize crime and deviancy, it is also possible to argue that they provide a unique opportunity to educate adolescents on the risk and protective factors associated with offending behavior and the potential consequences of engaging in crime. There are numerous studies to suggest that teens utilize movies as a source of information and use them to guide their behavior in the real world (Bandura et al., 1961; Gerbner, Gross, Morgan, & Signorielli, 1986).

While cultivation and observational learning theories have been primarily used to support the idea that viewers acquire unrealistic and unhealthy views of love portrayed in movies (e.g. Parry, 2018; Roach, 2016; Ward & Friedman, 2006), they can also be used to argue that audiences can learn vicariously through the characters and their situations. For example, both Tyler and Landon in *Step Up* and *A Walk to Remember*, respectively, are punished for their deviant and criminal behavior, with both receiving community service. Since both Tyler and Landon are punished, it is unlikely that adolescent viewers would idealize their criminal and deviant behavior. It is possible that they could learn from Tyler and Landon, and young offenders or those at risk of offending could begin their desistance process.

While it is gratuitous to assume that the presence of a romantic relationship is responsible for the transformation of a rebellious bad boy, desistance research has shown that romantic relationships can indirectly trigger the desistance process through their tendency to disrupt routine activities, discourage negative peer associations, and foster new social networks (Akers et al., 2016; Horney, Osgood, & Marshall, 1995; Knight & West, 1975; Laub, Nagin, & Sampson, 1998; Sampson & Laub, 1990, 1993, 2003; Warr, 1998). Scholars refer to this effect as "knifing off," in which new life transitions into different environments can create turning points and lead to new noncriminal life trajectories (Sampson & Laub, 1993).

While sanctions may be the primary cause of knifing off, research has found that creating strong social ties to conventional institutions can have a similar effect. Relationships that are perceived to be of high value become a new priority and individuals begin to restructure their activities in favor of these new relationships, which, in turn, reduces the time available to spend with delinquent peers (Simons et al., 2002; Theobald, Farrington, & Piquero, 2019; Warr, 1998). Horney Osgood and Marshall (1995, p. 671) liken the development of social ties to an investment process. The more an individual invests in conventional activities, the more they want to preserve their place in society, and the less likely they are to engage in deviance.

Romantic relationships have also been found to serve as an agent of informal monitoring which, in turn, fosters desistance. Significant others can play the role of a capable guardian which encourages conformist behavior (Laub & Sampson, 2009; Osgood & Lee, 1993). While community service operates as the initial disruption to Tyler and Landon's routine activities in the movies *Step Up* and *A Walk to Remember*, their interest and investment in their relationships with Nora and Jamie, respectively, encourage them to restructure their routine activities reducing the time spent with their deviant peers. Tyler (*Step Up*) commits to spending his free time rehearsing with Nora, which also leads to the development of additional prosocial relationships with other students, while Landon (*A Walk to Remember*) rejects his deviant friends in favor of altruistic activities and spending time with Jamie.

While disruption to routine activities and new prosocial relationships can encourage offenders to desist, it is still necessary for individuals to make a conscious decision to commit to change and rewrite their self-narrative (Maruna, 2001). Research found that offenders who have an optimist outlook and a sense of agency are significantly more likely to desist than offenders who have a fatalistic attitude (Giordano et al., 2002; Maruna, 2001).

One of the ways in which self-narratives have been found to change is through romantic relationships (Mattingly, Lewandowski Jr., & McIntyre, 2014). Research has shown that motivation to be romantically involved with a partner is sufficient to promote individuals to integrate new positive attributes of the partner into their own self-concept (Slotter & Gardner, 2009, 2012). When entering close relationships, the self becomes intertwined with a romantic partner, as each individual merges aspects of the other into their own self-concept and they begin to think of a collective unit rather than individualistically (Agnew & Etcheverry, 2006; Aron & Aron, 1986; Aron, Aron, Tudor, & Nelson, 1991; Slotter & Gardner, 2012).

Psychological research refers to this as the Michelangelo phenomenon, whereby romantic partners influence, or sculpt, each other over time toward what they consider to be their ideal selves. They do this by affirming a partner's positive attributes and rejecting their negative qualities (Mattingly et al., 2014). In *A Walk to Remember*, Landon's change in self-narrative is evident when he creates a list of future goals "examine moon rock, go to college, get into medical school." After his mother challenges his goals citing "you are going to have to work really hard," Landon responds with "I can do that" and further explains "Jamie has faith in me. She makes me want to be different. Better." It is worth noting, however, that not all relationships result in positive changes to self-concept (Mattingly et al., 2014; Slotter & Gardner, 2012).

Consider, for example, Sandy's transformation in *Grease* from good girl to bad girl. When motivations are strong, individuals may merge undesirable qualities of a partner with their self-concept in the interest of gaining their affections (Slotter & Gardner, 2009, 2012; Slotter & Lucas, 2012). As such, it is not simply love or a relationship that encourages desistance, rather it is the valence of a partner's self-concept that is important (Mattingly et al., 2014). In the movie *Step Up*, Tyler also experiences identity transformation. At the beginning of the movie, Tyler has a fatalistic outlook, a characteristic of persisters (Maruna, 2001). After Nora asks Tyler what he wants, Tyler responds:

For me, it's just better not to want anything. That way, if it goes away or doesn't happen, you know, it just doesn't matter.

However, a significant event, namely, Skinny's death, acts as a turning point for Tyler who, with the help of his friend Mac, recognizes that his deviant and criminal past is "a bunch of bull" after which, he creates a new self-narrative that sees him pursue his dream of dancing.

Conclusion

Much research has suggested that romance films distort understanding and experiences of love, romance, and relationships. Reverse Cinderella rescue narratives have been identified as deceptive, as they appear to promote the idea that love is magical and transformative. This chapter aimed to provide new considerations on romance films by examining the movies *Step Up* and *A Walk to Remember* through a life-course criminological perspective. Upon consideration, it is evident that such films do not necessarily cultivate and reinforce the common cultural myths of "love is all you need," "love conquers all," and "the love of a good woman." Rather, it is perhaps a lack of consideration on the part of the audience that is responsible for the espoused idealistic notions. Desistance is a relatively new concept, and as such, it is understandable that there is a lack of knowledge regarding its processes. Future research should consider examining perceptions of desistance to assess whether a greater understanding of the desistance process impacts viewers' ideas about common romantic myths presented in reverse Cinderella narratives.

Discussion Questions

1. Identify the three broad categories of life course and desistance theories and explain how each contributes to the desistance process. Is there one theory that is more important to the desistance process?
2. Identify other popular films that depict reverse Cinderella rescue narratives. How do these movies depict the desistance process? Are they an accurate representation of life-course criminology and desistance?
3. How do reverse Cinderella narratives, in which a woman rescues a man (e.g. *A Walk to Remember*) compare with traditional Cinderella narratives, where the man rescues the women (e.g. *The Last Song*), in their representations of the desistance process.

References

Agnew, C. R., & Etcheverry, P. E. (2006). Cognitive Interdependence: Considering Self-in-Relationship. In K. D. Vohs & E. J. Finkel (Eds.), *Self and Relationships: Connecting Intrapersonal and Interpersonal Processes* (pp. 274–293). New York, NY: Guilford Press.

Akers, R. L., Sellers, C. S., & Jennings, W. G. (2016). *Criminological Theories: Introduction, Evaluation & Application* (7th ed.). Oxford University Press.

Anderson, C. A., Berkowitz, L., Donnerstein, E., Huesmann, R. L., Johnson, J., & Linz, D. (2003). The Influence of Media Violence on Youth. *Psychological Science in the Public Interest, 4*, 81–110.

Aron, A., & Aron, E. N. (1986). *Love and the Expansion of Self: Understanding Attraction and Satisfaction*. Washington, DC: Hemisphere Publishing Corp.

Aron, A., Aron, E., Tudor, M., & Nelson, G. (1991). Close Relationships as Including Other in the Self. *Journal of Personality and Social Psychology, 60*, 241–253.

Bandura, A., Ross, D., & Ross, S. A. (1961). Transmission of Aggression Through Imitation of Aggressive Models. *Journal of Abnormal and Social Psychology, 63*(3), 575–582.

Berkowitz, L., Corwin, R., & Heironimus, M. (1963). Film Violence and Subsequent Aggressive Tendencies. *Public Opinion Quarterly, 27*(2), 217–229.

Burke, R. H. (2018). *An Introduction to Criminological Theory* (5th ed.). Routledge.

Center for Criminology and Public Policy Research. (2003). 2003 Annual Report to the Florida Department of Education: Juvenile Justice Educational Enhancement Program. Retrieved from http://criminology.fsu.edu/wp-content/uploads/Crime-in-the-life-course-ch-7-2003-annual-report.pdf

Chia, S. C., & Gunther, A. C. (2006). How Media Contribute to Misperceptions of Social Norms About Sex. *Mass Communication & Society, 9*(3), 301–320.

Coyne, S. M., Callister, M., & Robinson, T. (2010). Yes, Another Teen Movie: Three Decades of Physical Violence in Films Aimed at Adolescents. *Journal of Children and Media, 4*(4), 387–401.

Di Novi, D., Lowry, H. (Producers), & Shankman, A. (Director). (2002). *A Walk to Remember* [Motion Picture]. USA: Warner Bros.

Elder, G. H. (Ed.). (1985). *Life Course Dynamics: Trajectories and Transitions, 1968–1980*. Ithaca, NY: Cornell University Press.

Farrington, D. (1986). Age and Crime. *Crime and Justice, 7*, 189–250.

Feig, E., Gibgot, J., Shankman, A., Wachsberger, P. (Producers), & Fletcher, A. (Director). (2006). *Step Up* [Motion Picture]. USA: Summit Entertainment.

Franiuk, R., & Scherr, S. (2013). The Lion Fell in Love with the Lamb: Gender, Violence, and Vampires. *Feminist Media Studies, 13*(1), 14–28.

Galician, M. L. (2004). *Sex, Love, and Romance in the Mass Media: Analysis and Criticism of Unrealistic Portrayals and Their Influence*. New York: Routledge.

Galloway, L., Engstrom, E., & Emmers-Sommer, T. M. (2015). Does Movie Viewing Cultivate Young People's Unrealistic Expectations About Love and Marriage? *Marriage & Family Review, 51*(8), 687–712.

Garland, D. (1990). *Punishment and Modern Society*. Chicago: University of Chicago Press.

Gerbner, G., Gross, L., Morgan, M., & Signorielli, N. (1986). Living with Television: The Dynamics of the Cultivation Process. *Perspectives on Media Effects*, 17–40.

Giordano, P. C., Cernkovich, S. A., & Rudolph, J. L. (2002). Gender, Crime, and Desistance: Toward a Theory of Cognitive Transformation. *American Journal of Sociology, 107*(4), 990–1064.

Glueck, S., & Glueck, E. (1950). *Unraveling Juvenile Delinquency*. Cambridge, MA: Harvard University Press.

Glueck, S., & Glueck, E. T. (1930). *500 Criminal Careers*. New York: A.A. Knopf.

Glueck, S., & Glueck, E. T. (1937). *Later Criminal Careers* (Vol. 1). New York: Commonwealth Fund.

Hayes, H., & Prenzler, T. P. (2019). *An Introduction to Crime and Criminology* (5th ed.). Melbourne: Pearson Australia.

Hefner, V., & Wilson, B. J. (2013). From Love at First Sight to Soul Mate: The Influence of Romantic Ideals in Popular Films on Young People's Beliefs About Relationships. *Communication Monographs, 80*(2), 150–175.

Hirschi, T. (1969). *Causes of Delinquency*. Berkeley, CA: University of California Press.

Holmes, B. M. (2007). In Search of My "One and Only": Romance-Oriented Media and Beliefs in Romantic Relationship Destiny. *Electronic Journal of Communication, 17*(3), 1–23.

Horney, J., Osgood, D. W., & Marshall, I. H. (1995). Criminal Careers in the Short-Term: Intra-Individual Variability in Crime and Its Relation to Local Life Circumstances. *American Sociological Review, 60*, 655–673.

Hubbard, R. C. (1985). Relationship Styles in Popular Romance Novels, 1950 to 1983. *Communication Quarterly, 33*(2), 113–125.

Johnson, K. A. (2007). Unrealistic Portrayals of Sex, Love, and Romance in Popular Wedding Films. In M. L. Galician & D. L. Merskin (Eds.), *Critical Thinking About Sex, Love, and Romance in the Mass Media* (pp. 355–366). Mahwah, NJ: Lawrence Erlbaum Associates.

Kile, C. (1992). Endless Love Will Keep Us Together: The Myth of Romantic Love and Contemporary Popular Movie Love Themes. *Popular Culture. An Introductory Text*, 149–166.

Knight, B. J., & West, D. J. (1975). Temporary and Continuing Delinquents. *British Journal of Criminology, 15*, 43–50.

Laub, J. H., Nagin, D. S., & Sampson, R. J. (1998). Trajectories of Change in Criminal Offending: Good Marriages and the Desistance Process. *American Sociological Review, 63*(2), 225–238.

Laub, J. H., & Sampson, R. J. (2001). Understanding Desistance from Crime. *Crime and Justice, 28*, 1–69.

Laub, J. H., & Sampson, R. J. (2009). *Shared Beginnings, Divergent Lives*. Cambridge: Harvard University Press.

Laub, J. H., Sampson, R. J., & Sweeten, G. A. (2006). Assessing Sampson and Laub's Life-Course Theory of Crime. In F. T. Cullen, J. P. Wright, & K. R. Blevins (Eds.), *Taking Stock: The Status of Criminological Theory* (pp. 313–333). Transaction Publishers.

Le Blanc, M., & Loeber, R. (1998). Developmental Criminology Updated. *Crime and Justice, 23*, 115–198.

LeBel, T. P., Burnett, R., Maruna, S., & Bushway, S. (2008). The 'Chicken and Egg' of Subjective and Social Factors in Desistance from Crime. *European Journal of Criminology, 5*(2), 131–159.

Lombroso, C. (2006 [1876]). *Criminal Man*. Duke University Press.

Lövaas, O. I. (1961). Effect of Exposure to Symbolic Aggression on Aggressive Behavior. *Child Development*, 37–44.

Martin, K. A., & Kazyak, E. (2009). Hetero-Romantic Love and Heterosexiness in Children's G-Rated Films. *Gender & Society, 23*(3), 315–336.

Maruna, S. (2001). *Making Good: How Ex-Convicts Reform and Rebuild Their Lives*. Washington, DC: American Psychological Association.

Maruna, S., Immarigeon, R., & LeBel, T. P. (2013). Ex-Offender Reintegration: Theory and Practice. In S. Maruna & R. Immarigeon (Eds.), *After Crime and Punishment* (pp. 3–26). Cullompton, UK: Willan Publishing.

Mattingly, B. A., Lewandowski Jr., G. W., & McIntyre, K. P. (2014). "You Make Me a Better/Worse Person": A Two-Dimensional Model of Relationship Self-Change. *Personal Relationships, 21*, 176–190.

Matza, D. (1964). *Delinquency and Drift.* New York: Wiley.

Osgood, D. W., & Lee, H. (1993). Leisure Activities, Age, and Adult Roles Across the Lifespan. *Society and Leisure, 16*(1), 181–208.

Parry, G. (2018). Tainted Love: The Troubling Messages of Big-Screen Romance. *Screen Education, 90*, 58.

Quetelet, A. (1984). *Research on the Propensity for Crime at Different Ages* (S. Sylvester, Trans.). Cincinnati, OH: Anderson.

Roach, C. M. (2016). *Happily Ever After: The Romance Story in Popular Culture.* Indiana: University Press.

Rumgay, J. (2004). Scripts for Safer Survival: Pathways Out of Female Crime. *The Howard Journal of Criminal Justice, 43*(4), 405–419.

Sampson, R. J., & Laub, J. H. (1990). Crime and Deviance Over the Life Course: The Salience of Adult Social Bonds. *American Sociological Review, 55*(5), 609–627.

Sampson, R. J., & Laub, J. H. (1993). *Crime in the Making: Pathways and Turning Points Through Life.* Cambridge, MA: Harvard University Press.

Sampson, R. J., & Laub, J. H. (2003). Life-Course Desisters? Trajectories of Crime Among Delinquent Boys Followed to Age 70. *Criminology, 41*(3), 555–592.

Simons, R. L., Stewart, E., Gordon, L. C., Conger, R. D., & Elder Jr, G. H. (2002). A Test of Life-Course Explanations for Stability and Change in Antisocial Behavior from Adolescence to Young Adulthood. *Criminology, 40*(2), 401–434.

Slotter, E. B., & Gardner, W. L. (2009). Where Do You End and I Begin? Evidence for Anticipatory, Motivated Self–Other Integration Between Relationship Partners. *Journal of Personality and Social Psychology, 96*(6), 1137.

Slotter, E. B., & Gardner, W. L. (2012). The Dangers of Dating the Bad Boy (or Girl): When Does Romantic Desire Encourage Us to Take on the Negative Qualities of Potential Partners? *Journal of Experimental Social Psychology, 48*, 1173–1178.

Slotter, E., & Lucas, G. (2012). Validating a Measure of Self and Partner Change in Romantic Relationships: The Perceived Change in Relationships Scale. *Self and Identity, 12*(2), 177–185.

Tanner, L. R., Haddock, S. A., Zimmerman, T. S., & Lund, L. K. (2003). Images of Couples and Families in Disney Feature-Length Animated Films. *The American Journal of Family Therapy, 31*(5), 355–373.

Theobald, D, Farrington, D. P., & Piquero, A. R. (2019). The Impact of Changes in Family Situations on Persistence and Desistance from Crime. In D.P. Farrington, L. Kazemian & A.R. Piquero (Eds.), *The Oxford Handbook on Developmental and Life-Course Criminology* (pp. 475-494). New York: Oxford University Press.

Thornberry, T. P. (Ed.). (1997). *Advances in Criminological Theory: Vol. 7. Developmental Theories of Crime and Delinquency.* New Brunswick, NJ: Transaction Publishers.

Todd, E. (2013). *Passionate Love and Popular Cinema: Romance and Film Genre.* UK: Springer.

Van Riper, A. B. (Ed.). (2014). *Learning from Mickey, Donald and Walt: Essays on Disney's Edutainment Films.* North Carolina: McFarland.

Ward, L. M., & Friedman, K. (2006). Using TV as a Guide: Associations Between Television Viewing and Adolescents' Sexual Attitudes and Behaviour. *Journal of Research on Adolescence, 16,* 133–156.

Warr, M. (1998). Life-Course Transitions and Desistance from Crime. *Criminology, 36*(2), 183–216.

White, R. D., Haines, F., & Asquith, N. L. (2017). *Crime and Criminology.* Melbourne, VIC: Oxford University Press.

Zwier, A. J. (2012). *Just Another Teen Movie: Analyzing Portrayals of Teenage Romantic Relationships Across a Decade of Top-Grossing Teen Films.* Doctoral dissertation, Colorado State University. Libraries.

Labeling Theory and *Joker*

13

"Could You Introduce Me as Joker?": An Application of Labeling Theory to Explain the Creation of the Clown Prince of Crime

Shon M. Reed and Breanna Boppre

The 2019 film, *Joker*, provides an intense and moving backstory of the development of the popular DC comic book villain, the Joker. The film has since become the highest-grossing R-rated movie of all time and was the first to top $1 billion at the worldwide box office. *Joker* recently won two Golden Globe awards for Joaquin Phoenix's role as the main character, as well as the musical score, and has since received numerous other awards and nominations.

Few films in recent years, particularly comic book-related, have invoked such strong reactions as *Joker* (2019). Phoenix lost over 50 pounds for the role and gave an outstanding performance. Additionally, and uncommon to comic book films, the R-rating allowed for graphic emotional and physical scenes throughout the film, such that some have even cautioned that the film's portrayal of the Joker might incite others to commit violence.

Acting performance and societal controversy aside, *Joker* excited fans as it offered another origin story for the Clown Prince of Crime, a character whose origin is often debated. In this origin story, we see a protagonist named Arthur Fleck face deviant societal labels and stigmatization due to his mental health and profession.

S. M. Reed (✉)
University of Nevada, Las Vegas, Las Vegas, NV, USA
e-mail: Shon.reed@unlv.edu

B. Boppre
Wichita State University, Wichita, KS, USA
e-mail: Breanna.boppre@wichita.edu

© The Author(s) 2021
S. E. Daly (ed.), *Theories of Crime Through Popular Culture*,
https://doi.org/10.1007/978-3-030-54434-8_13

Following a chain of events that occur after Arthur starts committing violent crime, we see the character internalize these labels and become the Joker.

This chapter will apply Howard Becker's labeling theory (1963) to the *Joker* film. First, we provide a brief overview of the theory. Next, we discuss important scenes and apply labeling theory as an explanation for the development of Joker. Finally, we end with a discussion of our application and implications. We encourage readers to watch the film before starting this chapter.

Becker's Labeling Theory

Becker's labeling theory (1963) is a product of his graduate education as well as his life experiences. Being a student of the Chicago School of Sociology, Becker was inspired by the interpretive paradigm of Sociology, which emphasizes that what is deemed "reality" through social construction becomes real in its consequences (Thomas & Swaine Thomas, 1928). Becker relates his theoretical ideas to early anthropological work conducted by Malinowski (1926). In his studies of the native peoples of Trobriand Islands, Malinowski notes an incident when a young man commits suicide due to the societal repercussions of an affair with his cousin. Incestual relationships were not uncommon within this population, yet the social stigma attached to the affair was too much for the boy to handle. Becker associates this incident with the ways that society labels certain people and individuals as "deviant" within modern society (Becker, 1963). It was not the incident itself that guided the boy's behavior, but rather the social label and stigma associated with it.

For most of his life, and throughout his graduate career, Becker was a pianist that played at many locations both in and around Chicago, Illinois. According to Becker (1963), musicians are often seen as an "outcast" culture as they do not conform to the traditional Western ideals of mainstream employment. When he later interviewed his fellow musicians, many of them noted that they felt like they were separated from their audiences and the rest of the world (Becker, 1963). Being labeled as societal outcasts allowed these musicians to form their own culture where support was fostered from others who shared similar experiences and values.

During his interviews with individuals who used marijuana, Becker noted that a similar subculture occurred where the users were seen as "deadbeats" or "deviants" by society. Similar to musicians, these marijuana users began to associate with each other more frequently, as their behavior was not judged in the same way as it was by the general public. Through these narratives, Becker derived his theoretical framework which explains as to why it is that individuals join "deviant" or "outcast" subcultures.

According to Becker (1963), deviancy is any form of behavior which is not accepted by society in general. While many often attribute "deviancy" to illegal or criminal behavior, not all socially "deviant" behaviors are criminalized. Becker (1963) highlights that divergent forms of employment or sexuality may be considered socially deviant as they do not align with mainstream culture. For example, the jazz club musicians of Becker's study were often stigmatized for rejecting traditional forms of employment in favor of performing music.

Becker's theoretical framework of labeling begins with an individual engaging in some form of deviance, known in his framework as *primary deviance* (e.g., crime or drug use). According to Becker, the reason as to why this deviance occurs is unimportant, as the emphasis of the theory is focused around societal labels in reaction to the behavior. Following the deviant act, the individual is labeled by society as an "outcast," "deviant," "troublemaker," or other negative label. The label indicates that an outsider does not fit within societal norms. After this initial label, the individual continues to engage in *secondary deviance*, which is followed by continual labeling by society. Eventually, the "deviant" individual will internalize these labels until it becomes their *master status*. Once this process occurs, the individual sees themselves as the "deviant" or "outsider." They accept that they are no longer a part of general society and seek out a deviant or outsider subculture, which offers social support and acceptance. In turn, joining this group facilitates their *deviant career*, whereby they continue to engage in the deviant behavior.

With Becker's labeling theory in mind, we can now turn our attention towards Arthur Fleck, the main protagonist of the *Joker* film, who transforms into the Joker at the end of the film. How is it that a down-on-his-luck comedian becomes the Clown Prince of Crime? Through close observation of the dialogue and scenes in the film, we can clearly see how society's lack of empathy created one of the most infamous villains in comic book history.

Application to *Joker*

At the start of the film, we are introduced to Arthur Fleck who is both literally and figuratively beaten down by society. He sits in front of a mirror wearing clown makeup and is forcing his face into a smile. We next see Arthur dressed in his clown attire dancing with an advertising sign on the street. A group of teenage boys come up to Arthur and start making fun of his appearance. They then steal Arthur's sign and run across traffic into an alley. When Arthur tries to get the sign back, the boys begin beating Arthur up and ruining the sign. Arthur lays alone in the alley visibly in pain. By the end of the first major scene, we can tell Arthur is not appreciated or respected by the society he lives in, which sets the stage for the rest of the film and the application of labeling theory.

Another important characteristic of Arthur that we are introduced to early on is his struggles with mental illness, which includes a condition that forces him to laugh uncontrollably. Arthur carries around a laminated card describing his condition to avoid conflict with other when the laughing fits occur. Although Arthur presents this card to people when he has outbursts, the citizens of Gotham often treat Arthur poorly due to his unmanageable laughter. Early in the film, while on a bus, Arthur tries to make a young boy in the seat ahead of him laugh. The boy's mother turns around and confronts Arthur and he suffers from a fit of laughter. He hands the mother his card at which point she scoffs and turns away from him. Shortly after, Arthur meets with a caseworker regularly as a result of prior mental health institutionalization. Although he is on several medications, he is unsure if they help his condition as he is still depressed and suffers from uncontrollable laughter.

We learn that Arthur takes care of his mother, who refers to him by the nickname, "Happy," by himself in a seedy apartment. At this point in the film, we know nothing of Arthur's father and only see the relationship between him and his mother. His mother used to work for Thomas Wayne, the affluent mayoral candidate of Gotham city, whom she consistently sends letters to asking for financial help. Arthur fails to understand why Thomas Wayne is so important to his mother but still agrees to send her letters and check for Wayne's responses in the mail.

Arthur has dreams of becoming a stand-up comedian, but instead has a job working as an entertainment clown. While Arthur enjoys his job, many of his coworkers view him as "weird" or a "freak." Arthur is told by his boss that he is on thin ice when it comes to his work performance, which includes losing the sign at the beginning of the film. He will be fired if he screws up again. Following the assault by the teenage boys, Arthur is given a gun by his coworker to protect himself. Arthur carries this gun with him and accidentally drops the gun while he is performing for children at a hospital. This incident leads Arthur's boss to fire him due to his negligence.

During his commute home from the children's hospital, Arthur is assaulted by three affluent men dressed in suits on the subway, who we later find out work for Thomas Wayne's investment business. The men call Arthur a "freak" and make fun of his laughing condition. During the assault, Arthur draws his gun and shoots two of the men in self-defense. The third man attempts to flee the train and is shot in the leg by Arthur before he can escape. While attempting to escape the train station, Arthur follows the man and executes him.

The act of killing these men, namely the killing of the third man, is Arthur's act of *primary deviance*. While Arthur certainly killed the first two men in self-defense, the argument could be made that killing the third man was unnecessary, as Arthur would have been physically safe letting him escape. Following the killings, we see Arthur struggle with his emotions about murdering the men. This is evidenced by Arthur's dance in the public restroom following the killings, which is slow and somber.

In the days following the killings, media sources and public figures tied to the upper classes of Gotham begin to label the killer as a "coward," "outcast," and "freak," which reflects the next stage of Becker's theory (initial labeling). On the other hand, the murders also sparked "anti-rich" sentiment across Gotham and less wealthy residents began taking the side of the killer, according to the news. These reactions help validate Arthur's violence.

At this point in the film, it becomes clear that Arthur is beginning to internalize these labels. During a session with his caseworker, Arthur states that society is beginning to notice him. Arthur indicates that he feels he never really existed until now; stating that he is starting to become something "more." His caseworker dismisses his remarks and tells Arthur funding has been cut for mental services in Gotham and that he will not be able to get his medication. She implies that society does not care about people with mental health conditions, like Arthur.

Following this scene, Arthur attempts stand-up comedy for the first time, but he struggles to tell jokes due to his uncontrollable laughter. After the failed comedy act, Arthur sees in a newspaper that his actions are starting a social movement where the disenfranchised people of Gotham are protesting the upper classes of society using the likeness of the clown costume that he used for work. Immediately after, a taxi drives by with a passenger wearing a clown mask. Seeing this, Arthur smiles authentically.

Afterward, Arthur comes home and is in a very good mood. He dances around his living room with his mother. As his mother goes to bed, she asks him to mail a letter to Thomas Wayne. Arthur reads the letter and finds out his father might be Thomas Wayne, who is also the father of a young Bruce Wayne, who comic book fans will recognize later becomes the Batman. Arthur attempts to foster a relationship with Thomas Wayne throughout the movie, but his attempts are met with denial and threats. Even within his own family, Arthur struggles to fit in and be accepted.

We find out that detectives have been speaking to workers at the entertainment company about the murders. The detectives speak to Arthur's mother while he is away, and she has a stroke due to the stress associated with finding out that Arthur is a suspect. While at the hospital with his mother, he watches an episode of his favorite television show, *Live With Murray Franklin*. During the opening monologue of the show the host, Murray, plays a clip of Arthur's standup act and refers to him as a "joker." Arthur relishes the fact that his act is being broadcasted on Murray's show; he feels as though he is finally getting recognition for his comedy. While he may view this as a success, both Murray and the rest of the viewers are actually making fun of him (a further act of stigmatization). A few days later Arthur receives a call from the producers of Murray's show, asking if he would like to be a guest due to the popularity of his clip, to which he excitedly agrees.

While Arthur's mother is in the hospital, he finds out that she was institutionalized at Arkham Asylum for delusional psychosis and narcissistic personality disorder. After stealing her medical files, a further deviant act, he reads that he was adopted by his mother and faced severe neglect while her boyfriend repeatedly physically abused Arthur in his youth. In a flashback, his mother indicates that Arthur was always such a happy little boy. This is quite the juxtaposition to the Arthur we see throughout the film who is filled with sadness and melancholy. Also included in the file are adoption papers which indicate that Arthur was indeed adopted, as suggested earlier by Thomas Wayne.

Back in his mother's hospital room, the news about his abuse and adoption unhinges Arthur and, following a monologue where he discusses his mistreatment by her and society, he suffocates her with a pillow. The murder of his mother signifies the start of Arthur's *secondary deviance*. As Arthur has already been labeled, his violence escalates as he dives deeper into his outsider status.

The film then cuts to Arthur preparing for his television appearance. We see him dying his hair green, a feature of his prior clown costume, as well as a well-known feature of the character in the comics. He dances more sporadically and excitedly around the bathroom, which indicates his increasing excitement associated with this new identity. We also see Arthur practicing his stage entrance for the show and it appears as though he plans to commit suicide on the show by shooting himself with the same gun that he killed the three men with prior in the film.

While painting his face, two of his former coworkers show up at his apartment to offer their condolences about Arthur's mother passing away. Arthur tells them that he is not actually sad and is instead happy with how things are going, a sign that he is starting to reject societal norms. One coworker, who gave him the gun, tells him that detectives have been showing up at the office and asking questions about Arthur. Arthur brutally murders his coworker with a pair of scissors that he took off of his mother's makeup stand. He allows his other coworker to leave, without harming him, as the man was always nice to him while he worked at his old job. This interaction indicates that the way in which people treated Arthur has a major impact on his identity and feelings toward others in society.

Following the murder of his former coworker, we see Arthur for the first time in his full Joker persona. He is wearing a bright-colored suit, his hair is dyed green, and his makeup is done in a way that matches the clown look of the protestors. As Arthur heads to the television station, we see him dance in a way unlike any other time in the movie. His dance to the "Rock and Roll" song by Gary Glitter is filled with excitement and bigger, more exaggerated moves, like pelvic thrusts and punches. His dancing is interrupted by two detectives who had been looking for him.

Following a chase by the police, which leads to a riot on the subway by protestors, Arthur arrives at the television station. While in the dressing room, Arthur is visited by Murray and an executive on the show to let him know what to expect while he is on stage. After a brief discussion, Arthur asks Murray if he can be introduced as Joker, rather than as Arthur Fleck. When asked why, Arthur responds, "It's what you called me when you played my clip." At this moment, it becomes evident that Arthur has fully adopted his *master status* as Joker. He is no longer the timid Arthur Fleck; he is now a symbol of chaos and the rejection of societal norms.

As Arthur is introduced on stage and the curtain is drawn, we see him dance for one of the final times in the movie. This dance is slow and choreographed. Now that he has become Joker, he is calm and in control. While on stage, Arthur tells a distasteful joke and is ridiculed by Murray. The audience laughs at Arthur's expense. Discouraged, he admits that he killed the three men on the subway and that he is the true cause of the chaos in the city. Arthur then proceeds to tell a joke that starts, "What do you get when you cross a mentally-ill loner with a society that abandons him and treats him like trash?" He turns, shooting Murray multiple times on national television. Arthur is arrested and while in the back of the police car, he sees the chaos of the riots on the streets. He smiles in excitement as all of the chaos stemmed from his actions.

Following a car accident caused by one of the protestors, Arthur is taken unconscious out of the back of the police car and placed on the car's hood. Upon awakening, Arthur sees the protestors, all in clown attire, celebrating his actions. He stands on top of the police car and we see him use his fingers to create a bloody smile on his face and he begins to dance, again in a calm and calculated manner. Arthur has found his *outcast subculture*: a subculture of followers who embrace Arthur for who he is. He is now a member of a group accepts and reveres, unlike the rest of general society.

The film closes showing Arthur incarcerated in Arkham Asylum. He begins to laugh during a session with a therapist. When she asks why he is laughing, he tells her that he is thinking of a joke that she "wouldn't understand." This is a sign that

Arthur sees himself as an outsider and that she represents general society. The final shots of the film show Arthur walking down the hallway of the asylum, leaving bloody footprints as he goes, inferring that he killed or at least severely injured his therapist. These footprints signify that Arthur is now comfortable in killing or hurting others. He is no longer bound to societal norms. Now, Arthur is freely able to lead a *deviant career*, as he knows his followers accept him for who he is.

Discussion

There is much to unpack in the *Joker* film. Multiple criminological theories could be used to explain the evolution of Arthur Fleck to the Joker, including life course theory (Sampson & Laub, 2003; i.e., trauma and mental health leading to his violent crime later in life) or strain/anomie theory (Merton, 1938; i.e., the societal pressure and inability to achieve success leads to criminality). However, we chose to apply Becker's labeling theory as the theory best captures Arthur's full transformation.

Arthur starts the film as a man who is down on his luck and engages in *primary deviance* through the killing of the three men on the subway. Following this, Arthur is labeled as a "clown," "freak," and "outcast" by society. Arthur begins to internalize these labels as he is repeatedly mistreated by society and begins to view himself as a social "other." He later kills his mother and former coworker, two people who labeled and rejected him throughout the film. These occurrences function as his acts of *secondary deviance*. While Arthur may not be outright labeled prior to his adoption of "Joker" as his *master status*, it is clear that the societal uprising was representative of his actions, and that he was continually labeled as "deviant." Finally, the full theoretical framework comes to fruition at the end of the film when Arthur requests to be called Joker, revels in his prior violent acts, and commits a murder on live television which incites a riot among his followers. He is then able to pursue his *deviant career*, as evidenced by him killing, or at least injuring, his therapist in Arkham.

Hence, *Joker* provides an effective medium for the application of Becker's theory. The film provides multiple glimpses into Arthur's internal processing toward accepting his master status. More subtly, we see this through shifts in Arthur's dancing and laughter throughout the film. His dancing begins very slow and somber, but after murdering his mother and former coworker, his dances become more chaotic, joyful, and sporadic, a sign that he is becoming more comfortable with this transition toward his new master status and his excitement toward this new identity.

The final two dances are more rhythmic and calmer, insinuating that he is now in control of who he is and accepts his new deviant identity.

Throughout multiple scenes at the beginning of the movie, we see that Arthur suffers from fits of uncontrollable laughter. Oftentimes, his laugh leads to further social stigma. As the film progresses, we see that Arthur has laughing fits more infrequently as he has more control over them. These laughing fits may be a reaction to social stigma and his nervousness about interacting with others. Once Arthur stops caring about how society views him, the condition lessens.

Arthur's journey through his acceptance of master status as the Joker is extremely telling. Under Becker's labeling theory, individuals internalize and attach self-identity to the words, terms, and stereotypes used by others to define them. We see the harms of Arthur's labels throughout the movie in relation to stigma. Labels serve to dehumanize, vilify, and reduce a person's holistic identity to their criminal acts or defects (Boppre & Hart-Johnson, 2019). Criminal and mental health-related labels have very real consequences for system-impacted persons, including negative self-perception, decreased social capital, and barriers to socioeconomic opportunities (Decker et al., 2015; Hadjimatheou, 2016; Middlemass, 2017).

Given the potential harms related to the stigma of labels, person-centered language has gained popularity in recent years (Denver et al., 2017). Person-centered language seeks to dismantle the stigma associated with crime-focused labels that fixate on past behaviors or deficits (Boppre & Hart-Johnson, 2019). From a clinical perspective, focusing on one's past behavior does little to support or promote change in future behaviors (Willis, 2018). Instead, person-centered language helps foster desistance through empathy and respect.

Perhaps if Arthur were treated with decency instead of harmful labels and stigma, his journey may not have involved serious crime. As seen at the beginning of the film, Arthur initially did not desire to cause harm. He did not even fight back against the group of teens who assaulted him in the opening scenes of the movie. He was simply an individual who had struggled thus far in his life and was making the best out of a bad situation. While it was ultimately Arthur's decision to commit violent acts, society's labeling of Arthur and lack of social support fueled his deviance and led to major riots within the streets of Gotham. By labeling Arthur as a "clown," "freak," and an "outcast," society unintentionally cultivated an outcast subculture among the lower-class who were empathetic to Arthur's plight.

Another major outcome of Arthur's transformation was the subsequent murder of Thomas and Martha Wayne in Crime Alley by a protestor during the riot at the end of the film. As known by many comic fans, these murders lead to the development of the Batman, as Bruce Wayne watches his parents' death in Crime Alley. Unwittingly, society's attachment of social stigma to Arthur led to the creation of the Dark Knight (Batman). Throughout the comic books, there is a debate as to whether Gotham City is actually safer under the presence of Batman. Many comic book characters speculate that Batman may actually increase the number of super-villains within Gotham, leading to a never-ending cycle of crime in the city. If this is indeed the case, then Gotham's mistreatment of those who struggle in society, like Arthur, leads to a future of hardship, death, and crime in the city for decades to come.

Conclusion

This chapter presented an application of Becker's labeling theory to the controversial and award-winning film *Joker*. The film reflects a cautionary tale that echoes issues our own society must confront. Throughout the film, we see a lack of community services and support available to Arthur Fleck. *Joker* forces audiences to consider a larger question of whether the poor treatment and stigmatization of individuals in society labeled as "outcasts" contributes to crime. Ultimately, *Joker* is a call for empathy given the impact on individuals when society lacks it.

The U.S. and other nations have a long history of disenfranchising, labeling, and stigmatizing individuals who do not fit societal expectations of the political elite (e.g., the indigent, racial/sexual minorities). At some points in history, social movements have influenced and improved the treatment and social standings among those marginalized (e.g., the Civil Rights movement in the U.S.). Yet, the process of labeling largely pushes members of society further to the margins through criminalization and incarceration (e.g., Foucault, 1977; Liska, 1992; Quinney, 1974; Rusche & Kirchheimer, 1939). Arthur's story portrays how each of us should think more critically about how we treat and interact with others in society.

Discussion Questions

1. Summarize Becker's labeling theory. What are primary and secondary deviance? How does one adopt a deviant career and criminality as a master status? Use *Joker* to provide examples.
2. Thinking back to Arthur's journey, what are some potential points in his life where increased social support could have changed his journey?
3. Arthur's journey inadvertently led to a social movement among the lower-class in Gotham. Are there other examples in which labeling and societal responses to outcasts have led to social movements?

4. Scholars often debate whether nature (i.e., being born with inherent criminality) or nurture (i.e., being raised in a certain manner/environment) leads to criminal behavior. Do you believe that it was nature or nurture that led to Arthur's criminality? Explain your position.

References

Becker, H. S. (1963). *Outsiders: Studies in the Sociology of Deviance*. New York, NY: Free Press.

Boppre, B., & Hart-Johnson, A. (2019). Using Person-Centered Language to Humanize Those Impacted by the Legal System. Retrieved from https://prisonersfamilyconference.org/advocacy-in-action-coalition

Decker, S. H., Ortiz, N., Spohn, C., & Hedberg, E. (2015). Criminal Stigma, Race, and Ethnicity: The Consequences of Imprisonment for Employment. *Journal of Criminal Justice, 43*(2), 108–121.

Denver, M., Pickett, J. T., & Bushway, S. D. (2017). The Language of Stigmatization and the Mark of Violence: Experimental Evidence on the Social Construction and Use of Criminal Record Stigma. *Criminology, 55*(3), 664–690.

Foucault, M. (1977). *Discipline and Punishment: The Birth of the Prison*. New York, NY: Pantheon Books.

Hadjimatheou, K. (2016). Criminal Labelling, Publicity, and Punishment. *Law and Philosophy, 35*(6), 567–593.

Liska, A. E. (1992). *Social Threat and Social Control*. New York, NY: State University of New York Press.

Malinowski, B. (1926). *Crime and Custom in Savage Society*. New York, NY: Humanities Press.

Merton, R. K. (1938). Social Structure and Anomie. *American Sociological Review, 3*(5), 672–682.

Middlemass, K. (2017). *Convicted and Condemned: The Politics and Policies of Prisoner Reentry*. NYU Press.

Quinney, R. (1974). *Critique of the Legal Order: Crime Control in Capitalistic Society*. New York, NY: Transaction Publishers.

Rusche, G., & Kirchheimer, O. (1939). *Punishment and Social Structure*. New York, NY: Columbia University Press.

Sampson, R. J., & Laub, J. H. (2003). Life-Course Desisters? Trajectories of Crime Among Delinquent Boys Followed to Age 70. *Criminology, 41*(3), 555–592.

Thomas, W. I., & Swaine Thomas, D. (1928). *The Child in America: Behavior Problems and Programs*. New York, NY: Knopf.

Willis, G. M. (2018). Why Call Someone by What We Don't Want Them To Be? The Ethics of Labeling in Forensic/Correctional Psychology. *Psychology, Crime & Law, 24*, 727–743.

Hegemonic Masculinity and *Game of Thrones*

14

"Never Forget Who You Are": Game of Thrones's Ramsay Bolton, Hegemonic Masculinity, and Structured Action Theory

Jill A. Kehoe

Game of Thrones (2011–2019) is a television fantasy drama based on George R. R. Martin's book series *A Song of Ice and Fire* (1996–Present). Over eight seasons on HBO, *Game of Thrones* depicts the lives and struggles of the people of the ancient continent of Westeros, otherwise known as the Seven Kingdoms. With interwoven stories including those of dangerously freezing winters, zombie-like White Walkers attacking the living, and supernatural prophetic visions, much of the story focuses on the fight for the Iron Throne, the ultimate seat of power ruling over all the citizens of the Seven Kingdoms. A thorough examination of *Game of Thrones* in its entirety, even through the lens of a single criminological theory, would take a book, if not several volumes. As such, this chapter attempts to provide an analysis of one particularly dynamic character, Ramsay Snow/Bolton, using the updated framework of Connell's theory of hegemonic masculinity, and its application to the field of criminology, Messerschmidt's theory of structured action (Connell & Messerschmidt, 2005).

J. A. Kehoe (✉)
CUNY LaGuardia Community College, Long Island City, NY, USA
e-mail: jkehoe@lagcc.cuny.edu

© The Author(s) 2021
S. E. Daly (ed.), *Theories of Crime Through Popular Culture*,
https://doi.org/10.1007/978-3-030-54434-8_14

Theory: Hegemonic Masculinity and Structured Action

Hegemonic masculinity is a systematic sociological theory of gender based on the notion that the beliefs, practices, and norms of a society dictate the culture's notions of maleness and the criteria by which all men are defined. Each society possesses multiple forms of masculinity, with categorization based upon how an individual portrays himself according to the society's standards of gender and sexuality. Connell (1995) outlines four types of masculinities, specifying how each relates to one another in regards to social standing and power relations. One who personifies the honored characteristics of the hegemonic male places himself at the apex of the gender hierarchy and in a position of social dominance, yielding power over both females and subordinate males. Goffman (1963) describes the American culture's version of the hegemonic male as "a young, married, white, urban northern, heterosexual Protestant father, of college education, fully employed, of good complexion, weight, and height, and a recent record in sports" (p. 128). Qualities associated with the archetypal male include heterosexism, sexual prowess, strength, authoritativeness, control, endurance, competitiveness, aggressiveness, individualism, and independence (Connell, 1995; Connell & Messerschmidt, 2005; Messerschmidt, 1993).

Those who are unable to achieve hegemonic masculinity fall into one of the remaining three categories. Connell's second type of masculinity, complicit masculinity, includes most of the men in a given society. Complicit males do not embody the characteristics of the ideal male but consent to and participate in the systemic structure of hegemonic masculinity. Male complicity affords such benefits as the domination of women and avoidance of subordination (Connell, 1995). Men who, despite seeming physically able to aspire to hegemonic masculinity, do not present their male gender in accordance with the society's ideology fall into the third category. The subordinate type of masculinity include men who present with non-hegemonic masculinity in social settings, including in the realm of physicality, speech, dress, social roles, economics, and/or sexuality. These men are viewed by society as deviant in terms of their masculine identity and are thus relegated to inferior status, putting themselves at risk for criticism and loss of legitimacy (Connell, 1995). Lastly, marginalized men are those who are unable to participate in hegemonic masculinity due to a disqualifying factor such as being of a minority race/ethnicity and/or having a disability (Connell, 1995).

Reflecting the constructionist notion of "doing gender," it is not sufficient for an individual to rely on one's gender as a predetermined or static attribute nor is it sufficient for an individual to assert one's gender at one particular time or in one particular way (Connell & Messerschmidt, 2005; West & Zimmerman, 1987). Instead, it must be accomplished systematically through a lifetime of self-regulated conduct. In social situations, one must construct their own identity through their actions and interactions with others and their environment. Dimensions of one's identity must be accomplished and interpreted by others in accordance with society's approved standards of hegemonic gender. One's gender identity must be established and reestablished in the public sphere in order for an individual to be perceived as adhering to the norms of the social context. Those that perform gender successfully, in accordance with society's hegemonic masculinity, acquire membership in the highest echelon of the sociocultural hierarchy and are able to hold the most authority in the society's current power structure (Connell & Messerschmidt, 2005).

Messerschmidt's (1986, 1993, 2014) application of the concept of hegemonic masculinity to the study of criminology allows for an improved analysis of male perpetrated crime. Viewing male perpetrated crime within the framework of the sociology of masculinity provides a better understanding of why men commit a disproportionate amount of crime as well as why men, by and large, commit different types of crimes than women. Furthermore, crimes must not just be analyzed based on the gender of the perpetrator, but in regards to the structural conditions of the society in which they occur. According to structured action theory, individuals have varying avenues and capital for acting out and accomplishing masculinity based on membership to various interacting social categories. Decisions to engage in legal and/or illegal behaviors are influenced by the availability of socially appropriate opportunities. As described in Chambliss's (1973) renowned study of adolescent boys, white middle-class boys focused on constructing a form of masculinity based on academic success and athleticism, while white working-class boys opted to pursue masculine identities based on achieving occupations heavy in manual labor and engaging in adolescent rule-breaking such as vandalism, truancy, drinking, and physical aggression. Racial minority lower-working class boys, denied opportunities to achieve masculinity through social, academic, and occupational routes, resorted to violent behavior, street crime, and gang activity to assert masculine identities. Those in power have more opportunities to receive a quality education, obtain a high paying job, and attain elevated levels of social status through legitimate means. Without these pathways toward success, criminality becomes an alternative avenue toward achieving power.

Ramsay: The Worst Person on Television

Ramsay Bolton, nee Snow, serves as one of the most memorable villains in the *Game of Thrones* television series. In fact, more than 145,000 readers of *The Atlantic* (2015) voted and crowned Ramsay "the worst person on television" with the hashtag "#actualworst," beating out such infamous evildoers as Hannibal Lecter of *Hannibal* and Walter White of *Breaking Bad*. In its analysis of violations of international humanitarian law in *Game of Thrones*, the Australian Red Cross (2019) found Ramsay to be the most egregious offender of the first seven seasons. Ramsay's rap sheet memorably includes taking hostages, torture, sexual violence, and murder by a variety of methods including flaying his victims alive, feeding them to his pack of dogs, and hunting them for sport.

We are officially introduced to Ramsay in Season Three as the son of Lord Roose Bolton. While all of the citizens of Westeros must swear allegiance to the King or Queen who sits on the Iron Throne, each region of Westeros is governed by a Great House, a noble family in charge of both the land and its occupants. House Bolton is a moderately powerful house in the North of Westeros that controls a region of land east of its capital of Winterfell. Given Ramsay's status as the ultimate *Game of Thrones* villain, his tortured back-story should come as no surprise. (Note: While this analysis is strictly focused on the television series and not its literary inspiration, some additional details about Ramsay's birth are derived from the books as they coincide with the minimal information provided in the television series.) Upon hearing that a man had married without his permission, his father Lord Bolton murdered the man and raped and impregnated his wife. The unnamed woman brought the child to Lord Bolton shortly after his birth in order for him to acknowledge his son. Despite initially wanting to murder the child and whip the woman, he ultimately chose to raise the child as his bastard after realizing he was indeed biologically his. After the death of Lord Bolton's wife and older trueborn son Domeric, he is left with Ramsay as his only immediate blood relation. Raised in House Bolton, the second most powerful house in the North, Ramsay grows up with many of the advantages of the highborn. Noble houses control the land surrounding their castle, field moderately sized armies, collect taxes and tithes from the common folk, and retain a household of servicemen and women for domestic tasks such as childcare, cooking, and labor. Brought up with amongst the power, protection, and resources of House Bolton, Ramsey's upbringing is by no means deprived.

Despite his upbringing amidst the nobility of the North, Ramsay commits some of the most sadistic acts of brutality in a show already ripe with violence and suffering. His plotline is virtually bereft of anything other than acts of cruelty and carnage. Often with a smile across his face and a witty quip, Ramsay relishes inflicting pain upon both those who he deems his enemy and those who have done him no wrong. His exploits include the following noteworthy acts of violence.

The Torture of Theon Greyjoy

Ramsay takes Theon Greyjoy hostage at castle Dreadfort, meting out a series of psychological and physical torments including orchestrating fake attempts to liberate him and give him false hope of rescue, flaying and amputating his extremities, castrating him and pretending to eat his penis (it was actually a pork sausage), and mailing a box containing his severed genitals to his family. Ramsay relishes the power he has over Theon, perpetrating acts of intense cruelty with a smile on his face and delivering such memorable lines as "Let's play a game: which body part do you need the least?" and "If you think this has a happy ending, you haven't been paying attention" ("The Climb"). Ramsay's abuse is so intense that he is able to make his victim abandon his old identity as Theon Greyjoy, the youngest son of Lord Balon Greyjoy leader of the Iron Islands, and transform himself into Reek, a loyal servant to House Bolton unable to commit the slightest act of rebellion against his master.

Military Betrayals

In Season Two, Ramsay and his men siege castle Winterfell in an attempt to take it back from Greyjoy control and return it to their Stark allies. After his military victory, despite promising mercy upon surrender, Ramsay flays all of the soldiers alive and burns the city of Winterfell. In Season Four, Roose orders Ramsay to take Moat Cailin, an important base in the North, from the Greyjoys. Ramsay captures Moat Cailin, and again flays his surrendering enemies alive, violating the rules of Westerosi warfare.

Myrcella, Tansy, and the Girls of Dreadfort

Ramsay enjoys releasing women into the Bolton forests and hunting them down. In Season Four, Ramsay hunts down his lover Tansy for making his girlfriend Myranda feel jealous. Tracking her through the forest, he taunts her "If you make it out of the woods, you win" ("The Lion and the Rose"). After wounding her with an arrow he finishes her off by ordering his bloodthirsty hounds to attack her and eat her flesh.

The Rape of Sansa Stark

In an arrangement designed to placate the citizens of the North, Roose Bolton orchestrates the marriage of his son Ramsay to Lady Sansa Stark. After their marriage ceremony, Ramsay rapes Sansa and forces Theon, a brother-like figure to Sansa, to watch. Ramsay tells Theon, "You've known Sansa since she was a girl, now watch her become a woman" ("Unbowed, Unbent, Unbroken"). Suffering a series of rapes over the next few days, Sansa plans an escape. Upon learning of the escape plan, Ramsay flays Sansa's elderly handmaid and forces her to look at the dead body.

The Murder of Lord Roose Bolton, Lady Walda Bolton, and Baby Boy Bolton

Roose is upset with his son for allowing the escape of Sansa and Theon from Bolton custody. Shaming Ramsay for "playing his games" with them, Roose is disappointed at the loss of political leverage. Giving him the ultimate threat, Roose reminds Ramsay that without Sansa he will be unable to produce a legitimate male heir and Roose will have to rely on his new wife Walda to produce a male heir. Ramsay knows his position has sole male heir is fragile, telling his father "My position is quite clear. I'm your son until a better alternative comes along" ("Kill the Boy"). After being chastised by his father for his failed attempts at capturing Sansa, and hearing the news that Walda has delivered a healthy baby boy, Ramsay plunges a knife into his father's chest. Ramsay immediately calls for Walda and the baby to be brought to him, declaring "I am Lord Bolton" and sharing his preference for being an only child before siccing his pack of hungry hounds on them. Upon their deaths Ramsay assumes his father's titles and becomes Lord of Dreadfort, Lord of Winterfell, and Warden of the North.

Battle of the Bastards

In Season Six, Jon Snow and Ramsay Bolton go to battle against each other for domain over the North. With his father appointed Warden of the North by the Iron Throne, Ramsay claims to be the rightful ruler of the North, but Jon Snow looks to retake control in the name of the Starks. Ramsay writes Jon Snow a letter, insisting up the return of his bride Sansa or else face a series of terrifying threats.

> I will ride North to slaughter every wildling—man, woman, and babe—living under your protection. You will watch as I skin them living. You will watch as my soldiers take turns raping your sister. You will watch as my dogs devour your wild little brother. Then I will spoon your eyes from their sockets and let my dogs do the rest. Come and see. ("Book of the Stranger")

While a battle between thousands of soldiers is bound to be bloody, Ramsay once again manages to engage in despicable behavior beyond that of common warfare. Meeting across the battlefield, Ramsay presents his enemy Jon Snow with a captive Rickon, Jon's half-brother. Despite having the chance to kill him quite easily as Rickon is bound with ropes, he decides he would rather play a game. He instructs Rickon that if he is to successfully run across the battlefield to his awaiting family, he will be free. A desperate Rickon takes off running with Ramsay shooting arrows behind him. Ramsay, a skilled archer, strikes Rickon with an arrow just before he reaches his family, leaving him to die in the outstretched arms of Jon Snow.

Theoretical Analysis

Hegemonic Masculinity in Westeros

While it may be easy to pass off Ramsay's appalling acts of violence as a product of psychopathy, sociopathy, or some other form of severe mental illness, to do so would be to ignore the context in and the conditions under which Ramsay commits these actions. While Ramsay may indeed have a diagnosable psychiatric condition, his exploits are incontrovertibly rooted in his pursuit of hegemonic masculinity. Therefore, it is key to understand the notion of masculinity as it exists in Westerosi society, and how Ramsay fits into this concept, both as others see him and as he sees himself.

The role of the hegemonic male is largely influenced by two major factors of Westerosi life. First, the presence of a hierarchical and patriarchal structure dictates power relations within the Seven Kingdoms. The king sits atop the social hierarchy with wardens of provincial regions and lords of noble houses next in line. The common folk occupy the lowest rung of the ladder holding little to no power. In regards to gender, Westeros is a patriarchal society where men possess power over women, limiting the role of women in fulfilling sexual and reproductive needs. Secondly, as implied by the title of the series, *Game of Thrones* very much focuses on the political-military power struggles amongst the influential men and women of the Seven Kingdoms. The eight seasons of *Game of Thrones* take place soon after the Targaryen conquest and Robert Baratheon's rebellion, depicting the next sequence of contests including the Greyjoy rebellion and the War of the Five Kings. As Varys observes, "blood has never been in short supply here, ever since the First men carried a crown into Westeros" ("The Death of Kings"). In a civilization ripe with combat, hegemonic masculinity is irrefutably intertwined with prowess on the battlefield. Knights and sellswords with successful military records, noblemen with robust armies, and individuals capable of inflicting serious physical violence are glorified as power comes to those who can take it by force.

The hegemonic men of Westeros hold high social rankings, have a considerable amount of money, land, and resources associated with their family lineage and titles, secure marriages to respectable women, and offer a strong physical presentation capable of aggression. Some examples of hegemonic men include King Robert Baratheon, 17th ruler of the Seven Kingdoms, Ned Stark, Warden of the North and King Robert's trusted advisor, Stannis Baratheon, King Robert's brother and claimant to the Iron Throne, and Lord Tywin Lannister, one of the richest men in all of Westeros. Ramsay is not a hegemonic male in the same vein as these powerful men, existing much lower in social rank. Ramsay is also not a subordinate or a marginalized male. He does not present his gender incorrectly (like homosexual characters Renly Baratheon and Sir Loras Tyrell), nor is he part of a marginalized social group (like Varys the eunuch or the Dothraki men of color). Instead, he is complicit, observing, and participating in Westerosi gender norms with the ultimate goal of being hegemonic. What prevents Ramsay from achieving hegemony is his illegitimacy.

Bastardy: Baseborn Children

Vitally important to understanding Ramsay's masculinity, and ultimately his offenses and motivations for committing them, is his status as a Westerosi bastard. Children born out of wedlock, referred to as "baseborn" or "bastards" in the Seven Kingdoms, are subject to discrimination. Frequently, fathers do not acknowledge their bastard children, leaving them to be raised and supported by their mothers alone. Some fathers may send financial support while others will send the child to be raised away from his legitimate children. In extremely rare circumstances, as was the case of Ned Stark and his bastard son Jon Snow, bastard children will be raised alongside legitimate children, but with the lingering stigma and lowered social status of an illegitimate child. Despite choosing to raise Jon Snow with his legitimate children, even he yielded to the social norms of treating bastard children differently. As was evident during the visit of King Robert Baratheon and Queen Cersei Lannister to Winterfell, Jon Snow was banned from attending the celebratory banquet with the elite as to not offend them while dining.

Prohibited from using their father's last name, noble bastards must instead have a region-specific surname indicating their status as an illegitimate child. As Ellaria Sand explains, "A child born to a wife is a gift from the gods. A child born to a mistress or an obedient servant girl is a bastard, unworthy of its father's name" ("The Bastards of Westeros"). As a bastard child of the North, Ramsay's given surname is Snow (other bastard surnames include Flowers in the Reach, Hill in the Westerlands, Pyke in the Iron Island, Rivers in the Riverlands, Sand in Dorne, Stone in the Vale of Arryn, Storm in the Stormlands, and Waters in the Crownlands). The absence of an ancestral surname allows for society to properly identify bastards and treat them with the stigma dictated by their society. Furthermore, the use of an ecological surname suggests that bastards exist outside of the civilized world of familial bonds, and instead exist in the wild, uncivilized realm of nature. Tagging bastard children with nature-derived surnames is a reflection of the society's belief that illegitimate children are substantively inferior to legitimate children, born from impure relations and embodying the primitive ways of the elements. In a hierarchical society where one's place in the pecking order is determined by nomenclature, the bestowal of a bastard's surname is damning. In a heartfelt conversation with Jon Snow, Tyrion Lannister says, "Let me give you some advice, bastard. Never forget what you are. The rest of the world will not. Wear it like armor, and it can never be used to hurt you" ("Winter Is Coming"). Tyrion later states, "I have a tender spot in my heart for cripples, bastards and broken things," ("Cripples, Bastards, and Broken Things") further clarifying Westeros's position on illegitimate children by grouping them with other types of social outcasts.

From a legal perspective, following primogeniture, bastards are banned from inheriting their father's land, title, or house. Furthermore, bastards are officially prohibited from carrying the heraldry of their noble parent's house, a great honor and mark of class distinction in the Seven Kingdoms. Limited to noble members of the family and those bestowed with the privilege of knighthood, heraldic symbols may not be displayed by common folk or bastards as representations of themselves, but only to identify their side in battle. To claim some visual representation of noble status, bastards in Westeros may use the heraldry of their highborn parents with the colors inverted. In a conversation with his father, Ramsay declares, "The flayed man is on our banners," to which his father replies, "My banners, not yours. You're not a Bolton, you're a Snow" ("The Lion and the Rose").

Marriage proposals are also constrained by one's bastard status. Marriages based on love are far less common in Westeros than marriages arranged for political and financial purposes. As with the marriages of Khal Drogo and Daenerys Targaryen, Joffrey Baratheon and Margaery Tyrell, and Tyrion Lannister and Sansa Stark, alliances between houses are created and fortified through marital contracts. As a bastard, Ramsay is not particularly desirable as a marriage prospect. In Season One, Ramsay is in a relationship with a servant named Myranda. As the daughter of Bolton's kennel keeper, she does not have noble status and does not offer Ramsay wealth, political power, military strength, or the promise of highborn children.

Without the benefit of noble filiation, bastards are deprived of most of the Westerosi avenues of acquiring honor and status. Illegitimacy precludes a bastard from achieving social status, amassing material wealth, establishing alliances based on familial allegiances, and creating a family lineage of legitimate noble children. As multiple forms of masculinity are present in any society, Ramsay does have other options for establishing masculinity more open to men of illegitimate birth. Jon Snow, raised the bastard son of Ned Stark, chooses to join the Night's Watch as an alternative path. A military command in which the men do not marry, father children, possess land, or wear markers of class distinction, the Night's Watch defends the Seven Kingdoms from those that threaten from beyond its borders. Here, in its more egalitarian social structure, Jon Snow can escape the stigma of his bastard status and achieve the prestige bestowed on the men who protect the realm from foreign aggressors. As Ramsay optimistically reflects on Jon Snow's success in the Night's Watch, "Bastards can rise high in the world, like your half-brother, Jon Snow. Born the Bastard of Winterfell, now the Lord Commander of the Night's Watch. You didn't know? Yes, he's done very well for himself" ("The Gift"). Other avenues for bastards to pursue status are by knighthood, in which a man is able to gain land, titles, and a place in his liege lord's house, religious service as septons or septas in the Faith of the Seven, or training at the Citadel to join the intellectual order of the Maesters.

Ramsay is restricted in his efforts to achieve and maintain his masculine identity in Westerosi society due to his status as a bastard. Conventional avenues of doing gender, such as presenting oneself as a Lord of a titled house, securing marriage to an upper class, respectable woman, passing on one's noble surname to one's children, displaying traditional family heraldry, and inheriting family land, are not viable in his current circumstance. While avenues for pursuing alternative forms of masculinity were open to him, Ramsay makes a conscious choice to ignore those more conventional options in favor of cruelty and brutality. Ramsay chooses physical violence, sexual aggression, and psychological manipulation to compensate for his illegitimate status and attempt to seek a traditional embodiment of hegemonic masculinity.

Legitimization

An analysis of Ramsay would be incomplete without addressing the principle transformative moment in his life. In Season Four, satisfied with his son's military success, Roose presents Ramsay with a document legitimizing his son, changing his name from Ramsay Snow to Ramsay Bolton, and formally giving him all of the benefits afforded to a trueborn son. Kneeling before his father he says, "You honor me. I swear I will uphold your name and your tradition. I will be worthy of you, Father" ("The Mountain and the Viper"). Before his legitimization he is Ramsay Snow, the bastard son of Roose Bolton, burdened by stigma and unable to achieve the same successes and status of a legitimate son. After his legitimization he is Ramsay Bolton, the son of Roose and heir to House Bolton and all it rules over.

As Ramsay's illegitimacy is the chief impediment to his quest for hegemony, one may assume that his use of violence as an instrument for doing gender and asserting masculinity might wane in favor of more noble endeavors on his journey to hegemony. Prior to his legitimization, Ramsay is well aware that his identity as a bastard compromises his chances of acquiring honor. He resents the fact that he is not afforded the respect of a trueborn son. Disadvantaged in life by his illegitimate status and looked down upon by others, Ramsay seeks alternate ways of wielding power over people. However, after his legitimization, Ramsay is still insecure in his masculinity. His status as Roose's primary heir is tenuous for, as Sansa points out, "But you're a bastard, a trueborn will always have the stronger claim" ("The Gift"). Despite the legal decree and new surname, Ramsay's bastardy is not washed away overnight. His blood is not pure Bolton and the people of Westeros will forever view him as the former bastard.

Both before and after his legitimization, Ramsay's most useful tool in his arsenal is his ability to inflict brutal violence upon others with no remorse. He instrumentalizes violence to prove himself to his father and to himself as a man capable of attaining power and dominance. Ramsay is comfortable with the use of his sadism and violence as his primary method of achieving power over others. While other complicit males may opt to join the Night's Watch, religious service, or the

Maester's to portray their masculine identities, these enterprises do not afford Ramsay the same opportunity for acting out his resentment and bitterness nor appeal to the bloodthirsty nature of Westeros, his father, and himself.

In Westerosi society, it is crucial for men to present themselves as capable of violence. Similar to Messerschmidt's (1986) depiction of modern-day macho street culture, in Westeros, "most are forced to think only of fulfilling heir own needs the best way possible. A form of ruthless, egotistic, exploitative individualism becomes the norm" (p. 67). While becoming a Maester, septon, or member of the Night's Watch might allow him to escape the daily confirmations of his bastardy and its inherent inferiority, it would not grant him the access to the power that he, like most men of Westeros, desire.

Ramsay is constantly seeking approval and respect from his father. Roose regularly dispatches Ramsay into combat, with his son seeking victory to satisfy both the needs of House Bolton and his own need for validation. Ramsay admits that his father trained him to be aggressive, telling Theon, "My mother taught me not to throw stones at cripples…but my father taught me 'aim for their head" ("Mhysa"). Ramsay's excessive use of violence, even beyond what his father is accustomed to, is treated with surprising banality. Roose flippantly reflects, "But Ramsay…well, Ramsay has his own way of doing things" ("Mhysa"). Moreover, it is not a coincidence that Ramsay's preferred method of execution is flaying, the infamous centuries-old practice which House Bolton depicts in its heraldry. Roose Bolton retains his respect for the practice despite the North outlawing it, proudly stating, "Unlike some other houses, my ancestors earned the Bolton words: 'Our Blades Are Sharp'" ("House Bolton"). With his father basing his feelings toward his son on his military conquests and his fondness for his house's time-honored tradition of flaying, it is not surprising that Ramsay's acts of violence serve as a way to cultivate their relationship.

Identification as a second-rate citizen and a lifetime of inferior treatment leave Ramsay with a chip on his well-armored shoulder that a profession of scholarship, religious service, or protection could not resolve. Instead, perpetrating acts of violence allows Ramsay to lash out at the society that shamed him. It is through violence that Ramsay is capable of experiencing power, a feeling he truly takes pleasure in. Ramsay admits to this feeling as he flays the finger of a captive Theon, stating, "This isn't happening to you for a reason. Well, one reason. I enjoy it" ("The Climb"). He feels omnipotent when he exercises his decision to kill, experiencing, albeit temporarily, the ultimate power that he seeks. In addition to the power over life and death, Ramsay strategically utilizes his violence to deprive his victims of their other prized assets. He rapes women, both noble and common, taking advantage of their powerlessness and lack of autonomy to control their bodies and their sexuality. And with his most exhaustive act of torture, in transforming Theon into Reek, he deprives Theon of his physical strength, his sexuality, his ability to produce heirs to rule his Iron Islands homeland, his noble identity, and his humanity. "You don't look like Theon Greyjoy anymore. That's a name for a lord, but you're not a lord, are you? You're just meat. Stinking meat. You reek...Reek! That's a good name for you" ("Mhysa"). In a cruel twist of fate, Ramsay is bastardizing Theon.

Conclusion

Game of Thrones, with its seemingly endless list of characters, provides numerous examples of Connell's (1995) hegemonic, complicit, subordinate, and marginalized masculine identities. Situated in the medieval period's hierarchal and patriarchal social structure, *Game of Thrones* offers an uncensored look at the modalities of masculinity amidst the struggle for power in the Seven Kingdoms. Ramsay's physical and sexual violence against his military opponents, prisoners, common folk, lovers, and family members is a form of extreme exploitation. As a complicit male, he uses the bodies of those around him as disposable instruments in his nontraditional quest for hegemony and power.

While Ramsay may stand out for his unusually shocking acts of brutality, he is by no means the only person engaging in violence. Many male and female characters regularly engage in sexual and physical violence, highlighting its role in Westerosi life. Worthy of note is not the frequency at which *Game of Thrones* depicts of use the violence, but the fate of those who employ it. King Robert Baratheon, Ned Stark, Stannis Baratheon, Tywin Lannister, and many of the other men who embody hegemonic masculinity through the use of violence and aggression are short-lived. The women of Westeros who adopt hypermasculine characteristics, such as Daenerys Targaryen and Cersei Lannister, find themselves similarly condemned. With characters often destroyed by the wars and turmoil brought about by their quests for power, *Game of Thrones* depicts hegemonic masculinity as a destructive force for both those who embrace it and for those around them. In the final episode of the series, the remaining elite of Westeros meet to discuss the future of the Seven Kingdoms. Sitting in a circle are Robin Arryn, Gendry Baratheon, Yara Greyjoy, Tyrion Lannister, Prince Martell of Dorne, Yohn Royce, Davos Seaworth, Arya Stark, Brandon Stark, Sansa Stark, Samwell Tarly, Brienne of Tarth, Edmure Tully, and Grey Worm, all characters without a history of hegemonic masculinity. Some were more complicit in their masculinity than others; some were subordinated for their nontraditional presentation of gender, and others were marginalized for being disabled or men of color. Those who succeed at the "game of thrones" are not those who embody hegemonic masculinity, as those men and women effectively cause their own demise. George R. R. Martin admits it himself, "And if you look at the books, my heroes and viewpoint characters are all misfits. They're outliers. They don't fit the roles society has for them. They're 'cripples, bastards, and broken things'—a dwarf, a fat guy who can't fight, a bastard, and women who don't fit comfortably into the roles society has for them" (Hibberd, 2015, para. 4). A statement from the council reinforces the show's perspective on the harmful nature of masculinity. Davos Seaworth, reflecting upon the annihilation caused by previous leaders, demands, "We've had enough war. Thousands of you, thousands of them. You know how it ends. We need to find a better way" ("The Iron Throne"). The message is clear: The men and women of the Dragonpit Council, the surviving few and future of Westeros, did not and should not conform to the toxic notion of hegemonic masculinity.

Discussion Questions

1. Which characters from *Game of Thrones* embody hegemonic masculinity, complicit masculinity, subordinate masculinity, and marginalized masculinity? What characteristics do they present to merit classification at this level of the gender hierarchy?
2. Other than the actions of Ramsay, what crimes and acts of aggression do you think were influenced by notions of hegemonic masculinity? How?
3. How would Westerosi society need to change in order to eliminate the toxic consequences of hegemonic masculinity? Would you the society you live in need to change?

References

Australian Red Cross. (2019). *Game of Thrones: Violations of and Compliance with International Humanitarian Law*. Australian Red Cross.

Chambliss, W. J. (1973). The Saints and the Roughnecks. *Society, 11*(1), 24–31.

Connell, R. W. (1995). *Masculinities*. Cambridge, UK: Polity Press.

Connell, R. W., & Messerschmidt, J. W. (2005). Hegemonic Masculinity: Rethinking the Concept. *Gender & Society, 19*(6), 829–859.

Goffman, E. (1963). *Stigma: Notes on the Management of Spoiled Identity*. New York, NY: Touchstone Books.

Hibberd, J. (2015, June 3). George R. R. Martin Explains Why There's Violence Against Women on 'Game of Thrones'. *Entertainment Weekly*. Retrieved from http://ew.com/

It's Official: Ramsay Bolton Is the Actual Worst Character on Television. (2015, December 4). *The Atlantic*. Retrieved from theatlantic.com/

Martin, G. R. R. (1996–Present). *A Song of Ice and Fire*. (Vols. 1–5). New York, NY: Bantam Books.

Messerschmidt, J. W. (1986). *Capitalism, Patriarchy, and Crime: Toward a Socialist Feminist Criminology*. Totowa, NJ: Rowman & Littlefield.

Messerschmidt, J. W. (1993). *Masculinities and Crime: Critique and Reconceptualization*. Lanham, MD: Rowman & Littlefield.

Messerschmidt, J. W. (2014). *Crime as Structured Action: Doing Masculinities, Race, Class, Sexuality, and Crime* (2nd ed.). Lanham, MD: Rowman & Littlefield.

West, C., & Zimmerman, D. H. (1987). Doing Gender. *Gender & Society, 1*, 25–51.

Episodes and DVD Extras

Winter Is Coming (Season 1, Episode 1)

Benioff, D., & Weiss, D. B. (Writers), & Van Patten, T. (Director). (2011). Winter Is Coming [Television Series Episode]. In D. Benioff, B. Caulfield, B. Cogman, F. Doelger, D. Nutter, M. Sapochnik, C. Strauss, & D. B. Weiss (Executive Producers), *Game of Thrones*. New York, NY: Home Box Office.

Cripples, Bastards, and Broken Things (Season 1, Episode 4)

Cogman, B. (Writer), & Kirk, B. (Director). (2011). Cripples, Bastards, and Broken Things [Television Series Episode]. In D. Benioff, B. Caulfield, B. Cogman, F. Doelger, D. Nutter, M. Sapochnik, C. Strauss, & D. B. Weiss (Executive Producers), *Game of Thrones*. New York, NY: Home Box Office.

The Climb (Season 3, Episode 6)

Benioff, D., & Weiss, D. B. (Writers), & Sakharov, A. (Director). (2013). The Climb [Television Series Episode]. In D. Benioff, B. Caulfield, B. Cogman, F. Doelger, D. Nutter, M. Sapochnik, C. Strauss, & D. B. Weiss (Executive Producers), *Game of Thrones*. New York, NY: Home Box Office.

Mhysa (Season 3, Episode 10)

Benioff, D., & Weiss, D. B. (Writers), & Nutter, D. (Director). (2013). Mhysa [Television Series Episode]. In D. Benioff, B. Caulfield, B. Cogman, F. Doelger, D. Nutter, M. Sapochnik, C. Strauss, & D. B. Weiss (Executive Producers), *Game of Thrones*. New York, NY: Home Box Office.

The Lion and The Rose (Season 4, Episode 2)

Martin, G. R. R. (Writer), & Graves, A. (Director). (2014). The Lion and the Rose [Television Series Episode]. In D. Benioff, B. Caulfield, B. Cogman, F. Doelger, D. Nutter, M. Sapochnik, C. Strauss, & D. B. Weiss (Executive Producers), *Game of Thrones*. New York, NY: Home Box Office.

The Mountain and the Viper (Season 4, Episode 8)

Benioff, D., & Weiss, D. B. (Writers), & Graves, A. (Director). (2014). The Mountain and the Viper [Television Series Episode]. In D. Benioff, B. Caulfield, B. Cogman, F. Doelger, D. Nutter, M. Sapochnik, C. Strauss, & D. B. Weiss (Executive Producers), *Game of Thrones*. New York, NY: Home Box Office.

Kill the Boy (Season 5, Episode 5)

Cogman, B. (Writer), & Podeswa, J. (Director). (2015). Kill the Boy [Television Series Episode]. In D. Benioff, B. Caulfield, B. Cogman, F. Doelger, D. Nutter, M. Sapochnik, C. Strauss, & D. B. Weiss (Executive Producers), *Game of Thrones*. New York, NY: Home Box Office.

Unbowed, Unbent, Unbroken (Season 5, Episode 6)

Cogman, B. (Writers), & Podeswa, J. (Director). (2015). Unbowed, Unbent, Unbroken [Television Series Episode]. In D. Benioff, B. Caulfield, B. Cogman, F. Doelger, D. Nutter, M. Sapochnik, C. Strauss, & D. B. Weiss (Executive Producers), *Game of Thrones*. New York, NY: Home Box Office.

The Gift (Season 5, Episode 7)

Benioff, D., & Weiss, D. B. (Writers), & Sapochnik, M. (Director). (2015). The Gift [Television Series Episode]. In D. Benioff, B. Caulfield, B. Cogman, F. Doelger, D. Nutter, M. Sapochnik, C. Strauss, & D. B. Weiss (Executive Producers), *Game of Thrones*. New York, NY: Home Box Office.

Book of the Stranger (Season 6, Episode 4)

Benioff, D., & Weiss, D. B. (Writers), & Sackheim, D. (Director). (2016). Book of the Stranger [Television Series Episode]. In D. Benioff, B. Caulfield, B. Cogman, F. Doelger, D. Nutter, M. Sapochnik, C. Strauss, & D. B. Weiss (Executive Producers), *Game of Thrones*. New York, NY: Home Box Office.

The Iron Throne (Season 8, Episode 6)

Benioff, D., & Weiss, D. B. (Writers), & Benioff, D., & Weiss, D. B. (Director). (2019). The Iron Throne. [Television Series Episode]. In D. Benioff, B. Caulfield, B. Cogman, F. Doelger, D. Nutter, M. Sapochnik, C. Strauss, & D. B. Weiss (Executive Producers), *Game of Thrones*. New York, NY: Home Box Office.

The Bastards of Westeros. (2015). In *Histories and Lore, Game of Thrones: The Complete Fourth Season*. HBO Blu-Ray.

The Death of Kings. (2015). In *Histories and Lore, Game of Thrones: The Complete Fourth Season*. HBO Blu-Ray.

House Bolton. (2014). In *Histories and Lore, Game of Thrones: The Complete Third Season*. HBO Blu-Ray.

Critical Criminology and *Hunger Games*

15

Critical Criminology and State Crime in *The Hunger Games*

Jared M. Hanneman

Introduction

This chapter discusses the use of *The Hunger Games* to illustrate many of the concepts and categories that comprise critical criminology and state crime. Critical criminology is quite dissimilar from most of the other dominant theoretical paradigms that are used to explain the existence and persistence of criminality in society. A fundamental divide in criminological theory is between micro-level and macro-level theories. Many of the earliest criminological theories developed were at the micro-level, that is, those theories that use the characteristics, experiences, and interactions of individuals and small groups as their levels of analysis.

The classical criminological theories, which emphasize the importance of rational choice and deterrence, are micro-level theories that are generally approachable and make good common sense. Choices are made daily, and, intuitively, some individuals will make criminal choices. This certainty in explaining criminality will often last until students begin to explore the positivist biological, biosocial, and psychological theories that posit an empirical difference between the criminal and the noncriminal. Students (and social science) may not yet know exactly what such differences may be, but many are confident that such differences exist, separating the noncriminal from the criminal.

J. M. Hanneman (✉)
Thiel College, Greenville, PA, USA
e-mail: jhanneman@thiel.edu

This transitions seamlessly into the idea that criminals and noncriminals often interact with one another. This explanation is exemplified in theories grouped together as social process theories. Such theories explain human behavior as a result of the interaction between individuals and other individuals and social groups. The most empirically supported of the social process theories is the social learning theory. It stands to reason that just as a beginning piano student can be taught by an experienced player, so too can an inexperienced potential delinquent be taught by a career criminal. According to differential association theory, individuals with relationships with other actors who have pro-criminal attitudes, values, and beliefs are more likely to engage in criminality than individuals having relationships with law-abiding actors. Sutherland specified certain characteristics of an individual's relationships with pro-criminal actors, such as frequency, intensity, duration, and priority, will be more influential in contributing to criminal careers when observed in greater degrees in the associations. As an example of the importance of intensity, an actor is much more likely to be socialized into pro-criminal beliefs through interaction with members of a primary peer group, which is characterized by close, intimate relationships, than by interaction with larger and more superficial secondary peer groups. It is not just the quantity of an individual's relationships that is criminogenic, but the qualities of those relationships are also important (Sutherland, 1947).

Students also grapple with one of the dominant contradictions in the social process paradigm. Rather than the differential association of criminal influences pulling naturally conforming actors into a life of crime and deviance, control theory asserts that individuals are naturally inclined to deviant and criminal behaviors and that it is only the bonds that they have with conforming social institutions that prevent this lawlessness. Hirschi (1969, p. 16) identified four constitutive elements of these social bonds: attachment, commitment, involvement, and belief. When individuals have formed strong social bonds with the most significant social institutions—family, education, religion, and peer groups—then they are less likely to engage in serious criminal behavior. While both theoretical explanations emphasize the importance of social interactions, they differ in their fundamental assumptions about human nature. Social learning theory assumes actors must be socialized into deviance and criminality, while social control theory assumes the actors must be socialized into conformity.

In continuing to examine the effects of social interactions and relationships on criminality, Becker (1963) argued that, rather than individual relationships and associations of delinquents/criminals with other actors or social groups causing criminality, it was the weight of social judgment—through the institutional act of formal or official labeling—that led to a self-fulfilling prophecy of individuals labeled as criminal internalizing the label and engaging in acts of criminality.

This labeling theory and the theories discussed above are all fundamentally micro-level theories—that is, they are used to explain the criminality of individual actors. Some of the proposed variables affecting these actors may be their rationally calculated choices, fears of committing a crime, biological and psychological influences, or the effects of their interactions with other individuals and social groups. These theories may posit different explanations for individual criminality, but they all focus fundamentally on the micro-level of analysis, that is, on individuals or small groups.

Many criminology students gravitate preferentially toward these micro-level theories, particularly because they exhibit many attractive features. Micro-level theories' units of analysis are at the same level as the theories' audiences. Given the multitude of decisions that individuals make on a daily basis—many with great deliberation, many almost unconsciously, and still others somewhere along this continuum—it is understandable that students give credence to micro-level theories. When people experience the world at the micro-level, it may seem to be common sense that theories framed at the individual level of analysis seem more useful in explaining crime. While individuals may innately recognize the existence of the forest, they live amongst the trees.

It is this deviation from everyday perceptions of cause and effect that frequently challenge students' understanding of macro-level criminological theories. The social structural paradigm examines criminality in and across societies from a bird's eye perspective. Social disorganization theory (Shaw & McKay, 1942) describes enduring poverty and crime in geographic areas over long periods of time—patterns that persist even when individual criminal actors are aging out of crime, becoming incarcerated, or otherwise leaving the area. The crime rate remains stable while the experiences of individual criminals are anything but.

Other macro-level social structural theoretical explanations include Merton's (1938) theory of social structure and anomie, Cohen's (1955) theory of status deprivation and the delinquent subculture, Cloward and Ohlin's (1960) theory of differential opportunity and delinquent subcultures, and Miller's (1958) theory of focal concerns of lower-class culture. Each of these classic works examines the effects of social institutions and structures on aggregate measures of crime and deviance. The studies address the effects of, for example, strain and frustration in so far as some actors will adapt through conformity, innovation, ritualism, retreatism, or rebellion (Merton, 1938), but the greater explanatory power of these social structural theories is that they explain the stability of crime rates across geographic areas or social classes.

This shift from the micro to the macro can be a difficult change in perspective for many students. This difficulty is often brought into even sharper relief when examining critical criminology and state crime. It is for this reason that popular cultural artifacts often make effective pedagogical tools to illustrate more complex concepts to students in a format with which they already have some familiarity.

The Hunger Games

The Hunger Games is a trilogy of dystopian young adult novels written by Suzanne Collins: *The Hunger Games*, *Catching Fire*, and *Mockingjay*. These novels were adapted to feature films of the same name. The most notable difference is that events in the *Mockingjay* novel were portrayed over the course of two films.

The story is set in the fictional nation of Panem, which is comprised of the central Capitol and 12 (spoiler alert: actually 13) outlying districts. Each district is known for a particular exploited resource required by the Capitol. For example, District 4 specializes in fishing while District 12 specializes in coal. About 74 years prior to the events of *The Hunger Games*, the districts rebelled against the political domination of the Capitol in a conflict referred to as the "Dark Days." The Capitol put down this revolution and forced the districts back under its control, ending the Dark Days through the signing of the Treaty of the Treason, which marked, among other elements of political domination, the beginning of the Hunger Games.

The Hunger Games are an annual event in which 24 "Tributes"—a male and female from each of the twelve districts are selected at an annual "Reaping" and brought to the Capitol to compete in a televised battle royal to the death until only one remains as "Victor." Children aged 12–18 are eligible to be chosen as tributes. Most districts hold a lottery to determine who will be selected, though the protocol of the Reaping allows for the possibility for someone to volunteer as a tribute. This is the case for 16-year-old Katniss Everdeen who volunteers to take the place of her 12-year-old sister Primrose whose name was drawn in the lottery. The male tribute selected in the lottery is Peeta Mellark, a 16-year-old whose family owns a bakery in the district. The current year's tributes are mentored through the process by a previous victor from the tributes' home district. The only surviving victor from District 12 is Haymitch Abernathy, an alcoholic who is still suffering from the effects of post-traumatic stress disorder from his Hunger Games experience 14 years earlier.

Although Panem is ostensibly a single nation, there is very much an imperial quality to the relationships between the Capitol and the outlying districts. The political and economic relationships have much more in common with colonizing and colonized states. The colonizing nation typically acquires the resources that are needed to support their higher standard of living while the colonized people are left to utilize few of their own natural resources, all in return for the "civilizing" influence and "protection" of the colonizer, which is typically little more than the ideological justification for the occupation of the colony in the first place. The residents of the Capitol are depicted as wealthy and overly indulgent—some going as far as to induce vomiting in order to be able to continue eating at lavish parties. This wasteful opulence is visibly off-putting to Katniss and Peeta, as many of their friends and family struggle to keep from starving to death in District 12, much less gorge themselves on culinary excesses. There is a pronounced emphasis and importance placed on appearance and dress in the Capitol, where one's worth and status may be quite literally worn on one's sleeve.

In an additional literary allusion to decadence and excess, most of the Capitol residents have Roman names, for example, Caesar, Plutarch, Octavia, Flavius, Cinna, Claudius, and Coriolanus. The residents of the Capitol tend to look down on the people from the districts as a type of curiosity and as a second-class citizen. Collins drew much from ancient Roman history to provide a detailed foundation for the Capitol. The name of the nation itself—Panem—is the Latin word for bread and is derived from the late Roman empire practice of plying the masses with "*panem et circenses*," that is, bread and circuses, to keep them placated and compliant, which was derided by Juvenal (1992) in his *Satires* in which he vilified the abrogation of political responsibilities of the Roman citizens in favor of wheat doles and costly games and entertainment.

> Already long ago, from when we sold our vote to no man, the People have abdicated our duties; for the People who once upon a time handed out military command, high civil office, legions—everything, now restrains itself and anxiously hopes for just two things: bread and circuses. (10.77–10.81)

Even though the vast majority of the Panem population lives in the outlying districts, the events of the film are concentrated in either the Capitol, where the Hunger Games are annually held, or District 12, the home of the protagonists Katniss and Peeta. District 12 is depicted using imagery from both 1930s Depression era America and rural Appalachia. Because the district's main resource is coal, the majority of residents work in the mining industry, and the district has the feel of an early twentieth-century mining company town. At the beginning of the second film, Katniss and Peeta, having survived the 74th Hunger Game in the first film, are living in the upper-class area of the district, a gated community, of sorts, named "Victor's Village" where victors of the Hunger Games are permitted to live for the remainder of their lives. This is also reminiscent of the higher quality housing available to the executives and managers in a company town, separating them from the workers.

Katniss and her friend Gale (spoiler alert: who along with Peeta comprise the films' love triangle with Katniss) are accomplished hunters who frequently poach squirrel and other game on prohibited grounds to sell or barter at an illegal black market that is passively tolerated by the Capitol's "Peacekeeper" enforcement soldiers stationed in every district. Katniss hunts with a bow, which is symbolic of the early American conflicts between the indigenous Indian population and the British colonists and, eventually, the U.S. government. Katniss's skill with a bow becomes one of her trademarks during the Hunger Games competitions. This is in addition to a gold mockingjay pin that she received from her sister. The mockingjay is a bird that is indigenous to Panem that is known for its ability to mimic short melodies. This symbolization of Katniss as Mockingjay eventually comes to be representative of the rebellion itself.

I draw mainly from the film series for several reasons: (1) due to the significant popularity of the films, readers of this volume are more likely to have seen the films than to have read the books; (2) it is less time-consuming with respect to student workloads to devote one or two class sessions to showing a film—or requiring the film to be viewed as "homework", if class-time is at a premium—than to assign one or more books; and (3) specific film clips can be more easily introduced during class lecture or discussion to highlight a concept or issue. All quotations cited in this chapter are taken from the films rather than the novels.

Critical Criminology

Critical criminology is a relatively recent theoretical addition in the field of criminology. The origins of critical criminology are found in the writings of Marx and Engels, who analyzed the industrial revolution and capitalist expansion, particularly with respect to the degree to which both depended upon the exploitation of the proletariat working class for the benefit of the bourgeois, capitalist, upper class. Marx (1887, 1964, pp. 158–160) and Engels wrote very little about crime specifically, but they generally asserted crime was best understood as the result of law enforcement and criminal justice policies, that is, that the upper classes, by virtue of controlling the criminal justice institutions, labeled certain acts, particularly those of the lower classes, as criminal. They also highlighted the connections between criminality and the inherent inequality and exploitation in the capitalist mode of production. Engels (1958, pp. 242–243), in particular, identified crime as a sort of unconscious, pre-critical expression of rebellion against the exploitative nature of capitalism.

The mid-twentieth century was marked by the emergence of a number of breakdowns in social stability. World War II and the accompanying deaths of millions of people, including soldiers as well as even greater numbers of civilians, led into the Korean Conflict, the Vietnam War, and the Cold War. This same time period also included the antiwar protests, protests against nuclear proliferation, Civil Rights movements, women's rights movements, and various other reactions against religious or political conservativism. Much in the way that the early twentieth-century Structural-Functionalist domination of sociological theory ceded academic legitimacy to conflict theory, symbolic interactionism, and late modern perspectives, such as the positions advanced by Foucault, Bourdieu, and others, the criminological theory that had been dominated by the classical, positivist, social process, and social structure theories ceded a measure of explanatory authority to conflict theory, feminist theory, critical race theory, and critical criminology.

Critical criminology most successfully advanced as a subfield of criminology after the publication of Taylor, Walton, and Young's *The New Criminology* in 1973. Siegel (2012) writes that in the wake of *The New Criminology*, "there has been a tradition for critical criminologists to turn their attention to the field itself, questioning the role criminology plays in supporting the status quo, and aiding in the oppression of the poor and the powerless" (p. 270). Critical criminologists also examined the contemporary operations of the American political system and American influence in other nations. The role of corporate power, especially at the expense of a decreased role of government in the provision of social services, is an additional area of inquiry. Critical criminology also analyzes the misuse of power by state and/or corporate institutions and actors. It is this examination into state power that I focus on in this chapter.

State Crime

William Chambliss (1989) made specific mention of "state-organized crime" in his 1988 presidential address to the American Society of Criminology in which he identified acts by representatives or office-holders in state governments as potential objects of criminological inquiry. State or political crime can be understood as criminal acts by individuals or groups who oppose a government or its practices, for example, terrorists, or as criminal acts committed by elected or appointed officials in the government, law enforcement, or criminal justice system. Ross (2003) identified four categories of state crime: (1) illegal domestic surveillance, (2) human rights violations, (3) state-corporate crime, and (4) state violence. In this section, I introduce and illustrate each of these categories with examples from *The Hunger Games*. Many of the examples from the films will be clear and obvious illustrations of the four categories. Some of the examples, due to the incomplete depiction of every aspect of Panem governance and its various legal codes, may require some inductive reasoning or inference in order to connect the dots between the events of the film and the elements of state crime.

Illegal Domestic Surveillance

This type of government surveillance occurs when officials read mailed letters and other correspondence, search shipped packages and parcels, listen in on and/or record telephone conversations, or read/copy or intercept emails and text messages. This surveillance can also include the ubiquitous presence of surveillance cameras, global positioning system (GPS) monitoring of mobile communication devices or vehicles, and the specific electronic tracking of individuals, whether knowingly or not. Other surveillance technologies include facial recognition software to track the locations or movements of specific individuals and license plate readers that can scan all vehicles near an operating officer or passing through a toll stop, an exit ramp, or geographic border. With increased technological advancement there is increased potential for electronic surveillance.

During the Hunger Games competitions, the tributes are required to have a GPS tracking device implanted into their arms. In addition to constant tracking of their position and movements, nearly the entire area of the Hunger Games arena is being surveilled and recorded by hidden cameras. Ostensibly this is to ensure that the audiences viewing the Games are not going to miss any of the "action," but these cameras also allow the Gamemakers to introduce new dangers or obstacles, direct tributes toward or away from other areas, or otherwise direct or influence the outcome of the Games.

Outside the context of the Games themselves, there is a significant implicit use of surveillance in the Capitol and the outer districts. Often the cameras or drones are not conspicuously placed, so the viewing audience does not necessarily observe constant use of surveillance, but when riots and other forms of domestic unrest begin to break out in the districts, Katniss is able to surreptitiously observe the Capitol's video footage of the events. Additionally, at the beginning of the first film, when Katniss and Gale discuss running off and leaving District 12, Katniss dismisses the suggestion, saying that they [the Peacekeepers] would catch them. This degree of certainty presupposes the extensive use of state surveillance.

In the 74th Hunger Games contest shown in the first film, Katniss and Peeta are able to manipulate Seneca Crane—the head Gamemaker—into permitting two victors (if both are from the same district) by pretending to be in love with one another, though Peeta is not pretending. Katniss thinks that this deception will eventually pass, and they can just return to their previous lives, but this proves impossible. Victors of the Hunger Games are something akin to reality television stars in Panem. They are also obliged to serve as mentors to the tributes from their home districts, as Haymitch did for them, in all future Hunger Games. While Katniss believes that their deception will be eventually be forgotten, she is wrong in that the narrative of "star-crossed love" between Katniss and Peeta will be broadcast and discussed anew with every future Hunger Game. By surviving the Hunger Games, Katniss and Peeta's social roles have been irrevocably changed. This is true for all of the victors of the Games, but even more so for them, because there had never before been two victors, in addition to the compelling story of their doomed love.

Compounding this wrinkle in their plan, their strategy to portray themselves as star-crossed lovers in order to survive is also perceived by some dissident groups and districts as a statement against the totality of the authority of the Capitol. President Snow threatens Katniss with the wholesale destruction of District 12 if, while on their required public relations victory tour through the twelve districts, they fail to convince the masses, and thus President Snow, of the sincerity of their love. When President Snow confronts Katniss at her home to impress upon her the importance of a convincing portrayal of love, he also shows her surveillance footage of her and Gale sharing a kiss. This allows a fair conclusion that at least Katniss, if not the whole of District 12, is under extensive surveillance.

A final example of illegal domestic surveillance, coupled with the abrogation of civil liberties, is the actions of the Capitol's Peacekeepers, who are deployed in the outlying districts. They are seen searching district residents' homes for contraband without presenting a warrant or other form of authorization for their actions. The Peacekeepers are also depicted seizing property and destroying it in public conflagrations. In the course of the Peacekeepers' crackdowns on black market gatherings and other forms of political dissidence, they also detain and take into custody numerous district residents, again without offering any official authorization to do so. Many of these detainees are never heard from again. This dovetails with the second category of state crime.

Human Rights Violations

There are a variety of state actions that fall under the umbrella of human rights violations. Siegel (2012) lists the extreme use of corporal punishment, torture in interrogation, the denial of civil rights, detention without trial or due process, the use of hard labor or torture to punish dissidents or others accused of political crimes, the utilization of prisons run by authoritarian regimes in order to circumvent domestic laws mandating the humane treatment of prisoners, the exploitation of forced or captive labor, the "disappearing" of arrested activists, dissidents, or political opponents, and summary executions.

The most extreme example of human rights violations comes at the end of *Catching Fire*. After the rebels, who infiltrate the Capitol and plant an infiltrator as the head of the Gamemakers' staff, free Katniss and facilitate her escape from the Capitol, President Snow follows through on his earlier threat to see "thousands upon thousands…dead. This town reduced to ashes…buried under radioactive dirt as if it never existed." As President Snow warns, District 12 is bombed into nothingness, killing hundreds of thousands as punishment for the rebels' actions. This is not the first time that the Capitol took such action, as it was the destruction of District 13 that brought an end to the Dark Days, beginning the Hunger Games era.

As another example, in the confusion surrounding the rescue of Katniss from the 75th Hunger Games contest in *Catching Fire*, Peeta is left behind in the custody of the Capitol. During the months of his detention, he is tortured and subjected to a brainwashing technique that causes him to become enraged when he is in the presence of Katniss. There are a few instances in which he violently attacks her, trying to kill her. Peeta is only one of many individuals who have been tortured in one manner or another by the Capitol.

The Hunger Games in and of themselves are an egregious example of human rights violations. The Capitol mandates a lottery, overseen by Peacekeeper soldiers, in which 24 teenagers are to be selected to compete in a contest in which there is only supposed to be a single survivor. The winner will be hailed as the Victor for that year, but the cost of victory is almost always extraordinarily high. Haymitch, the District 12 Victor from the 50th Hunger Game, states in *Catching Fire* that "nobody ever wins the games—period. There are survivors, but there's no winners." The use of human sacrifice in any sort of state ritual has been long outlawed as a violation of the inherent worth and dignity of all individuals. Of course, a number of states still retain sufficient monopoly over the use of violence to make some crimes punishable by execution, but this practice declined notably over the twentieth century—the United States being a prominent exception.

The Hunger Games are not just a danger to the tributes but, indeed, to their families, friends, and coworkers. None of the characters are more aware of this than Haymitch, who was the Victor in the 50th Hunger Games contest by utilizing the force-field surrounding the gaming arena in an unexpected manner, causing a weapon thrown at him to bounce back and hit the last remaining tribute. As punishment for his tactic, the Capitol murdered his mother, younger brother, and girlfriend a few weeks after the Games concluded. Not even Capitol citizens or Gamemakers themselves were safe from state retribution. Following the conclusion of the 74th Hunger Game from the first film, in which Katniss and Peeta are both declared Victors, as punishment for that outcome, President Snow had Seneca Crane—the Head Gamemaker—confined to a room with only a bowl of the poisonous berries. In some respects, this parallels the sentence of execution given to Socrates in which he was forced to ingest hemlock as punishment for his defiance of (city-)state authority. The second film makes reference to Crane having been hanged, so there is some discrepancy as to his actual cause of death. There is no confusion that he is executed by the Capitol as punishment for his failure.

State-Corporate Crime

There are fewer examples of state-corporate crime as a category of state crime, though such instances frequently have extremely significant costs. A first example is the use of some or all media outlets as an extension of the state. This phenomenon is extensively observed in *The Hunger Games*. The second dimension of state-corporate crime encompasses the granting of special privileges to specific private corporations and not to others, often based on some degree of conflict of interest or outright bribery. There are many methods by which this can occur. The state might grant exclusive leases or rights of access to resources such as minerals, oil, or natural gas located in public land to some corporations and not others. Another example may be differential enforcement by the state of environmental protection regulations; antitrust, securities, and exchange violations; and/or occupational safety or other labor violations against some companies and not others.

In *The Hunger Games* series, the media plays a vital role in promoting the interests of the Capitol and downplaying or ignoring entirely any reports of political dissidence or uprising. The Games themselves are elaborately crafted as a glorious contest in which the tributes are fighting for their personal honor as well as the honor of their district. Always implicit is that such beneficence is granted by the generosity of the Capitol. Caesar Flickman is the most prominent media personality in the series. He presides over a number of televised programs in which the tributes are paraded into the Capitol and then interviewed about their lives and expectations for the Games. All of these presentations are designed to portray the Capitol in the most flattering light while simultaneously generating as much excitement as possible in the audiences, particularly the Capitol audience. Collins and the filmmakers clearly draw on many U.S. reality television programs in their portrayal of both Flickman and his Hunger Games television productions.

Plutarch Heavensbee—the Head Gamemaker in *Catching Fire* (spoiler alert: and secret rebel agent)—is certain that the media would be a powerful weapon in the state's efforts to put down the rebellions that begin to spring up in the aftermath of Katniss and Peeta's joint victory. Many of these uprisings are influenced by Katniss and her portrayal as the Mockingjay. In the exchange between President Snow and Heavensbee, the president is quite telling about the Capitol's intended role for the media and explains that because she is a symbol of hope, she needs to be eliminated.

Heavensbee is intuitively cognizant of the Thomas theorem, proffered by William I. and Dorothy S. Thomas (1928), which states, "If men define situations as real, they are real in their consequences." The state plans to sow discord and rancor among the districts and against Katniss as the symbol for the rebellion. Whether the programming is true or not, Heavensbee asserts that the repetition of the message will eventually be effective in marginalizing Katniss's symbolic influence and popularity with the masses.

State Violence

The final category of state crime that is illustrated by *The Hunger Games* series is state violence. There is some overlap in categories, particularly between human rights violation and state violence, but there are enough notable distinctions to make the use of different terms appropriate. Examples of state violence include death squads, that is, armed unofficial groups, though frequently acting on the behalf, if not at the behest, of the state, that kills suspected political dissidents or opponents or other undesirable or marginalized social, racial, or ethnic groups. Death squads have historically been responsible for assassinations, kidnappings, disappearances, and other violent methods of public intimidation.

The Hunger Games series of films demonstrate numerous examples of state violence. The Peacekeepers used by the Capitol share much in common with death squads, although there are some notable differences. During the public relations tour that Katniss and Peeta are obliged to perform at the beginning of *Catching Fire*, an older man in District 11 interrupts their prepared speeches and performs the three-fingered salute that has been a symbol of discontent toward the Capitol from the beginning of the first film. This prompts the entire crowd to perform the salute. The Peacekeepers break up the gathering immediately. They then drag the old man up on the raised platform and summarily execute him by shooting him in the head.

Later in *Catching Fire*, the Peacekeepers are breaking up the black markets in District 12 and confiscating people's belongings to be destroyed. Gale attempts to prevent a man from being beaten by a Peacekeeper. As a result, he is detained by the Commander of the Peacekeepers, tied up to a pole in a town square, and whipped repeatedly until Katniss and Haymitch intercede on his behalf. The Commander relents but threatens that the next time it will be a firing squad. This harkens back to a scene from the first film, referenced above, when Katniss and Gale discuss running away. Katniss says that they would catch them and "cut out our tongues... or worse." As another example of corporal punishment, in retribution for Cinna—Katniss and Peeta's stylist—giving her a dress that is contrary to the design intended by President Snow, in the moments before Katniss was to begin the Hunger Game in *Catching Fire*, her entry to the game arena is delayed while she is forced to watch Cinna being brutally beaten in front of her. The use of state violence is a universally acknowledged phenomenon in *The Hunger Games* series.

Conclusion

For many criminology or criminal justice students, critical criminology theory can be one of the harder theories to grasp. The majority of the classical, positivist, and social learning criminological theories assert the factors—varied though they may be—that contribute to crime and deviance within the individual actors. Labeling theory and the social structural theories recognize the importance of institutional and organizational factors in contributing to delinquency. Critical criminology, with its Marxist influence—particularly its emphasis on the role of inequality and state actions—often proves challenging for undergraduate students to easily grasp. *The Hunger Games* films make a very useful illustration of the four most common categories of critical criminology and state crime. The film series was extremely popular when it was released, so there should be a low entry barrier to encourage students to engage with the films. Many students will have already seen them previously, and a number of events in the film already exist as cultural touchstones. The books and films certainly were popular with young adult audiences at the times of their release from 2008 through 2015, but they also had significant reading and viewing audiences with older generations as well. The trilogy of novels sold more than 65 million copies and the films earned nearly \$4 billion at the box office, making them a worldwide phenomenon. Due to their significant presence in contemporary popular culture, the films are an excellent vehicle to present examples to students of critical criminology and state crime.

The constant monitoring and tracking of tributes during the Games, as well as the near omnipresence of video surveillance and Peacekeeper troop patrols, are examples of illegal domestic surveillance. The wholesale destruction of District 12 at the end of *Catching Fire* and the holding of the Hunger Games themselves, where Panem citizens are sacrificed in satisfaction of the Treaty of the Treason, are examples of human rights violations. The use of the media to serve as the mouthpiece for the Capitol as well as to function as the source of the dissemination of propaganda are examples of state-corporate crime. Finally, the whippings, beatings, kidnappings, and summary executions of Panem residents by the Capitol's Peacekeeper soldiers are examples of the frequent incidents of state violence that occur regularly throughout *The Hunger Games* series of films. The nation of Panem exists in a violent world, and the Hunger Games contests serve well to depict the critical criminological explanations for these numerous instances of state crime.

Discussion Questions

1. *The Hunger Games* are generally classified as "dystopian fiction," which are works typically set in worlds marked by significant amounts of social strife and problems. Can you think of examples of state crime from other fictional works that take place in less extreme settings?
2. What are some examples of current events of state-corporate crime? Are you able to find more or fewer examples compared to instances of state violence or human rights violations?
3. What are some parallels between Heavensbee's plans to pillory Katniss in the media and the use of propaganda by political campaigns or administrations in order to sway public opinion on candidates or issues?

References

Becker, H. (1963). *Outsiders: Studies in the Sociology of Deviance*. New York: Free Press.
Chambliss, W. (1989). State Organized Crime. *Criminology, 27*(2), 183–208.
Cloward, R., & Ohlin, L. (1960). *Delinquency and Opportunity*. Glencoe, IL: Free Press.
Cohen, A. (1955). *Delinquent Boys*. Glencoe, IL: Free Press.

Engels, F. (1958). *The Condition of the Working Class in England* (W. O. Henderson & W. H. Chaloner, Trans.). Oxford: Basil Blackwell.

Hirschi, T. (1969). *Causes of Delinquency*. Berkeley: University of California Press.

Juvenal. (1992). *The Satires* (N. Rudd, Trans.). London: Oxford University Press.

Marx, K. (1887). *Capital: A Critique of Political Economy* (Vol. 1, S. Moore & E. Aveling, Trans.). London: Swan Sonnenschein, Lowry and Co.

Marx, K. (1964). Theories of Surplus Value, Vol. 1. In T. B. Bottomore & M. Rubel (Eds.), *Karl Marx, Selected Writings in Sociology and Social Philosophy*. New York: McGraw-Hill.

Merton, R. K. (1938). Social Structure and Anomie. *American Sociological Review, 3*, 672–682.

Miller, W. B. (1958). Lower Class Culture as a Generating Milieu of Gang Delinquency. *Journal of Social Issues, 14*, 5–19.

Ross, J. I. (2003). *The Dynamics of Political Crime*. Thousand Oaks, CA: SAGE.

Shaw, C., & McKay, H. D. (1942). *Juvenile Delinquency and Urban Areas*. Chicago: University of Chicago Press.

Siegel, L. J. (2012). *Criminology* (11th ed.). Belmont, CA: Wadsworth.

Sutherland, E. H. (1947). *Principles of Criminology* (4th ed.). Philadelphia: Lippincott.

Thomas, W. I., & Thomas, D. S. (1928). *The Child in America: Behavior Problems and Programs*. New York: Knopf.

Radical Criminology and *Star Wars* 16

"I've Got a Bad Feeling About This": *Star Wars* and Radical Criminology

Andrew Wilczak

With its film premiere in 1977, *Star Wars* launched what would become, possibly, the largest and most recognizable science-fiction franchises in the world. Over 40 years later, the *Star Wars* universe has produced 11 feature-length movies, 4 animated television series, 2 popular web series, and innumerable adult and young adult novels, graphic novels, and video games, most of which are accepted as canonical lore in the larger *Star Wars* universe. While, on the surface, all of this might seem like it amounts to nothing more than a cyclical story of good versus evil with lots of exciting space battles and laser sword fights, nothing in this galaxy can exist without a foundation of violent oppression—the exact sort of thing that the larger field of critical criminology and its various offshoots focuses on in the real world.

Star Wars is a story about good versus evil, to be sure. However, it is a conflict based in a fascist dictatorship that is ruthlessly capitalistic, overtly racist, and covertly theocratic, where genocide is perfectly acceptable, the military-industrial complex is highly organized and extremely powerful, criminal syndicates are permitted to engage in a variety of illicit activities, and political dissent is punishable by death or enslavement, much of which is done purposefully by a single sociopathic tyrant.

Sound familiar?

A. Wilczak (✉)
Wilkes University, Wilkes-Barre, PA, USA
e-mail: andrew.wilczak@wilkes.edu

© The Author(s) 2021
S. E. Daly (ed.), *Theories of Crime Through Popular Culture*,
https://doi.org/10.1007/978-3-030-54434-8_16

In this chapter, we're going to examine the *Star Wars* film franchise as we examine the field of critical criminology. Critical criminology, also referred to as conflict criminology or radical criminology, is a theoretical discipline that challenges us to think about crime and justice in terms of power dynamics in society. Specifically, critical criminology draws heavily on Marxist thought and the idea that society is structured in such a way as for the upper-class to perpetuate their power and privilege through the unending exploitation and oppression of the classes beneath them. For our purposes, the criminal justice system and the rule of law are two ways that this power and control have been perpetuated over time. Historically, critical criminology tends to focus solely on the role of social class structure and the ways the wealthy upper-class benefits from the criminal justice system. In this chapter, we're also going to include elements of critical race theory and feminist theory in the discussion. Marxist thought is exclusively focused on social class stratification; we're going to open the radical umbrella and include race and gender as well because, as we'll see, these core elements of social structure matter and are just as relevant in today's world.

A Primer in Radical Criminology

The first thing we need to consider when talking about radical criminology—and I want to be clear that we are talking about this branch of criminological theory in very broad strokes—is that it differs from other types of theory in terms of application. No doubt, other theories that you have read about in this book so far focus on the explanatory power and the different variables employed to demonstrate the theory's ability to tell us how and why criminal behavior occurs. Many of these theories are used quantitatively, and there are mountains of research in support of these arguments.

This is not typically the case with much of radical criminology.

Instead of thinking about why crime happens in terms of patterns that emerge in the data, radical criminology wants us to think about the relationship between the powerful and the powerless in society and how this dynamic is related to the creation and application of checks on deviant behavior via the use of different norms (informal checks) and laws (formal checks). Radical criminology also wants us to think about why this power is used and the abuse that power creates; it challenges us to look for social problems that exist but do not receive attention from those in power, question why the people suffering in these situations do not receive any attention or assistance and what that means for their place in the world, and what benefits those in power might receive by failing to attend to their needs.

Critical criminology has its roots in the work of Karl Marx (1818–1883). Marx comes to criminology through its connection to sociology; in his original works, Marx had very little use for the criminal underclass, which he termed the lumpenproletariat. Marx viewed the lumpenproletariat as being nothing more than a drag on the inevitable socialist revolution; these were people who were incapable of developing any sort of class consciousness, people who were unable to develop any kind of positive bond to their community or their neighbors and so these were people who were not capable of making meaningful contributions to the good of the people. Since his death, Marxist thinkers have modified this theory and have a different view of the criminal underclass today—rather than viewing them as a group with nothing to offer, some began to see them as the vanguard of the revolution and as members of the working class pushed to the brink by an unfathomably powerful system.

A major turning point in Marxist sociology broadly, and perhaps the creation of Marxist criminology specifically, was in the work of Richard Quinney. Quinney argued that the purpose of the criminal justice system was not to create an actual just society, but rather to enforce the will of the powerful (Quinney 1977). In this way, the criminal justice system is a cudgel used by oppressive forces within society to beat back the revolution. This requires us to think about crime, not in terms of good or bad behavior or good or bad people, but in terms of the presence or absence of power in a given moment. In other words, if there was a robbery—was the victim someone with privileged status? If they were, then the system might move Heaven and Earth to try to find justice. Was the robber someone with privileged status? If not, we will gladly throw them into the meat grinder of the criminal justice system because the system has to be fed.

Today, radical criminology challenges us to think about crimes committed by the powerful and how powerful people use their positions of authority to construct and enforce narratives around the "true" problem of crime in society as a means of deflecting from their own wrongdoing. In practice, this means focusing on white-collar crime and state and political crime, human rights violations, and general ways in which the system is constructed to oppress those not in power. Currently, we can think about critical theories of crime as encompassing not only social class, but race, ethnicity, and gender as well.

Let's talk about race and ethnicity first. Thinking about crime critically from this perspective, we're focusing on how the system is set up to create and perpetuate a system of white supremacy. We see this manifest throughout the American criminal justice system. Michelle Alexander's book *The New Jim Crow* (2010) argues that the War on Drugs transformed the American criminal justice system into a form of social control inflicted almost entirely on the Black community. Alexander

(2010) argues that the War on Drugs was the logical step in a system in a series of policies that originated with chattel slavery and turned into Jim Crow style laws following the end of Reconstruction until the end of Jim Crow in 1965 with the passage of the Voting Rights Act. Essentially, Alexander is arguing that though these two massive forms of social control—chattel slavery and Jim Crow—were overthrown, neither the racist ideals behind them nor the racist legislators responsible for implementing them, were removed from American life. The victories of the Civil Rights movement may have secured a new form of equality for Black Americans, but the system was able to adapt to this, creating a new language of colorblind racism. This allowed those who would seek to control and destroy Black Americans to construct a new system of justice that didn't explicitly target Black people in its mission but, by designating Black communities as high crime areas, brought nothing but pain and misery to much of Black America. Further, Alexander (2010) argues that similar to past systems of social control, American politics and American media have consistently jumped to the defense of this new form of oppression; happily, gleefully parroting stereotypes about Black people, poor people, and drug use. This created, for example, the stereotype of the "crack whore" and "crack baby" who were allegedly commonplace in Black neighborhoods—women whose morality had been sacrificed by drugs, children born addicted to crack who needed white America to step in and save them. It is a language almost identical to the language used to perpetuate slavery and to encourage the genocide of Indigenous people. This level of control, and the mythology justifying it became so entrenched in the criminal justice system that the U.S. Supreme Court created new precedents for the system to further abuse their power in the quest to rid the streets of these foul drugs; and if a few Black people got sent to prison indefinitely, all the better.

With regard to gender and critical theory, we want to think about how the system treats men and women. This is not necessarily just an issue of how the system creates and perpetuates sexism, though that certainly has been a problem, it's also a case of thinking about equity in terms of the types of crimes that rise to the attention of the system. In other words, if the criminal justice system is truly fair, then anyone, regardless of class, race, or gender, will receive identical treatment. This is the idea that justice is blind and, therefore, fair. In practice, we know this couldn't be further from the truth. Early feminist criminologists approached the issue of gender and crime from a couple of different angles. On one hand, theorists like Freda Adler (1975) argued that crime was related to masculinity, and perceived increases in the number of women committing crimes were tied to the women's liberation movement—that it had become socially acceptable for women to assume roles that had traditionally solely belonged to men, and it was thought that this was causing women to adopt other masculinity traits, including a greater propensity to commit a crime. Classic interpretations of this theory suggest that women are committing crimes because they're behaving in more masculine ways, but Hunnicut and Broidy (2004) argue that what we're really seeing here is a connection between independence and economic marginalization and that increases in women's crime were, therefore, connected to a need to survive more than a desire to adopt masculine behavior.

A more useful paradigm for feminist criminology, and one that I think pairs well with the other theories presented in this book, is the work done by Daly and Chesney-Lind (1988). In their work, they argue that we should not treat sex and gender as the same thing, rather, to make distinctions between the biological (sex) and the social (gender). For our purposes, we will be thinking about how gender is socially constructed and how those in power might try to reduce social issues into a single biological one. When I say that gender is socially constructed, I want you to think about the ways in which you perform your gender identity: the ways in which you show to the world that you are masculine or feminine or something in between. How do you dress? How do you wear your hair? Do you wear makeup? Do you shave? Beyond personal appearance, what types of jobs have traditionally been associated with masculinity or femininity? Why? What about college majors? Why? If you hear yourself saying that it's just the way it is, or that this is because of some biological difference, you're playing into the hands of oppressive systems because you're taking a social process (gender) and reducing it to biological explanations. Gender, like race and social class, is socially constructed by our interactions with each other and the values we project onto others' behavior.

Taking this idea a step further, we can argue that the powerful in society have the ability to influence the social construction of reality in some pretty major ways. We've already talked about the role of the media in the spread of mass incarceration and the War on Drugs—this is how powerful media and government entities worked together to influence the social construction of race and drug use, according to this perspective. If the same thing is happening regarding women and femininity and crime, where do you think we see examples of it?

Daly and Chesney-Lind also argue that knowledge itself is gendered in that so much knowledge has been produced by men, who create it from a distinctly masculine viewpoint, and therefore have centered masculine ideals while pushing femininity to the sidelines (1988). Indeed, this is why the idea of objectivity in research itself is problematic: the critical perspective would argue that when we say research should be objective, what we really mean is that it should conform to masculine values. In an applied sense, this means that we've got programs and policies in place that focus on extreme forms of masculinity and male behaviors, disregarding everyone else who fits into that box. Why do we assume that the police, prisons, and courts are absolutely objective? Why are we so hellbent on finding a one-size-fits-all system that might not actually exist? Why not explore methods of policing or punishment or legal systems that actually benefit the communities they exist in, rather than forcing the same broken, violent system on everyone? Because "objective" and "fairness" really equals masculinity.

In sum, the critical approach to crime overall challenges us to think about the ways in which social class, gender, and race and ethnicity are weaponized by the system as a way of oppressing powerless groups within society. In an American context, this means we need to think about how the criminal justice system is weighed against people living in poverty, people who are nonwhite, and ways in which it reinforces toxic masculinity. We need to look for the multitude of ways that the system isn't concerned with justice but with upholding the status quo. And, having identified the inadequacies of the system as an institution meant to serve the people, we need to work toward either reform or abolition, to create true systems of justice that heal individuals and communities.

A Long Time Ago, in a Galaxy Far, Far Away

Before we get into the ways in which radical criminology is demonstrated in the *Star Wars* franchise, I suppose it is necessary to take a moment to run through what this story is all about; for those of you who are uninitiated and don't have the time to watch all of these movies right now (though you totally should. Go ahead. You deserve a break). Not only is there a lot to watch, but the movies also weren't released in chronological order, meaning that if you watch the movies in the order they were released, the story will jump back and forth in time, and there's a lot of fan debate about what order they should be viewed in. So, let's try to make things as simple as possible and proceed through the story chronologically. As the opening crawl goes, this is a story set a long time ago in a galaxy far, far away...

The first chronological series of movies come in what is typically referred to as the prequel trilogy. Here, we are introduced to the Galactic Republic: a bloated, toothless bureaucracy that has existed for over 1000 years spanning much of the known galaxy. Peace is kept by the Jedi Order, an organization of people capable of wielding The Force: the unseen and infinite power that binds the universe together. The Jedi represent the Light Side of the Force (they're the good guys). In the first trilogy, we see the death of the Republic at the hands of a man named Sheev Palpatine. Palpatine single-handedly manipulates the Republic and those who disagreed with the Republic, as well as the Jedi Order, into collapsing into an all-consuming Civil War. Palpatine himself is the leader of both the Republic and the Separatists, though few (if any) know the extent of his duplicity. Palpatine uses this war to create a massive military infrastructure and erode any and all democratic institutions, as well as completely eradicating the Jedi Order in the process. His coup-de-grace is convincing one of the most powerful Jedi, a man named Anakin Skywalker, to betray the Order and join him. Anakin gives in to the rage we have seen building in him, attacking his pregnant wife, Padme, and his best friend and mentor, Obi-Wan Kenobi, after obliterating everything and everyone in his path. Anakin is defeated by Kenobi and left for dead. He is revived by Palpatine, now Emperor, and transformed into the iconic black-armored warrior Darth Vader. Without their knowledge, Kenobi and others put his newborn children into hiding as Padme has died in childbirth. There are two new Skywalkers in the galaxy, hidden away from their father and his puppet-master.

The second chronological trilogy, commonly known as the original trilogy, picks up roughly 30 years after the conclusion of the prequels. Palpatine and Vader have transformed the Republic into something wholly unrecognizable: the Empire. The films begin as Palpatine prepares to gain complete control over the galaxy via the threat of his world-destroying space station despite the continued annoyance of a growing rebellion, led by who we find out are Vader's children: Princess Leia Organa, political wunderkind and thorn in the Emperor's side, and Luke Skywalker, hot-tempered doofus farm boy. Luke has been watched over by the exiled Obi-Wan Kenobi, who becomes his mentor after Luke is orphaned a second time at the hands of the Empire. Through this trilogy, we see Luke grow in power considerably, and despite the best machinations of the Empire and all their world-destroying power, Palpatine is defeated when Luke's persistent unconditional love for his father destroys Vader and Anakin is redeemed, at least metaphysically. We are left hoping for a future controlled by the Second Republic.

The third trilogy again jumps ahead in time roughly 30 years and shows how history repeats itself. We find out that the Second Republic struggled to eradicate the last remnants of the Empire, and a new version of Palpatine's dream has manifested in the form of an organization called the First Order. The First Order is able to amass a sizable military and its planet-destroying arsenal, crushing the Second Republic and shattering these new institutions easily during the first two films of the sequel trilogy. Most of our old heroes are dead or lost, and there is little hope for freedom in the galaxy. As of this writing, the final movie in this trilogy has not yet been released, so I am unable to provide you with any sort of definitive conclusion to this iteration of the franchise but suffice it to say that I have no reason to expect it to deviate from the themes of the previous films.

Two standalone films have also been released designed to fill in some of the gaps between the prequel and original trilogy. For brevity's sake, I'm not going to go into much detail about them here, though the larger issues of imperialism and crime are central to both movies. In *Rogue One: A Star Wars Story*, we see the Empire's destruction of a sacred Jedi temple in the name of rooting out rebellious forces and the first major action by the rebels to coalesce into a more organized revolutionary group. In *Solo: A Star Wars Story*, we learn more about the backstory of Han Solo, a central figure in the original trilogy and the beginning of the new trilogy, whose attempt to live the life of a roguish outlaw brings him up close to the oppression of the Empire and the toxicity it has created, hinting at his future as a key figure in the rebellion.

The *Star Wars* films are about the ongoing battle of good versus evil and right versus wrong, but they're also movies about political corruption and the crimes of imperialism. We see the rise and fall (and potential rise again) of the Emperor, and the total devastation caused by his quest for power. Palpatine is emblematic of everything critical criminology and similar radical perspectives teach. Through these films, we see connections between imperialism and genocide, the ways government uses and abuses its ability to control narratives of crime, its relationship with and ability to destroy dissidence, and, more broadly, its ability to divide and conquer.

Government Controlled Narrative

Another important aspect of critical criminology is the idea that the state is responsible for creating narratives around crime, using their power and authority to distract the public from the crimes they themselves are committing. The War on Drugs is again an excellent example of this: when President Nixon announced new federal policies targeting street drugs in the United States, there was no real street drug problem. Certainly not the scourge of the streets like he wanted people to believe—and if there was ever a President who wanted to distract the public from his own criminal misconduct, it was Nixon.

We see this idea of the government manipulating the public through its control of the narrative throughout the *Star Wars* prequel trilogy, especially *Episode II: Attack of the Clones* and *Episode III: Revenge of the Sith*. These movies cover the period in the story known as the Clone Wars, the Civil War between the Republic and the Separatists created entirely by Palpatine to create an enormous military apparatus and install himself as Emperor. To accomplish this, Palpatine has to overcome both the Galactic Senate and the Jedi Order, institutions which have existed since time immemorial. Palpatine is the head of both the Republic and the Separatists because he is also secretly a Sith Lord, with the Sith representing darkness, the enemies of the Jedi, protectors of the light. No one knows that he is a Sith Lord, or that a Sith is responsible for the Separatist movement—this is hidden from the public.

To accomplish this, Palpatine begins a campaign to cast both the Jedi and those Senators who disapprove of his totalitarianism as treasonous enemies of Democracy which no right-minded person would agree with. We see his whisper campaign against both the Jedi and the Senate operate through his relationship with Anakin Skywalker, himself a Jedi. Though we know that Palpatine is evil, Anakin doesn't, and our knowledge that Anakin is also being manipulated by Palpatine somehow makes his venom that much more toxic. We see him telling Anakin how the Jedi Counsel does not trust him [Palpatine] and how they're seeking power for themselves—that they want to overthrow him and take control of the government for themselves. The Senate votes to give Palpatine increasing power and those Senators who push back against this are also branded as traitors.

On the other side of things, as shadow leader of the Separatist rebellion, Palpatine's minions brand the Republic as hopelessly corrupt and the enemy of freedom. We're not able to spend a lot of time on this idea in the prequel trilogy itself, but this is a major theme of some of the *Star Wars* content outside of the movies: the Separatists claim that the Republic is antidemocratic while being extraordinarily antidemocratic itself. By occupying these two positions of power (whether or not we can really think of them as two separate jobs), Palpatine is able to make everyone paranoid about security and democracy while simultaneously eroding public trust in the two major institutions designed to provide democracy and security in the galaxy.

Once he successfully destroyed that trust, it's time to destroy those institutions themselves. By the end of *Revenge of the Sith*, the Jedi Order has been almost completely destroyed and its surviving leadership forced into exile. The Senate has been transformed into nothing more than an extension of Palpatine's power, and we know that in the next 30 years the Senate is dissolved completely as Palpatine further consolidates his power.

Palpatine is, in many ways, a representative of the worst fears of radical criminology. Indeed, it is not hard to believe that this fictional character might represent the worst of what men like Karl Marx would have feared in governmental authority. Palpatine creates divisions where there are none, he backs his opponents into one winless situation after another, and does both in the short- and long-term (as of this writing, *Episode IX: Rise of Skywalker* has not yet premiered, but we do know that Palpatine is featured in this film, which means that his manipulations might extend for another 30 years after his supposed death).

So, let's look at the social problems coming out of the Separatist movement and Palpatine's government: the war, the corruption, and the lack of democracy. Though these are most certainly problems to be taken seriously, their sources are completely fictional—in other words, these were intentionally designed to create tacit support for an authoritarian government. Further, the government that results from Palpatine's maneuvering is itself corrupt and antidemocratic, using an enormous military to enforce his every whim. From a critical perspective, there are very obvious parallels here to the American government post-9/11: terrorism perpetrated by people we're responsible for creating is happening because they hate our freedom, our government, and our way of life, and so in response, we are going to eliminate freedoms and change our way of life and our philosophy of government that makes it inherently less-democratic. Where Palpatine said anyone challenging his authority was an enemy of democracy, major government figures up to, and including, the President have alluded to the fact that resistance to them or the security apparatus in their control is to be un-American. As of this writing, the President has been engaged in a very public feud with four Congresswomen whom he has accused of hating America while doing everything he can to threaten war with multiple countries and consolidate his own power through strengthening the executive branch of the government while simultaneously diminishing the power of the other branches of government through the installation of his own cronies, toads, and yes-men.

Using the Law to Root Out Political Dissidence

Let's continue with this idea that freedom-is-slavery, slavery-is-freedom that a critical perspective would argue is inherent to both the government central to the story told in *Star Wars* and to the modern American government and justice system. While many fans have been attracted to the franchise because of the more spiritual battle of good versus evil, at its heart, *Star Wars* is a franchise about political and social upheaval and the ways fascist, totalitarian governments attempt to perpetuate their power. In *Star Wars*, this is the conflict between the Empire and the Rebel Alliance in the original trilogy and the First Order and the Resistance in the new trilogy. For purposes of discussing political dissidence, let's focus on the original and most recent trilogies, progressing through the story chronologically.

In *Star Wars Episode IV*, we are told that there is an ongoing rebellion against the authority of the Emperor, that the totalitarian government he created at the end of the prequel trilogy is facing some resistance. We're told about it in pieces—Darth Vader accuses Princess Leia of being part of the Rebellion very early in

Episode IV. During her arrest and subsequent torture, Leia reveals the location of the rebel base, and when Imperial scouts find that she has lied and sent to them a recently abandoned site, the Empire responds by destroying her adopted home planet of Alderaan in front of her. The message couldn't be clearer: this government does not, and will not, tolerate any resistance to its authority.

Because this is a story where we know the good guys will win (distinguishing it from real life), the existence of this super-weapon ends up being the thing that galvanizes the rebellion. Knowing that their actual literal destruction is imminent, they organize an attack on the Empire designed to destroy this new weapon (appropriately called the Death Star) and cripple the Empire's authority. They are successful, of course, and for the first time in the chronology of the story, we see Palpatine defeated. He is not going to take this defeat lightly. In the following film, we see the Empire push back against the rebellion in a major way—first by the attempt to murder Luke Skywalker (this includes one of the most famous scenes in American cinematic history when Anakin as Darth Vader reveals to Luke that he is his father and then Luke begins screaming about how that's impossible) and then by the capture and imprisonment of Han Solo, General in the Rebel Army (Vader assists in the capture of Solo and sees that he is frozen and given to a crime lord whom Solo was indebted to). Following this film, we see how the rebels are able to recover and rally their forces against the creation of a second Death Star. Here, Palpatine has laid a trap for Luke Skywalker, hoping he will kill Anakin and become his new apprentice (similar to how Anakin killed and replaced his former apprentice. It's a thing with this man). Luke, remarkably, does not fall for this trap and instead is able to free Anakin through his faith in him. Anakin then kills Palpatine, throwing him into the Death Star's reactor. The newly reunited Skywalkers are able to escape the Death Star before the rebel fleet destroys it, though their reunion is short-lived, as Anakin died shortly after the battle. Though their reunion is short-lived, as Anakin dies shortly after the battle. The original trilogy ends with the Empire presumably destroyed, and a new day dawning on the galaxy.

The conflict between the Empire and the Rebel Alliance is laid out in relatively simple terms for the sake of the story, but there are parallels to events in recent American history. In fact, I would argue that the FBI's Counter Intelligence Program (COINTELPRO) operations targeting various civil rights groups across the United States is a perfect example of this. COINTELPRO was designed to enforce the status quo in the United States at all costs. If there was an organization of people threatening to disrupt any aspect of business-as-usual in the United States, they were infiltrated with the express purpose of dividing and destroying them. COINTELPRO began as an intelligence program focused on the Communist Party in the United States, at least in part due to ongoing fears of communism resulting from the cold war (but likely also connected to the larger history in the United States between socialism and anarchism and the government). This fear of communism soon resulted in COINTELPRO being focused on any and every sizable organization or charismatic leader within the United States who might be disruptive in some way.

It's hard not to overstate how terrified the federal government was of communist infiltration of the United States. Anything that threatened the status quo was viewed suspiciously as if it were part of a larger communist plot. Every person involved in the civil rights movement was viewed with suspicion, up to and including Rev. Dr. Martin Luther King, Jr. While the FBI insists COINTELPRO was ultimately one small part of their work (according to their website, it amounted to 0.2% of their total workload over the 15-year period the program was in operation (https://vault.fbi.gov/cointel-pro, accessed September 12, 2019)), the damage COINTELPRO caused to organizations around the country is almost immeasurable. Arguably, the reason civil rights in the United States are so far from where they should be is the direct result of COINTELPRO disrupting and destroying these organizations.

"You Know About the Rebellion Against the Empire?" Rebellion as Radicalism

Because *Star Wars* is fiction, we know that despite the Empire's best efforts, the Emperor is going to lose because the good guys have to win in the end. And lose he does, being murdered by Anakin Skywalker at the conclusion of *Episode VI: Return of the Jedi*. But how does this franchise compare to actual radical revolutions that've happened during the course of human history?

Theda Skocpol, in her case studies of revolutions from a Marxist perspective, writes:

> Revolution itself is accomplished through class action led by the self-conscious, rising revolutionary class (i.e., the bourgeoisie in the bourgeois revolutions and the proletariat in socialist revolutions). Perhaps the revolutionary class is supported by other class allies such as the peasantry, but these allies are neither fully class-conscious nor politically organized on a national scale. Once successful, a revolution marks the transition from the previous mode of production and form of class dominance to a new mode of production in which new social relations of production, new political and ideological forms, and, in general, the hegemony of the newly triumphant revolutionary class, create appropriate conditions for the further development of society. In short, Marx sees revolutions as emerging out of class-divided modes of production, and transforming one mode of production into another through class conflict. (2018 [1979], p. 8)

How well does *Star Wars* depict a Marxist interpretation of the ways revolutions occur? The application of Marxist historical theory to the film franchise is tenuous at best. First, it's difficult to see the Rebel Alliance as possessing anything resembling class consciousness at the macro level. There is an allusion to entire planetary systems pushing back against the Imperial structure, but we're never given any more information on that. The piece of the rebellion we are exposed to is a fractured and thrown together band of soldiers led by a vanguard whose political stance is defined only as their opposition to the tyranny of the Empire (because the leadership of the Rebellion is Senators from the Party in Opposition, we may be able to infer that this is a more bourgeois liberal revolution, which would be consistent with the culture of the late 1970s and early 1980s when the original trilogy was released). Supposing we can frame the economy of the Empire as centered entirely on the production and sustainability of the military-industrial complex and the Rebels attack the Death Star(s) as symbols of rejection of that economic structure, then maybe there's something here we can work with.

As the war with the Empire intensifies, we see the leadership of the rebel vanguard take on military titles—specifically General—to reflect their own status within the Alliance military. None of these characters have significant military training that we know of, but they are given this command position regardless. We might think of this as a parody of the existing military structure in the film, as the characters build their own organizational structure in defiance of the Empire. This includes one of the main characters—Leia Organa, herself a Senator when we first meet her—adopting the title of General. This parallel military command structure makes me question whether or not the rebellion in *Star Wars* is a rejection of the Imperial military-industrial complex, and not an attempt to overthrow Imperial authority and replace it with a liberal one (and, obvious to fans of the films, the government that replaces the Empire is referred to as the Second Galactic Republic, so there's that).

In reality, the revolution depicted in *Star Wars* is not in line with the ideas presented by Marxist historians. There is no well-defined class gaining consciousness and rising up to overthrow the existing regime. There is no shift in economic structure and possibility spurring the revolution on; the Empire is not a barrier to the beginning of a new age in the galaxy. But there may still be some Marxism here to be found yet.

Contemporary critical criminology has reimagined Marx's idea that revolution will be brought on by the working class. This philosophy views revolution as something perpetrated by the truly undesirable in society: its criminals. Viewing crime as an act of rebellion allows us to reframe and reconsider what revolution might look like. Crime is, by definition, a challenge to and disruption of state authority; if the state is now working against the best interest of its people, then its authority shouldn't be considered legitimate, and therefore, people breaking the law and challenging the system are actually actively rebelling against that authority. There's even language worked into the system—charges like "resisting arrest"—that lend credence to this viewpoint. In this way, then, the political dissidence discussed in the previous section are themselves acts of revolution according to a Marxist criminological standpoint. The authority of the Empire is eternal and unlimited: challenging that authority, or even testing the boundaries of that authority, is an act of revolution.

The Power of the Dark Side: Internalized Oppression and Self-Negation

The last idea I want to talk about in this chapter has to do with the ways that oppressive systems are able to perpetuate themselves over time. As we talked about earlier in this chapter, in her book *The New Jim Crow*, Alexander (2010) argues that the system of mass incarceration created by the War on Drugs was able to sustain itself through the use of stereotypes surrounding race and drug use, creating so much animosity in the community that voters were happy to continue electing politicians who would continue this oppression.

The question that comes from this, though, is how was the system able to prevent any meaningful resistance from the communities affected by it, and how individuals who may have much in common with those victimized by the system become either passive or active supporters of it. In other words, how does the system convince people it's likely to harm that this is the best for everyone? There are a couple of things happening here. On the individual level, we have the ideas of internalized oppression and self-negation. When someone who is a part of a minority group begins to internalize stereotypes about themselves and act as if they are true, turning society's hatred for them into hatred of themselves, they're engaging in self-negation. If what they say about us is true, then certainly we deserve the punishments and abuses hurled at us, because that's what happens to bad people. This is how pervasive and persuasive systems of oppression often are—taking otherwise intelligent people and turning them against not only the communities they live in but their own families and their own selves.

It is difficult to point to instances of self-negation and internalized oppression in the *Star Wars* films. Other than those background characters we see who have signed onto work for the Empire's war machine, there aren't really instances of people whose lives have been ruined by the machine openly advocating for it (we could say that by definition, the machine has made most people's lives worse, and anyone not openly fighting back against it is engaged in some form of internalized oppression). Instead, I want to focus on one of the main characters: Anakin Skywalker.

Anakin Skywalker might be the most fascinating character in these movies, and I would be remiss if I did not take time in this chapter to talk about him. In the prequel trilogy, we meet Anakin when he is a child, a slave on the desert planet that would one day be the home of his son and best friend in exile. Anakin's potential is recognized almost immediately, and he is selected for Jedi training—because there is a prophecy stating that he is going to bring balance to the Force. As Anakin grows up during the prequel trilogy, we see both his ability as a leader and a warrior and his rage grow exponentially. By the beginning of the third movie in the prequel trilogy, *Episode III: Revenge of the Sith*, Anakin Skywalker is the most powerful Jedi in existence. Anakin's betrayal of everyone and everything he stands for comes about as a result of his volcanic rage being manipulated by Palpatine. Palpatine has convinced him that the world—the galaxy—is out for him, that Palpatine is the only one he can really trust. When Anakin realizes what's going on, it's too late. He's gone too far. He can't turn back. He is Palpatine's weapon, now. When Anakin is almost killed at the end of *Episode III* and transforms into the monster Darth Vader, a literal shell of his former self, is when we see a form of self-negation at play: he has lost everything, he is irredeemable, he is a plaything for the Emperor. Everything he was taught about himself and his role in the world was turned upside-down because of the oppressive force around him; he became a part of that force rather than fighting back against it, as he was taught to. It's not until he finds out that his children are alive that he finds the strength of purpose to finally do the right thing and fight back, killing himself in the process.

Beyond that, there is another idea that Alexander (2010) talks about regarding the ways communities do, or do not, respond to mass incarceration: pluralistic ignorance. To Alexander, one of the barriers against toppling this system of mass incarceration is directly related to the shame families feel about shouldering the burden of a loved one—or ones—incarcerated. She argues that there are communities where people don't know the true extent of harm that mass incarceration has inflicted on them because they're not willing to talk openly about their private struggles. This way of keeping everything private, be it because of self-negation or shame or both or something else, plays directly into the hands of the ruling class, according to critical criminology. By not talking openly about one's problems with the system, knowledge isn't spread through the community, and if that knowledge isn't spread, then there is nothing to counteract the messaging of the system and the status quo remains in place.

In the *Star Wars* franchise, there is nothing as specifically oppressive as the War on Drugs and mass incarceration. The films tend to dole out oppressive circumstances in much broader strokes: genocide, slavery, planetary destruction. But, as there is a growing rebellion against the Empire, we know that there are pockets of resistance throughout the galaxy. In *Episode IV*, we are introduced to the rebellion via Luke Skywalker, a clueless farm boy who has dreams of escaping the tedium of his life and joining this larger movement. His sister, Princess Leia, threatens Vader that the tighter the Empire's grip, "the more systems will slip through your fingers," which can be interpreted as a growing awareness of, and frustration with, the tyranny of this government. In *Rogue One*, we learn that this rebellion is fractured, but by the time Luke has joined, and we meet him and Leia as adults, the movement has crossed the point of no return and he has no choice but to make a strike against the Imperial forces.

Genocide and the Erasure of Unwanted Peoples

A constant thread throughout the *Star Wars* films, especially the first two trilogies, are questions of personhood and genocide. In the prequel trilogy, we see a galactic Civil War that is fought almost entirely by intermediaries: A Droid army deployed by the Separatists, and a Clone army by the Republic. Throughout the films (and supplemental material), it is made abundantly clear that the beings in both armies, though sentient and intelligent, are completely disposable. Because we're seeing much of the narrative through the heroes, this means that we're hearing from them that these beings are less than they are. At the beginning of *Episode III: Revenge of the Sith*, Obi-Wan Kenobi chides Anakin Skywalker for wanting to save some of the clones fighting alongside them, who will surely die so that they can continue the mission. It's a moment meant to echo other war movies—that these are soldiers who knew what they signed up for and are willing to give their lives to the greater cause—except in *Star Wars*, virtually no one fighting this war actually had a choice in the matter.

Following the end of the Civil War and moving into life in this new Empire, as depicted in the original trilogy, these beings who had been an integral part of three movies are now no longer visible: the clones are gone, replaced by authentic humans, the droids used for military service have disappeared completely (though droids remain an important part of this world, and are still treated as objects and not lifeforms well after the Civil War). The Geonosians, a race of sentient insects that was also a major part of the Separatist cause, are also erased from existence, never to be seen or heard from again (and in case it wasn't clear, or to fill in a plot hole, this erasure is explained in supplemental material as another genocide that followed their enslavement).

One of the more overt themes in the *Star Wars* films is their depiction of genocide. Because we're in a science-fiction setting, writers have been able to approach genocide from a variety of different angles. Thinking of one's planet of origin as a form of ethnicity, we see genocide in the destruction of Alderaan by the Death Star (*Episode IV: A New Hope*) and the multiple planets destroyed by Starkiller Base (*Episode VII: The Force Awakens*). We also see the Death Star used to eradicate a city that had once been a Jedi holy place (*Rogue One: A Star Wars Story*). These are military actions done with the explicit purpose of terrorizing the population at large, forcing them to submit to the will of the Empire lest they meet a similar fate. The genocide of the clones, the droids, the Genosians, and other races in the *Star Wars* universe is much more subtle, happening off-camera and with indicators to the audience that these people don't matter. In this way, the fictional depiction of genocides here mirrors genocides that have happened historically: we are told these people do not matter, their very existence impedes the progress of civilization, they and their culture must be dealt with immediately, and we will spare you the details.

Focusing again on policies and practices in the United States, we've seen genocide play out in different forms, dating back to the colonization of these lands. Clearly, the almost total obliteration of Indigenous Nations, their peoples, and their culture that existed here before colonization is an example of genocide. That this eradication happens gradually doesn't make it any worse; if anything, it shows how nefarious politicians can be and the lengths they—and their constituents—will go to demonize an entire group of people to justify their near-total elimination. The end result of federal policies toward First Nations can be seen in just how little we know about them, their language, and their religion, and their cultural practices have been wiped from existence, and now few people in mainstream American culture care that this ever happened.

In addition to the Native American genocide, chattel slavery in the United States was also certainly bordering on genocidal. Though the economic structure of the American South was dependent on the dehumanization and forced labor of Blacks to survive, and therefore the total eradication of Blacks was never the ultimate goal, it should be obvious that slavery destroyed everything about the lives of the enslaved up to, and including, their bodily autonomy. Countless stories of the enslaved being separated from their children, banned from learning to read or write, and being hunted down and captured for daring to escape to freedom.

More contemporarily, we see practices that are at best genocide-adjacent happening in places throughout the country. School districts that restrict the language of their students, faculty, and staff to American English are practicing a form of genocide because they are actively and intentionally erasing the culture of the community. We've seen schools attempt to do this in California, Arizona, Texas, and Nebraska, to name a few (https://www.edweek.org/ew/articles/2003/10/29/09spanish.h23.html, https://www.foxnews.com/world/texas-principal-put-on-leave-for-banning-spanish-in-school, https://www.latimes.com/politics/la-pol-ca-proposition-58-bilingual-education-20161012-snap-story.html, accessed September 17, 2019). Returning to the work of Michelle Alexander (2010), the era of mass incarceration could also be viewed as genocidal, because while federal drug policy isn't specifically calling for the execution of people involved in the drug trade, the myriad ways these policies exclude people from society is tantamount to genocide. Presently, the policies of the Trump administration including but not limited to forced family separation of immigrants applying for asylum and then putting their children up for adoption is most certainly something consistent with genocidal regimes.

Conclusion

The *Star Wars* film franchise is more than a story about the ongoing battle of good versus evil and the unknowable forces that may (or may not) guide human behavior. These are movies about oppression and revolution, injustice, and survival. We see the gradual, unimpeded rise of an authoritarian hyper-militarized dictatorship and the very sudden collapse of that dictatorship. We see the vanguard of revolutionaries responsible for the collapse of the Empire scattered to the wind and the gradual re-emergence of the same authoritarianism, a counter-revolution that shatters everything that generation accomplished.

Critical criminology asks us to think about how the state is responsible for the crime happening within its borders and challenges us to think of all of the ways the state either perpetrates crime itself or influences the popular narrative surrounding the crime, or both. We've seen countless historical examples of this in the United States, ranging from the genocide of Native Americans and the near-total destruction of Indigenous culture to the ongoing War on Drugs and the ways it has destroyed communities throughout the country.

Viewing these films—themselves released over a period of more than 40 years—through the lens of critical criminology is illuminating. This is a story about trying to find peace in one's life in times of tremendous social and political turmoil. It is a textbook example of the many, many ways a government can intentionally work against the people, as powerful political actors manipulate their surroundings to maximize their own political strength and longevity. It is a blueprint for the ways an authoritarian government can use the military to control as much of society as possible. Additionally, it is a template for political and social resistance, as a random collection of heroes and martyrs as diverse as real-world revolutionaries rise up against this authority and smash it, making incredible personal sacrifices in the process.

That said, critical theory would also want us to think about the ways in which the *Star Wars* films present a message that itself is in line with contemporary political ideology. Though critical theory argues that crime itself can be thought of through a revolutionary lens, crime in *Star Wars* is more in line with how Marx himself viewed this aspect of society—as the lumpenproletariat, a drag on the momentum of the actual revolution, nothing to be valued. The *Star Wars* films are rife with portrayals of criminal gangs, crime lords, gambling, slavery, and so on, all of which are tied to a more conservative rational choice, low self-control perspective on crime. The rebellion depicted in the films is not one that rises out of a unified working-class consciousness but rather one led by a vanguard of liberal thinkers and their allies whose primary aim is to overthrow Imperial tyranny and restore "freedom" in the vaguest sense. In other words, the Rebel Alliance couldn't have risen up and installed a socialist or even democratic socialist government, because that was something too antithetical to the existing U.S. government: Reagan's America isn't going to allow the rebels to create their own Commune or Politburo.

Still, the good far outweighs the bad with this franchise. There's redemption in this story, which is something desperately lacking in the criminal justice system. The story of Anakin Skywalker is a heartbreaking tragedy, and if we can accept that if even the greatest hero of his generation can be nearly completely ruined by an oppressive, villainous system, then so too are the everyday people who have to live in it.

Discussion Questions

1. What are times in your life when you've had authority figures in your life (parents, teachers, etc.) tell you that certain behavior was bad? Why did they tell you that?
2. A major theme of *Star Wars* is that the things that matter most—independence, freedom, happiness, love (familial, sororal, fraternal, romantic, platonic)—are no match for the combined forces of capitalism and the military-industrial complex. How can this theme be applied to your own life?
3. How are the decisions of the characters in *Star Wars* the result of what they think they have to do, instead of what they want to do? What constraints are put

on them in how they make their decisions, and why? How does this mirror the major decisions you've made in your own life?

4. What is the status quo in your society? How does the law help enforce it? Can there truly be justice?

5. One lesson *Star Wars* teaches us is that oppression has a cascading effect in our lives and the ways our ancestors were harmed by the system end up harming us, too. Think of how Anakin Skywalker had his life destroyed by the Emperor, how that destruction ended up defining the lives of his children and grandchild. Apply this to your own life: can you see ways your family was affected by the current power structure that has changed your own life?

References

Adler, F. (1975). *Sisters in Crime: The Rise of the New Female Criminals*. McGraw Hill.

Alexander, M. (2010). *The New Jim Crow: Mass Incarceration in the Age of Colorblindness*. The New Press.

Daly, K., & Chesney-Lind, M. (1988). Feminism and Criminology. *Justice Quarterly, 5,* 497–538.

Federal Bureau of Investigation. (n.d.). COINTELPRO. Retrieved September 12, 2019, from https://vault.fbi.gov/cointel-pro

Fox News. (2013/2016). Texas Principal Put on Leave for Banning Spanish in School. Retrieved September 17, 2019, from https://www.foxnews.com/world/texas-principal-put-on-leave-for-banning-spanish-in-school

Hunnicut, G., & Broidy, L. M. (2004). Liberation and Economic Marginalization: A Reformulation and Test of (Formerly?) Competing Models. *Journal of Research in Crime & Delinquency, 41,* 130–155.

Quinney, R. (1977). *Class State and Crime: On the Theory and Practice of Criminal Justice*. New York: McKay.

Skocpol, T. (2018 [1979]). *States and Social Revolutions: A Comparative Analysis of France, Russia, and China*. New York and Cambridge: Cambridge University Press.

Ulloa, J. (2016). Bilingual Education Has Been Absent from California Public Schools for Almost 20 Years. But That May Change Soon. Retrieved September 17, 2019, from https://www.latimes.com/politics/la-pol-ca-proposition-58-bilingual-education-20161012-snap-story.html

Zehr, M. A. (2003). Classroom Ban on Spanish Protested. Retrieved September 17, 2019, from https://www.edweek.org/ew/articles/2003/10/29/09spanish.h23.html

Index

© The Author(s) 2021
S. E. Daly (ed.), *Theories of Crime Through Popular Culture*,
https://doi.org/10.1007/978-3-030-54434-8

Made in the USA
Coppell, TX
21 January 2021

48581913R00144